OVERCOMING SMUT

SUE BRAZEAL

OVERCOMING SMUT

Acknowledgments

I want to thank my sons, David and Brian who have given me the desire to reach as far as I could to improve myself. Upon reflection, I see that my parenting skills were not the best at times as I was dealing with many issues of my upbringing. Many memories were overwhelming at times especially while living with their father. "I did the best I could at the time" is a quote that I like to use. Thankfully, I had my sons, and many times they taught me the lessons of life. They gave me a focus which I needed. Over time they were my justification for the many challenges I had to handle, and how I chose to handle them at certain periods in my life.

Judy Bowles McComas has been such a strong support for me during this endeavor. Reconnecting with her after fifty-three years has given me a background in which she filled many gaps into my memories. I am so thankful that Judy gave me an insight of me through her eyes; which actually helped me see, me.

Janice D'Amore has helped me with the structure and synchrony of this project. We've been friends for a long time and she is steadfast in her beliefs and loyalty. Her time and honesty have always been valued by me and I'm sure it will always be the case in our friendship.

My friend Martha Mahon has been the cheerleader in my life. She has reached out to me when I needed someone who truly understood many of my struggles. She always shared a laugh with me when I needed a laugh—especially, a good old belly-laugh with a snicker or two.

Joanna Sieberg came into my life after I started my story. She spent hours editing and clarifying what I wanted to say. A gentle soul with a tactful manner without ever being judgmental is how I would describe her. I truly appreciate her perspective.

Kali Browne I've met through the work on the story of my life. She has treated me professionally and I am indebted for her direction and input.

Never has my life been short-changed with my sons and my women friends. Thank you.

Introduction

Biographies and memoirs have always been my favorite genre. One that made a strong impression with me was Anthony Quinn's autobiography. His words, "When one writes his story then one can let it go." This rang true for me years ago and still stands true today. I was not able to write all my words down until my third attempt. It has taken me years to accept certain painful facts. I still work at accepting that the abuse I suffered was not my fault. I was not the adult—I was the child. Every survivor has to accept this "truth."

Perpetrators will put the blame on the children they abuse. Many enablers will turn their heads and live in denial before, if ever, they come to terms with the bitter truth. Perpetrators and deniers aid each other to the detriment of the victim or the child.

This attempt I will succeed to tell my story. I've always admired writers who are honest and truthful with the reader. Hopefully, I will do his—even though I may not be seen in the best light at times. I no longer hide from myself.

Table of Contents

Acknowledgments — i

Introduction — iii

OVERCOMING SMUT — 1

WEST VIRGINIA — 2

Norfolk, Virginia — 36

The Long Trip — 39

NEW MEXICO — 45

CALIFORNIA — 77

My Step-Siblings — 93

Jackie* — 99

Bob and Brothers* — 103

NEW MEXICO AGAIN — 119

The Same Decision, Again — 134

College, You Say — 134

On to Hobbs — 159

Classroom Learning the Hard Way* — 213

The Rest of My Dog Tales — 218

Senior Olympics* — 227

Thelma and Louise go to West Virginia — 232

Dave and I Are Off to West Virginia — 239

My Politics — 241

#MeToo — 243

Hard Work Ahead — 244

Reading Coach / Board Member — 248

Final Thoughts — 249

OVERCOMING SMUT

The first setting of my life was in the mountains of West Virginia. As I write the state's name I feel a pang of pain and joy at the same time. John Denver's song, "Take Me Home, Country Roads," brings a nostalgic longing, and pride whenever I hear his beautiful words. That place where my life began held for me much pain—then again, much joy.

Fifty-two years ago, I was dealing with my life's challenges and circumstances in a vacuum. I was hiding from the world and myself, daily, every day. I just didn't know it. One day as I was walking through my small apartment in a small town in California, the "Oprah Winfrey Show" was on the television. She was speaking about the sexual abuse she had experienced at an early age. I was spellbound! Was it possible that someone as famous as she was had a background with a similar "secret as me?" That day I realized for the first time that I was not the only one who had been suffering in silence. This hidden, dirty, shameful, unspoken subject had only been spoken by me twice in my life. Both times that I spoke of the "secret" were to my young friends, and some trauma had just occurred. I was suffering, but not sure that anyone could tell. Not that I hid it well. People including family members just don't want to see this kind of abuse as they will have to deal with it. My mother simply ignored it. I finally accepted that fact when I was in my forties. Following Oprah via her television show over the years has brought so many victims to their own awareness concerning this issue. Thankfully, I was one of those who was helped by her reaching out to other victims of abuse during her television shows.

WEST VIRGINIA

My family would be classified as barely, low-functioning at best. As a matter of fact, all my family ties were lacking throughout my life. I was raised with three boys and one girl until I graduated from high school. They were younger than me, and we shared the same mother. I also have a half-brother and a half-sister who are older than me. I got most of my information about my mother by eavesdropping when she talked to her friend, Jean. At the age of fifteen my Aunt Nina would give me information which would make my world as I knew it then, implode!

Mom had at least nine children, and at least two that I know of were self-aborted. One infant was buried under the house in the holler. A clothes hanger was the instrument she used for aborting that one, not sure about the other one. Birth control was not an option for women back when I was born other than for douches. Once, while visiting my mother in the hospital, she made a comment while we were watching a commercial about condoms. Her arm trembled as she pointed to the screen. Barely being able to point, she said, "Sue, if they had condoms back when you were born you would not be here today." I totally understood what she meant.

Aunt Nina shared with me that Mom always had a low self-esteem growing up. She said Mom would bind her breasts so that she would look flat-chested, that way she wouldn't have to suffer comments and stares from men. As an adult, she wouldn't attend any of my school functions, even when I begged her to. She had dropped out of school in the eighth grade and had ran away and married her sweetheart at fifteen. When she ran away with Raymond, Grandpa told Mom to never darken his door again. I never heard why Grandpa hated Raymond so much. Mom had a picture of Raymond. She also had a picture of the two children she had with him. I remember looking at those pictures many times while I was growing up.

Many times, laws were interpreted in the remote parts of WV by a constable. I was told Mom was not notified of the court date of her child custody case. My aunt said the constable in that area was Mom's husband's friend. She explained that was the reason the father, Raymond, was given custody of the children. Another aunt told me that Raymond ran her off. As Mom was going down the road, he pointed a gun towards her and said if she looked back he would shoot her; she kept going.

Being without any means of support, Mom went to live with her aunt, Grandpa's sister, Bertha. That was in the 1940's, during the war. According to my aunt, Bertha ran a house of prostitution and Mom became one of her girls. There was a male teacher who visited Mom and she became pregnant with me. Mom was angry as he had said he was incapable of having kids. No one knew about any other offspring he had. Not sure he had any besides me. He was sixty-three when I was born. I was delivered on a riverbank my aunt told me. Maybe, Mom had another abortion planned.

During my childhood, Bertha would visit us sometimes. We were living with Mom's new man, Gabe. Bertha would always search me out and tell me that I would be rich someday. I never understood her interest in me, and she always seemed to be so secretive when she spoke to me; she would say confusing things to me. I never liked her—I would try not to be around her alone as she made me so uncomfortable.

Aunt Mina said my father had been quite wealthy. I was told he came to see me once and had brought many gifts for me. Aunt Nina said that Mom started cussin' at him and she threw all the presents over the bridge into the creek.

When I was around ten years old, Mom, all the kids and me were sitting in front of the Big House, a popular beer joint. We were waiting for Gabe, Mom's new man. He was inside with the local "whore," Mary Jug. I was sitting in the back seat directly behind Mom, who was behind the steering wheel. A man came around the car and addressed Mom, "Mary, is that her?" He was looking directly at me. Mom went into a roaring tirade! She used a barrage of curse words, and she attacked him hard. I was stunned listening to her. She had always been colorful with her 'cussin' within the family, but this was a stranger. Luckily, the man walked off just in time. Gabe came out a door with Mary Jug hanging on his arm, and the two were laughing for some reason. That was the first and last time I remember seeing my father.

Looking back, I'm sure every adult knew about my mother's circumstances and past. Mom didn't share them, but I'm sure Grandpa did. Most of the drinking coal miners would share many a lurid tale over their drinks after spending their shift deep underground. Most of the people Mom knew were mostly illiterate. Reading was definitely not a source of information for the coal dusted figures—that left gossip mostly for their entertainment and news source.

Mom could not take care of an infant, as she couldn't even take of herself, during the war. Also, I had whooping cough and Mom was worried I could die without a doctor's care, I was told. She took me to my grandparents' home and begged them to take me in and care for me. They said they would, but she still was not welcomed back to their house. My grandparents raised me until I was three or four. Their house was on top of a mountain called Dartmont. I remember Grandma was always working in her garden. There were other little houses around us and our neighbors were the "hunkies." Hunkies is an ethnic slur for Polish and Hungarian people. Every time anyone would say the word "hunkies" all the adults would snicker. I thought for a long time it was a curse word. "Hunkies" were made fun of I was told, because they stunk from their body odor. I guess their habit of eating garlic all the time was the reason for that odor.

Mom came and got me from my grandparents when she started living with her new man, Gabe. I do not remember any of the departure from my grandparents' house or meeting Mom's man. We were going to live in a little white house by a creek across from a little church.

The first memory I had living in that little white house was being afraid I was going to die. From Mom's cursing and thrashing I deduced I had started a fire. There was always a container of matches on the wall by the coal cooking stove, and I guess I got some matches and started a fire in an old cooking stove stored under the porch. Funny, she was the one beating me, and it was the first memory I had of any physical abuse... Surprisingly, Gabe was trying to get her to stop the blows while he continued laughing. Over the years, Mom would not beat me so much, but I had to be on guard constantly for her backhand.

Another early memory I had, took place in a Presbyterian Church. I was sitting on a wooden pew wearing a dress. I did not have any underwear or shoes on, and I smelled of my own urine. The dry crust was on my elbows and my ankles, because I rarely had a bath or even a good sponge scrubbing so, I knew the body was mine. The preacher, Reverend Brown was giving a sermon behind a pulpit. High over his shoulder was a stained-glass depiction of Jesus. That work of art was the most beautiful thing I had ever seen. Strange, that I was in a Presbyterian Church. Mom had a philosophy about churches. She said if you had money or a job other than mining, you went to the Presbyterian Church. If not, one would go to the Baptist Church. Guess I hadn't heard that before or had forgotten it, as I found myself in the Presbyterian Church that day.

She had a similar theory about politics, too. If you had money and a job other than mining you would vote Republican. Of course, the rest of us were Democrats. Another one of her assertions had to do with churches and unions. "Churches and unions are great unless a "poor" person needs either one of them, and then that person is just "shit out luck" she would say. Most all the miners belonged to the union. I never saw Mom in a church until she was in her late fifties.

Election day was an exciting time back when I was thirteen or fourteen. I don't remember a presidential election but there were elections for the sheriff, and other local positions. A man would come and pick Mom and Gabe up and take them to the polls. They were given directions on how to cast their vote. "Countdown four lines and put an 'X' in the box," the man would tell them. Mom could read and write some but Gabe was illiterate. After they voted, Mom would get a dollar, and Gabe would get a pint of whiskey. Everyone involved in that road trip that day came back in a good mood, just as if they had gotten away with something.

There was a large house behind the little white house that we lived in. The large house had steps that seemed really high to me. I just knew if I got on the highest step and jumped off I could actually fly. When I felt my ribs, I visualized wings just below my skin. I just knew the height would automatically bring them to the surface and I could soar to the clouds. It never happened, but I spent hours trying to prove nature wrong. Daydreams and my imagination were very important to me. I used both of them to escape my reality.

Mom was always angry with me. When the sun came up I was out walking through the coal camp. I remember walking door to door to see what was going on or looking for something to eat. Once, I came to my friend Alice's house, and her mother was frying chickens. The mother asked me if I wanted to eat some chicken with them. My reply was, "For breakfast?" Well that lady chewed me out right and left. She wanted to know who I thought I was, refusing an invitation which she had offered. After all, I was the little pest who was at her door every morning wanting food. You would think I would have learned to be more tactful or mannerly but it would take years for that to happen.

One other time we were visiting a family and the mother asked me if I wanted to eat with them. I asked, "What are you having?" Mom backhanded me so hard I hit the wall! Another time she slammed me so hard my ears had a ringing in them. The reason that time didn't have to do with food, though. The radio was playing music and I started dancing. She grabbed me by the hair and slapped me hard. "Don't let me ever catch you dancing to church music!" she yelled. Well, she never did catch me doing that again. It's like every time she saw me happy she had to squelch it, but I was one stubborn kid. Maybe, I would be diagnosed as oppositional defiant today, but I developed a lot of grit and defiance. Self-preservation, I guess.

I've since learned that I was disassociating a great deal during those years until I was in the sixth grade. My mind would let me escape the torment, but the time frame varied each episode. It was like a thick fog would cover me, and it would dull the pain I was living in. My memory had so many gaps; I can only remember instances of what happened. I was at a loss for any semblance of a timeline. The abuse I had to endure took so much energy, and I fought to survive all of it, all the time, it seemed like.

Abusing me was a source of sick entertainment for Gabe. I was a little bastard and I was reminded of that constantly, even by Mom. I guess that was their excuse for the torment I had to endure. There were sexual, emotional, and just any other source of cruelty Gabe could think of directed at me. One scene I remember happened regularly. It was the tradition of some miners to bring home a token of food from their lunch, which they kept the tidbits in their metal lunch buckets. When Gabe got home from the mines he would have us kids line up in a row. I was always last in line. Gabe would make a big deal of passing out a treat to everyone real slow. When it was my turn for a morsel, he would snicker and say, "No more, Smut," holding his coal covered hands in the air. I still don't understand why that hurt so much. I guess it was just plain mental cruelty to play on a kid. Not sure on reflection, which of the abuses was the most hurtful. It's hard to assign a degree of pain when you are a kid and you hurt all the time.

I don't remember first or second grade at all. Third grade had a lot of bright spots though. I think the reason for that, was the teacher. She was young, single, and she laughed a lot. For some reason, while I was in her class I had a fascination for gypsies. When I came to school dressed in a garb, she would just tease me in a gentle way. I was used to cruel taunting, and her teasing was in a loving way, and I enjoyed that. I'm sure someone must have told me about gypsies as we did not have a television or books in the house. Many days before school I would dress up in Mom's skirts, and I would tie a scarf around my head. Of course, hoop earrings hung at my ears, and I would be filled with confidence immediately. Those mornings I would go through Mom's purse and steal her change. Somehow, I knew gypsies were known for thievery, so I was playing the role to the hilt. I also remember stopping at the company store and buying everyone candy; I used the change I had taken from Mom's purse. I don't remember ever getting caught taking the money. Years later, I saw a documentary about gypsies, and it stated that gypsies traveled through the coal camps. Perhaps I met a band of gypsies, but I would only be speculating as I don't remember.

Another exciting thing happened to me in third grade; I got glasses! The optometrist told Mom that I couldn't recognize my best friend across the street. We were at the county seat of Boone County— there were streets by his office. So, I had a point of reference for his statement. What visions I saw all at once. Trees were no longer green globs. There were individual limbs supporting leaves of different sizes and colors. I was in a state of awe as my world had suddenly taken shape with vivid colors. It was as though, I could see my world for the first time and all my senses responded to the sights.

Remembering fourth-grade is totally a blank. I was shown a photograph once of my fourth-grade male teacher. At the sight of him I found myself shuddering. My gut actually tightened when I saw the image of that man for some reason. In fifth and sixth-grade I started using fantasies to feel empowered, I guess. I would visualize taking a butcher knife and sticking it in Gabe's gut, twisting it, and watching his entrails fall out one by one. The most gruesome visuals I made in my mind, the more I felt in control of my life. Hopelessness was my plight, and I struggled to find a whisper of hope somewhere.

I had the same teacher in fifth and sixth grade. Her name was Mrs. Eastep. I watched her walk down the railroad tracks every morning coming to teach us. Her husband ran a store and the post office. He was always trying to grab me. I kept my distance and was constantly looking for an opening so I could get away from him. Looking for an escape route became an obsession for me. I guess I was an easy target for some of the men living in those hollers. Mom was openly mean to me, and showed little interest in my whereabouts, and everyone knew it. There weren't any deterrents for them to watch their comments towards me, nor their actions. I've learned that sexual predators groom their targets, and I'm sure I let my guard down on more than one occasion. Once I found myself with an old man under a porch, and he had my hand on his penis. Not sure how that happened. Maybe he bribed me with candy, or he was just nice to me. I tried to get away from him, but he was moaning—he had a tight grip on me.

"Sandra Sue," I heard Mom's angry voice yelling for me. I knew I was getting my ass beat as she used my first and middle names! Being more afraid of Mom than this person gripping me, I twisted and somehow bolted away from him. Every morning that man was with a group of men sitting on the landing by the railroad tracks. Along with the other men he would hiss and yell out obscenities at me as I passed by. I just lowered my head, looked at my feet, and hurried down the railroad tracks. I needed to get to a safe distance where I couldn't hear their hisses and sneers anymore.

Once Gabe was drinking, whispering, and snickering to a father of one of my friends. They were on the back porch, and I did not like the sound of their snickering and cussing. The screen door opened and Gabe's drinking buddy was passing by where I was washing dishes. He rushed towards me from behind and grabbed my breasts. I grabbed a butcher knife and jabbed at him towards his crotch. "You son-of-a-bitch, you let me go or I will cut your balls off!" I screamed. He staggered backwards as he released his hold. I was so indignant and caught off guard by his actions! I was sure Gabe put the man up to fondling me, but I wasn't having any of that shit. It was bad enough I had to suffer this behavior in my own house. I for sure wasn't going to tolerate it from my friend's dad!

Mom wasn't home one time and Gabe chased me to the corner of the room. I looked him square in the eye and told him what I fantasized about many times before. "I'm going to catch you drunk or asleep and I'm going to stab you so many times your guts are going to fall out!" I threatened.

"Oh yeah, and who is going to feed you little bastards," he jeered. "Your mom ain't got any money."

I'm not sure where I got the nerve to stand up to him as I was just thirteen at that time. Maybe, I saw Mom fighting with him like that so much—I was just mimicking her. I did sense he was afraid of me when I had the knife though. I would keep that knife close by me all the time, even under my pillow when I went to bed. Many times, Mom would curse me out for wetting the bed. Waking up in a wet bed was normal for me until the seventh grade. I was just afraid of waking Gabe up, but Mom accused me of just being lazy. Once, when Mom and I were moving my bed around she saw the knife. She didn't say anything but I quickly told her I took it with me when I went to the outhouse at night because I was afraid of snakes.

Mom never held a job while we lived in WV, but that didn't mean she didn't work. She had at least two nervous breakdowns while we were in that state. She went to see a psychiatrist for a period of time. When she was leaving for an appointment Gabe would taunt her and say, "You going now, Crazy?" When there were thunder and lightning storms she would gather all the younger kids and huddle in a corner.

She would wail every time it thundered or the lightning struck! Gabe would call her "crazy" and make fun of her all during the time they were hunkered down in the corner.

Gabe accused Mom constantly of having an affair with his dad. His dad was called "Old Man Albert." One of the younger boys had a breathing problem—Mom fretted over him a lot. Gabe would say she was a whore, and she had been screwing Old Man Albert, while he was away working. He said there was no way he could have had a little bastard who looked and coughed like that little heathen in that crib. Later, Mom would call her own toddler, "Old Man Albert." I guess Mom was sleeping in the bed that she was accused of making for herself. That was Grandpa's prediction of the life she had chosen, when she was fifteen and ran away with Raymond.

One day, Mrs. Eastep, my fifth-grade teacher, asked me to stay in at recess so she could speak to me. I was in trouble a lot that year, and I thought she wanted to talk to me about a fight I had been in. As she entered the room she asked me if I knew my sister, Karen. I told her Mom talked about her, but I never knew her. She told me that Karen was going to our little school now. I was elated. Having an older sister was very exciting for me. We could share secrets, laugh, and giggle together and that would be fun.

It was easy to find a new girl on the playground as I knew everyone and there were only eighty students in the whole school. I went up to Karen and told her who I was. We hugged and held hands everyday when we saw one each other. She was always asking about Mom, and she wanted to know everything about her. I'm sure I did not tell Karen how mean Mom was, as I had not come to terms with that truth myself.

Karen wanted me to go home and ask Mom if she could come and visit. Well, I knew that was not going to be an easy matter. When I asked, Mom went in a tirade and started cursing and swearing which was her usual response to anything she couldn't handle. Of course, the answer was in effect, "Hell no!" Later when my aunt told me bits of my Mom's life she had said Mom cried herself to sleep every night for a long time because she had lost her kids. Not sure how Mom cut out those feelings and emotions for her kids. I think it was self-preservation. Probably, she thought she deserved a life of hell. Maybe, it was because she was regularly beaten when Gabe came home drunk. Whatever the reason it had made her mean.

One day I went to school and Karen wasn't waiting for me by the bridge. Her dad had been in the hospital and she had been staying with his relatives. For a couple weeks I had a sister older than me, a friend. I would never see her again but I thought of her many times over my lifetime.

I was usually around when Gabe was on a drunken tear. I had to endure the same treatment as Mom. Once, he made me get out of bed, and he immediately started taunting me. Not sure what I said, but rarely was I at a loss for words. He hit me with his fist as I stood before him, and I was knocked over a gas floor heater. I caught myself bent over backwards with my hand for support from the wall. I've wondered many times if I could have survived intact if I hadn't been such a tomboy. I had quick reflexes. I could outrun most of the boys. I saw what kind of life Mom had and I shared her hell for years. I did not want a life like hers, so I started deciding what I did not want in life. That seemed much easier than having dreams. Besides, I thought dreams would be denied to someone like me anyway.

Mom had a friend, Jean, and she was a nurse for the doctor who tended the coal miners' families. She was the only educated woman I knew besides the teachers. She had a hearty laugh, and Mom was happy when she was around. Her family included a husband, John, and five kids; four boys and a girl. The girl, Kathryn, was born with special needs, physically and mentally. I never saw Jean beat any of her kids but John did, constantly. He always wore a huge, thick belt with a monstrous, metal buckle. He would go to the back porch then whistle for those boys when he was ready to leave, and they had better get to him immediately. If they were not fast enough, he would take the belt and start giving the stragglers lashes as if he was showing off for anyone who was watching his cruelty. Those boys were tough, and they were afraid of their dad; Jean never seemed to be concerned with the beatings. I always wondered about that.

Overcoming Smut

The Brooks' family lived in a coal camp called Bricktown. When we started visiting them Mom did not have a driver's license. She had me go to the top of the mountain and see if the constable was home. If he was home, Mom would load us kids up and off we would go. She wouldn't drive around while the constable was on the hardtop road driving. He knew all the drivers who had a license in those hollers. If I saw his vehicle parked at his house I would rush down the mountain to let Mom know it was safe to drive. Gabe was at work while we did that. Besides, he hated John. Truth be known though, he hated all the people Mom knew or liked.

Tommy was the second oldest boy of Jean and John's. We became friends and we decided we were going to run away. The reason we had for that plan was that we both were beaten and mistreated constantly. We made our plans. We stashed food, blankets, pans, and matches. We had located a cave in some rocks that were atop one of the mountain ridges. After we had made the plan to run away then "when" became the problem. When I would decide to run away, it seemed Tommy would not agree. Then he would decide to run, and I would argue that things were going pretty well for me at that time. So, we kept putting it off. The truth was that we were both two scared kids. Soon, the summer was over, and we were still in our abusive homes, and wishing we had taken the risk and had run away during the past summer.

One day after church I decided to go to our hideout, and it was in the dead of winter. I had a dress on with slippers on my feet. Snow covered the ground and briar bushes were hidden below the snow. It was a hard climb to get to the place that had been so glamorous during the summer. While walking on the top of the ridge towards the cave, I looked down and what I saw was a shock! There were big tracks of a cat, and they went right to and into our cave! I had an eerie feeling that eyes were watching me. I bounded down that mountain as fast as I could. I fell in briars and my dress and coat were ripped—soon I was covered in blood. My legs were bleeding all over. Making it safely to the house I decided running away to the mountains may have not been a great idea after all, for sure not in the middle of winter.

Gabe, Mom's significant other, had a hard life growing up. He dropped out of school in third grade to go to work in the coal mines. He couldn't read nor write. He used a "X" when he signed any papers. He couldn't get a driver's license, nor fill out the paperwork to apply for a job. Mom had to go with him and do the talking and writing for him during interviews. His mother had died when he was young, and his father was known to have been very mean and cruel. Gabe had been drafted and was stationed overseas in Korea. Mom said every time he got a leave, he would go AWOL. They would have to drag him out of those mountains and take him back to somewhere, to a place he couldn't even name.

Gabe had a brother and a sister who left White Oak when they got older—they married each other and lived in Ohio. Gabe's favorite sister came to visit us once. Her husband carried me around while fondling me right in front of Mom. Ralph was Gabe's younger brother and he visited us a lot. He had a woman, Betty, but I'm sure they never married. They had three kids, two boys and a girl. He beat all of them constantly. I never remember him ever trying to touch me sexually, though. When I was sixteen Mom got a letter from someone and the letter said that he had tried to rape his nephew. After many years of these assaults, the boy fought back and killed Ralph right in the middle of the road! The boy was imprisoned a time after that, but later released.

There was another sister and she was the mother of the nephew who was the target of Ralph's abuse. She had the cleanest house of anyone we ever visited. Her daughter was confined to a wheelchair for years. Not sure what her condition was, but we called her a "hunchback." Her mother contracted tuberculosis and she went to a sanitarium for long periods of time. When she came home for a visit everything she had used, worn, or had eaten from, had to be burned. The mother died when we moved away. Once, we went to visit them and the girl was out of the wheelchair, wearing shorts and a cigarette was dangling from her fingers. I cringed when she called her father "Honey". Questionably, I looked at Mom. She only shrugged her shoulders and turned towards the door. It was as though she was saying what could anyone do anyway.

Jean and John Brooks moved their family to a holler after they had lived in the coal camp of Bricktown. I just remember visiting them in the holler once. Mom decided we should move to the Day Hollow after they moved to New Mexico. There was a house, a smokehouse, a chicken house, a dilapidated barn on the property and of course, the outhouse, which was across the creek. Not sure of the acreage but mountains surrounded the place on three sides. Eventually, I learned about every tree-bearing fruit tree, and where the coal mines were on the sides of the mountains. I would enter those mines and cool off in the water pools in the mines, during the heat of the day. There were wild strawberry patches, mulberries, walnut and pawpaw trees, and I learned where they all were. Of course, there were poison ivy vines and I would get a bad case of the itch from those vines, every year. I would wake myself every night having a fit from the itching. From the scratching I would be bloody all over. Gradually, I would get comfortable somehow or get plain exhausted, and then go back to sleep. The worst place to get the poison ivy was between my fingers and toes, but anywhere on my body was miserable.

When I went exploring in the mountains I always had my dog. I think I named three dogs that I owned "Lassie." Dogs were my total confidants and comfort, the many times I had been abused. They were my total means for affection, usually. I sure didn't get any attention from my family, well the right kind anyway. I had one dog which would go "mad" occasionally. Gabe wanted to put a bullet in his head, but because the dog had seizures and wasn't mean, I guess Mom pleaded my case. Once when my dog was having a spell, Mom called me. I had watched him many times just walk off a ten-foot porch. He would foam at the mouth, as his body was in the process of having seizures. I would hold him until his body quit jerking, and I could see that his eyes had gradually cleared. I had never heard the word veterinarian before. We kids were never afforded medical care so it was unheard of, maybe unthought of, to get care for an animal, in my family, anyway.

Once, there were two puppies to give away. Mom said I could have one, but the other one had to go. One was a beautiful female and the other one looked like a typical black and white, male coon dog. Gabe kept his coon dogs chained up and they were usually mean and tried to bite us kids when we got too close to them. I·chose the puppy which looked like a coon dog because I thought it would be easier for someone to love an attractive dog. I am still pleased with myself for making that decision, not sure where I got the lesson that attractive things were easier to love. It was not unusual for Gabe to kill kittens by drowning them. He shot the dogs. He would tell us kids about the acts of the killings, and as he did, he would laugh like he was insane. I think he wanted to scare us, but mainly, he wanted to terrify me.

One morning I woke up and decided I would track down the source of the creek which ran past our house. With a cold biscuit spread with blackberry jelly, Lassie and I proceeded to climb the mountain which laid before us. That day was so special to me. To say it was beautiful would not begin to speak of its incredible loveliness and splendor. Being barefoot just added to the scene for my sense of touch. Birds were singing just for me; I heard them as if a chorus was performing. Eventually, I came to flat, long rocks which were spread across the creek bed, just before there was another steep incline. The rocks were covered with moss, and the feel of the coolness and the softness of the natural lush greenery on my bare feet was such a pleasure I will never forget. A spring was gushing out the side of the mountain and it was the source of the wide creek which ran by our house. Looking ahead I saw the sun coming through the trees, and the sun seemed to project a light appearing like dancing stars which were being reflected in the water mimicking diamonds. "God is that you?" I talked to God a lot in those days. If I ever had a religious feeling it was on that day. I've read when you are in so much pain that you can truly have the highest joy which comes opposite of the pain one is suffering. Maybe, it was a message from the Creator that I can handle the bad with a hint of the good, occasionally, anyway.

American Bandstand became more important to my friends and me than church eventually. Two sisters, their brother and I would take turns meeting at each other's houses. We would watch American Bandstand every weekday and then practice new steps to the dances we watched on the show. We got really good at making fudge from the recipe on the cocoa can. We would make fudge for our younger siblings so they would leave us alone while we did the jitterbug, the twist and the waltz. Twice we climbed across two mountains to go to a sock hop. Now that was a special occasion for all of us.

In fifth grade the school had a talent show. I danced with a little chubby guy, and boy, could he dance. I had spent hours dancing with a bedpost while watching the dancers on American Bandstand. On the day of the contest Jerry Lee Lewis sang as we did the Jitterbug to Great Balls of Fire! We won first place, and we were so proud of our prize, five new pencils. When the kids clapped and encouraged us with cat calls it was as if something had clicked in my brain. I craved attention, and this was the best kind I had had so far. I wanted more.

I kept hearing about this guy, Elvis, from the older girls in school. I don't exactly remember how my crush on him evolved...but it certainly did. I use to wonder if he ever said the word "Sue." Not sure of the movie, but I heard him say the word "Susie," and so that was close enough for me. In eighth grade I remember getting in a shouting match with a couple of seventh grade girls. They were saying Ricky Nelson was a better singer than Elvis, and I blew my top! How-in-the-world could they think such a thing? I was ready to fist fight them over their poor judgment, but eventually we all cooled off, called a truce of sorts, and continued to walk to school together.

We got a black and white television when we lived in the holler. One evening I rushed home from playing to watch Elvis on the Ed Sullivan Show. Settling in on the couch I looked behind me, and I saw Mom standing in the doorway—she was actually smiling. At that moment in time we shared a smile, and a giggle or two, while watching Elvis on television. I guess it was two females appreciating one handsome man, who could sing and writhe on a stage. Whatever it was I know it was a great memory for me.

Mr. Elkins was the name of our principal at Brush Creek School. He was also the seventh and eighth grade teacher. I had talked to him when I was in fourth grade. I had been taken to him because I had passed out. I hadn't eaten in a couple of days, and I was famished. Mr. Elkins took me to the kitchen and I was given potato soup and a peanut butter sandwich by the cook, Mrs. Kinder. She started asking me questions like what I had for breakfast, and what time was my bedtime. I was very suspicious of all the questions that she wanted answered. Kids might know they are living in hell, but to them it is better than the unknown "hell" someplace else. Mom had told us we were not to tell anyone anything, anytime, as it was our own "dirty laundry," and it was no one else's business. It would take me years to overcome this philosophy or the BS she had laid out for us.

When I entered seventh-grade Mrs. Kinder offered me a job. I was to come to the kitchen early, eat my lunch, and wash dishes for the eighty students who had eaten. She would pay me a dollar a week...I was excited but I had a problem with my new found-employment, as I didn't want to miss any road trips going to other schools and playing against the girls there in volleyball... I loved that game! Mr. Elkins would coach us, and we were taught many strategies and drills while he pushed us hard; we loved it. I told Mrs. Kinder that if I worked in the kitchen for her I would miss the trips with Mr. Elkins. It was an all-day trip and I couldn't see how I could do both—work and play volleyball. Mrs. Kinder thought for a while and said she would get someone to step in for me on those days, and she did. She sure took an interest in me, and I will never forget her for her kindness.

I missed a lot of math in my seventh and eighth grades. I kept leaving the classroom earlier and earlier to get out of doing the math. I hated washing dishes, but I hated math more! I felt that I missed so much in my foundation of math due to my home life that I couldn't seem to get caught up. Mr. Elkins told me that he would double promote me, but I was so weak in math that he didn't think that was a good idea. I was more disappointed that a boy I had a crush on had went to a higher grade. He got double promoted. Since he was gone though, I became the smartest student in our class. Truthfully, I was rather proud of my new status. The first compliment I remember which I took to heart, was from Mr. Elkins. Out of the blue one day, he said, "Sue, I want you and Billy May to get married." Confused, I stared at him and I asked him why. He said, "You're both smart and you could send your smart kids to school here, and I could teach them."

Mr. Elkins became a focus of my life. He spent hours on the volleyball court with the girls and one small boy, Marshall. That boy loved volleyball as much as we did. He would throw himself at the ball, then dive head first in a defensive mode that was a sight to see. We readily accepted him there, and he would wait so patiently until Mr. Elkins would tell him to enter the game.

When I was coached in the drills which were shown to us I was a bit unorthodox in my movements. During that time, I learned to contort my body so I could complete the drills he wanted us to do. It was sort of compensating for being shorter than the other girls and being comfortable with my body in space is the best I can describe it.

The girls' volleyball team won county championship at least once, but I think it was twice for Boone County. We became quite cocky and full of ourselves after claiming our trophy. Mr. Elkins had a lesson for us; "It's easier to be a good loser than a good winner," he lectured us one day. He meant that we were getting the "big head" and becoming braggarts and show-offs. I've reminded myself of his words many times. I became disillusioned with several of my friends over the years who had not learned this little life's lesson. I definitely saw many female athletes turn into obnoxious prima donnas when they were on a winning streak. I'm glad I had a heads-up warning about not being one of those.

There was a lot of criticism at home for my new passions; volleyball, and academics at school. School was my haven and I paid attention! Mr. Elkins was a storyteller. He would rear back in his chair with his feet propped on his desk and he gave me visions I could not discern—like a banana split. I had never seen a banana in my life, and how could someone split one? State and county lines were something else I could not visualize. The nearest vision I came up with was an airplane pouring flour down to the ground in a line for the state and county lines. That was my explanation for boundaries, well, to myself anyway.

Another life lesson I learned was given to me from Mr. Elkins during a classroom session. He was giving a test and he gave the directive "no talking" or we would be given a zero. Not sure why I answered someone who was asking me something...and being me, I just blurted out something. Mr. Elkins gave me "the look" and my knees buckled. I fretted over a week trying to decide if he would follow through with his threat. I was the top student and he liked me, surely, he would forget to give me a zero. Well, the report card came and I had the dreaded "U" that I had so feared. The "U" stood for Unsatisfactory. Finally, I rationalized that if he hadn't given me that grade I would have been more disappointed. This was the first time I saw that someone kept their word and followed through with a discipline that was fair. I was even thankful for that lesson.

Perhaps the most meaningful lecture our teacher gave us was to be proud of who we were. He explained that people would put us down and talk about us because West Virginians were said to be "dumb hillbillies." He assured us that no one was any better than we were, and we could do anything we wanted to do. I took that philosophy to heart many times over my lifetime. I have succeeded in many attempts in different areas of my life. I know I need to give Mr. Elkins much credit for that personal self-esteem insight.

There were going to be tryouts for a cheerleading position in a couple weeks. The five who held the position already were considered to be the most popular girls... well, by me anyway. I wanted to be a cheerleader so bad that I was wound up tighter than a rubber band waiting for the day of the tryouts. I begged Mom to come and watch the tryouts, but she told me she didn't want anyone staring at her.

The day finally arrived; I wanted to look my best. Can cans were very popular at that time. Can cans were slips or petticoats which were heavily starched, and they would make our dresses or skirts flare out. The further they stuck out, the better we thought we looked. I had borrowed a couple extra can cans from my friend who went to high school. I took a shoestring and tied the stiff fabric of the can cans around my waist. I was ready! I no longer remember the words to the cheer, but I remember feeling very confident. Finishing the cheer from a kneeling position and listening to the applause I was elated, but only for a split second. Somehow the strings had loosened from my waist, and all the can cans were lying at my feet. Everyone on the hill watching the tryouts began laughing. I was humiliated! I ran to the school and hid in a stall in the bathroom kicking anything that my foot could reach. I didn't want to be a damn cheerleader anyway!

I heard the door close and heard my name, "Sue?" It was Lucy, the sweetest girl in the school. "Mr. Elkins sent me to tell you that you are now a cheerleader."

I practically fainted! I got the position even with all the laughter from the hill. I guess Mr. Elkins knew how hard I worked and how badly I wanted the position. Truthfully, I didn't care why he gave me a break—I was just happy he did.

The cheerleaders got to go to games and traveling twenty miles was a big deal for me. I had also earned the chance to enter the Boone County Spelling Bee. My life was looking up. On one of my trips a boy came over and said he was my cousin. He was my aunt's boy whom she had given custody to the boy's father. His mother would be the one who would give me many pieces to the puzzle that made up my life so far.

One of my most painful memories was listening to the taunts and threats of Mom and Gabe one day. There was a girl we knew and her name was Smut; she was from a dirt-poor family. Smut had been sold to an old man by her parents. The reason being it was said, was because the old man had a social security check coming in monthly. Smut's parents benefited from the old man's charity every once in a while so, there was an agreement made. That check was the only income for the older miners. One day while visiting next door, I heard Smut's little brothers and sisters yelling and screeching excitedly because Smut was coming to visit them with her with her old benefactor. She had a wooden container which contained ice cream packed in dry ice. No one I knew had a freezer nor a refrigerator at that time. The ice cream was bought at the dago store down the mountain, and Smut had rushed it to her siblings before it had melted. We only had ice cream on the 4th of July in our house. I stared at those small, unbathed bodies crawling on the dirt floor each with a spoon. Clutching their spoons, they were fighting and wrestling for another taste of that sweet concoction. It was funny and sad at the same time but I was mesmerized watching them.

Mom and Gabe told me they were going to sell me to an old man someday! Mom called me 'Smut' all the time. Guess she had considered that scheme in her imagination for me. Many a night I would lay awake worrying if I was going to be sold. I was told as an adult, Smut, had several kids but she gave all of them away for someone else to raise. Sad, that some parents in those mountains held the thought that kids were so dispensable. Now I know that the mountains are not the only place which have people who share that same value system for kids. I have had dealings with foster care in two other states, and there were many reasons for parents to put their kids out of their sight. Usually, finances or the lack of them figured into the equation somehow.

Mom was a name caller for sure. She was actually trying to make herself appear a bit "uppity" I guess. She would somehow see us better than another family. We were all white, but she would look for an excuse to look down on other people. The reasons I remember were that they were lazy or filthy. Human nature seems to want us to elevate ourselves over others. Sometimes it's an obvious reason such as skin color but if that is not evident, than people will make up other reasons like Mom. She would usually assign us—the kids' names of a particular family. I remember being called 'Marlene' interchangeably with Smut. Marlene was from a family that Mom considered to be "filthy trash." Marlene was killed by her husband as an adult I later found out from a friend. Mom called all of us, her kids, "little bastards" a lot—I will find out that that nickname was true for all five of us.

Carol was my friend and she had two brothers, Cecil and Greg. Cecil, the one with thick glasses was a nice guy. Greg, his brother was always making lewd remarks towards me and he was always trying to touch my breasts or pat me on the rear. I always wondered if they did the same thing to Carol. Once when I had been sexually abused by Gabe I ran to Carol and asked her to take a walk with me up the mountain. When we had gone a safe distance, I blurted out what Gabe had done to me. She laughed. I was so hurt and ashamed! I started screaming in my hands. Carol was the closest friend I had, and if she laughed what would others do? Of course, as an adult I know I overwhelmed her as she was just a kid herself. Maybe, I felt that those things were being done to her, and she would understand. Later in my life, she wrote me and then called me, and wanted to know if I was okay. She said she remembered what I told her that day on the mountain. I told her I remembered that day too. I told her I remembered her laughing, and that I began screaming. She denied that she laughed. Maybe, she didn't, perhaps that was just what I expected her to do. Anyway, I was touched that she reached out to me after all those years. I assured her I was okay.

Mom had some strange hobbies. I was her designated accomplice, until I got old enough to babysit and stay home. She liked to go to graveyards and collect the artificial flowers which were displayed on the graves. Of course, I had to be on the lookout for her. I was to keep watch—then alert her if anyone was driving around the curve. Guess her conscience bothered her some as she didn't want anyone to see her collecting the floral arrangements from the graves.

Another outing she enjoyed was going to the Danville dump. The younger kids would hit that dump running to see if they could find some worthwhile trash to play with. I hated going to the dump! I was afraid someone would see me there in that awful stinking place. The dump was always smoking from the fires which had been set by the town to burn the combustible trash. The damp, wet garbage had a clinging, putrid, smoky smell and it would seem to get in our pores and clothes. One day I met a girl, a teenager who lived right by the dump. She had a lean-to shelter, and she got most of her food from the trash people threw away. In a strange way, I identified with her. I thought this could me maybe, if I didn't want to live with an old man. For some reason she never said a word. I talked to her all the time. Not sure if she even understood me but she smiled a lot. I liked her company, maybe because she was a good listener. I never knew whatever happened to her and I often wondered about her.

Eventually, Mom used me for a built-in babysitter. I would much rather oversee the kids than go with her to her choices of entertainment. Cemeteries, garbage dumps, blackberry patches, where snakes were always feasting on the sweets were not on top of my list for enjoyments.

I went a time or two, sangin' with Mom and Grandma. We would go in the mountains and look for ginseng. Ginseng was a prized root which the people sold for extra money. It was used by some, for a sore throat. They would chew on the root and it would relieve the rawness of the throat. It was used for medicinal purposes by the hunters of the roots and they would sell the rest. China bought a lot of ginseng from West Virginians who went hunting for it. I was told China still buys it from the state.

When I was in sixth grade, there was a girl who bullied me after school. She was a big boned, red-headed girl with a cruel laugh. She would be waiting for me by the creek, and I was afraid of her—I always felt to be at her mercy! After she hit, kicked and mauled me I would end up with my clothes wet and torn, because she threw me in the creek when she was through with me. One day, Mom asked me about my clothes, and I broke down and told her that Judy Workman was beating me up after school. Well, Mom told me if I didn't stand up to that red-headed bitch, I would get the beating of my life. I was familiar with Mom's beatings so the decision in what to do was not that difficult. The next day I told Judy if she touched me again I would beat the hell out of her. I guess she was convinced I would, too. We became friends later when we started playing volleyball. That experience convinced me of two things. First, I was more scared of Mom than anyone else in the world! Second, stand up for myself when it comes to bullies. Life's lessons 101.

In every picture I have seen of myself I had a youngster on my hip. All of my younger siblings have told me stories about my harsh discipline, but I really can't recall. The story they told most often was me sending them to a corner for a punishment. I loved playing school. I do know I had four students built right in the house, so I made good use of them.

I remember seeing Dora and Fred being born at home in Mom's big bed. When her labor started, she would send me to go get the doctor. I would head out the door running. I had to cross a couple of mountains to get to the doctor's office. He would get his bag, and I could watch him from the top of a mountain as he drove the winding road and turn into the holler. I would beat him getting to the house every time to get back to Mom and tell her he was on his way. She had me on a riverbank, and the youngest boy was born in the hospital, but the other three kids were born at home.

Before she went in the hospital to have her last baby she got us a babysitter who was supposed to cook for us, also. The girl had the same first and last name as me. She was a teenager at the age of fifteen or thereabouts. Once, I walked into Mom's room to get something, and Gabe had the girl pinned in a corner, and was grabbing at her. He laughed and let her go when he saw me, and I saw the relief flood over her face. Not long after that she left and went home.

When Mom got home she was furious after discovering that Sue had left. She yelled for me and told me to get my ass out to the road, catch the school bus, and go to Sue's house. I was to tell Sue that Mom had paid her, and she was a thief for keeping the money and not taking care of her kids. I didn't know what to say, but I knew the reason Sue left, but there was no way I was going to tell Mom. Getting off that bus and walking to the broken-down door and knocking on it, was one of the hardest things I had ever done in my young life. Sue and her mom were the only two living in the shack. I guess they were having dinner. In each plate was one over easy fried egg and nothing else. Sue's mom was very firm in telling me that my daddy was grabbing Sue constantly and Sue was afraid of him. I knew the feeling, and I knew it was true. Sue's Mom handed me some money and told me she kept some as Sue deserved something for the anguish she had been through. I did not argue—I accepted her words as factual as I knew them to be true.

When I drug myself up that holler to relay all that information to Mom, I knew it was going to be hard on Mom and us kids, too, and it was. Mom stayed in the outhouse for hours and wailed, screamed obscenities, and moaned. She did that for three days. I tended the baby and took care of the other three kids. They were no trouble during that time as we all recognized pain and were used to it. Gabe worked on his old car and muttered, "Crazy bitch," occasionally and that was the only words I heard him say.

Mom had another friend and her name was Janet. We would visit her at Rumble. Janet had a daughter, Brytha and was I ever jealous of her. She was a knock-out! She was very aware of how good looking she was, too. I remember walking down the hardtop road with her and some boys one day, and the boys were enthralled with Brytha. She talked about her tits and her ass like the subjects were something she knew about and she was proud of them. I had never heard that kind of talk before from a girl.

Brytha and Janet really liked Mom and the feeling was mutual. Mom would sit at their table with a cigarette dangling from her fingers telling some of the funniest stories I ever heard. Janet and Brytha would laugh in that earthy way that only females can. While they were laughing they would be begging Mom to tell another story. I remember thinking Mom never told me stories. The only time she even talked to me was when she was cussing me out for something I had done or something I hadn't done. I became aware of Mom's storytelling talent when she was talking to them and I saw how happy she was doing it.

Brytha died when she was a teenager and I never found out the reason. I'm sure Janet was devastated over that sad time in her life. That mother and daughter sure were close—I was envious.

When it was time for school in the fall, we would get a pair of new shoes. Mom would take an old Sears catalog tear out a page and trace around one foot. She would then send it off to Sears, and we would get our new shoes in the mail. I usually got saddle loafers and I hated them, as they lasted until summer every year! Since we only got the one pair, we had to go barefoot the rest of the year. During the hot days called "dog days" we would swing from the grapevines. Later we walked through the places in the creek which still held water to cool ourselves off. Sometimes when I got out I had the strangest feeling on my legs. Leeches would have themselves wrapped around my legs and they would be sucking blood from my legs. I had learned to sit down and cut them in two pieces, before they would let go of my skin,

Of course, we had an outhouse and we would walk on the ground where the old outhouses had stood before. When the waste would get even to the ground the men would knock the building over and cover the waste with dirt. I remember having ringworms several times during those years. While sitting on the wooden toilet those worms would just hang out of my rectum. It was really scary and I would scream and grab a Sears catalog page and pull them out...utterly disgusting. I don't remember Mom treating us for them, but I don't remember having those parasites after we left the holler.

We eventually got evicted from the house in the holler. We could no longer afford the twenty dollars a month for the rent. Gabe wasn't working at the time. Mom had spotted a house up the road in a bottom by a coal mine. Mom went to the beer joint to use the telephone and

called about that place. The coal company didn't even know there was a house on their property. They said they didn't have a problem with us moving in the house and they told us not to worry about paying any rent. Mom was told to just keep an eye on the place by the coal company. We lived there my seventh and eighth years of school.

We had all of our furniture repossessed two different times. The mines were union, and they were told to "strike" until their demands were met. The poor mining families had to scrape by the best way they could, while the big union guys still had money rolling in. Anyway, this was Mom's version of our condition. And I guess it proved Mom right about unions back then. They weren't concerned with the workers at all, and they didn't give a damn how much the poor people were hurt. When the company store came and got our possessions Mom sat in a corner and wailed with the little kids huddled close to her. All the kids looked confused I remember. They were trying to figure out what was going on. Truthfully, I was too.

We raised chickens and hogs. Of course, the men would hunt wild game. A couple of times I got up from bed and would look under a tub and an opossum would be staring back at me. They sure were scary. After looking at them in the face I literally peed on myself a time or two. Well, that saved me a trip going to the outhouse anyway. I spent many nights up pulling my baby teeth and arguing with myself whether I was going to look under the tub or not. Maybe, I was getting a thrill of getting scared like people do at scary movies. Squirrels and rabbits were another source of meat. I hated them all! Anything wild I could not gag down. Not sure where I got that aversion. We didn't have any milk cows, but my friend had fresh milk and butter all the time—I loved visiting her.

I was glad when we moved from the holler. Gabe got away with abusing me and beating Mom on a regular basis in the holler. It was so remote and far from the main road. There was no one to stop him or to hear our yells there. Once I remember Mom had chased him around the house while shooting at him. Not sure what he had done that had her so angry. I remember thinking that I was really disappointed when she missed him with every shot.

Mom sewed all our clothes, and she used feed sacks for the fabric. She bought them from a lady who raised chickens. When the lady sold all the feed in the sacks she would turn around and sell the sacks to women for fabric. Mom gave me some money one evening and told me to go to the lady's house and buy some feed sacks. For some reason the lady did not have that many, so I had quite a bit of money left over. So, I stopped at the beer joint and bought some candy. I must have been gone for a long time as it was getting dark. As I was going home Mom and the kids were in the Ford Model A coming to find me. When she asked me for the rest of the change, I lied. I told her that I must have lost it. Not sure why she didn't believe me, but she didn't. That was the night I thought I was going to die! She started beating, slapping, kicking, and calling me names. She said she was going to go get a butcher knife and cut my heart out! I started begging her not to get the knife, but she was hell bent on doing so, or so I believed. Lonnie, the oldest boy was so upset and he must have believed her, too. All the kids were crying and screaming as he crawled out of the car. He begged Mom not to hurt me anymore, and finally she relented, and we all got in the car and went home. I still shudder from the memories of that night. Mom had a nervous breakdown right after that.

"She goes to bed with the chickens and gets up at the crack of dawn!" I heard Mom say many times about me. If I got up early no one would be yelling at me or slapping me around—a safe time. House cleaning was something I enjoyed, but many a morning I was cursed and accused of doing something. Usually, Mom accused me of trying to kill everyone from the fumes of the polish I used on the furniture. When I was being criticized or swung at by Gabe I would head for the hills because I knew it would just get worse. There, I would fantasize about finding a white stallion, taming him, and make my escape from the demeaning treatment I was suffering. The only horses I had ever seen were plow horses used for plowing people's gardens in the spring. Horses fascinated me, so in my mind I turned a plow horse into a mythical, white stallion. I guess I got the white stallion idea from school.

Usually I was alone, but somehow, I picked up a version of "God" from church. I would spend most mornings talking to him and asking him to prove to me that he was real. I would ask him to shake a limb of a tree for instance. Then if I blinked I just knew he shook the tree while I blinked. I would play this game with "God" day in and day out while sitting on the back porch.

Going to church was something I did every week. I went alone and it was not always a good experience, but not always bad one, either. Other than school it was the only organized place to socialize. There were three churches within walking distance from where I lived. One church I went to for a short time was because of a boy. He would ride the school bus to a friend's house and attend the church down the hill from the Eastep store. He would send a note via a friend to tell me if he was coming to church that night. There was a teenager who went to that church we called Joey Boy. Joey Boy had a high-pitched voice and he was the brunt of much ridicule and cruel teasing. One night the boy who I sat in church with and several other bigger boys had coaxed Joey Boy to go behind the church with them. The group had pulled Joey's pants down and they reported Joey had a girl's and boy's sex organ. My boyfriend told me what they did. I proceeded to break up with him that night. There was no reason I could see for anyone to be so cruel.

Reverend Brown from the Presbyterian Church came to visit one day; that was a rare oddity as I was the only one who attended church at that time. The only visitors we ever had were the Brooks family and Gabe's drinking buddies. Not sure how it was decided but Reverend Brown had come to ask Mom if I could go to the church camp which the church sponsored. It cost twelve dollars and he said the church would cover the cost of camp for me since I attended the church regularly. Otherwise, I'm sure I would not have been allowed to go because of the expense. After I was given permission to go, I panicked! I had a problem and not sure what to do about it. One of the older girls said there were showers at the camp. I did not know what that was, exactly, as we never had indoor plumbing and I had never seen a shower before. Once I spent the night with a great-aunt and she had a bathtub indoors. I was afraid of using the bathtub there though. Once during a discussion in the classroom, Mr. Elkins told us about a radio falling in the bathtub and the person bathing got electrocuted! After investigating and assuring myself that there were no radios in the bathroom I took a bath, and it was one great experience!

Another girl told me we all had to take our clothes off and stand under water which came from the ceiling. The problem; I had hair growing in my groin area and I was terrified that someone would see it! What would my friends think? So, the day before I left for camp I shaved all the hair off the best I could. Finally, the time had come to enter the shower naked! Having my back turned from the other girls I finally peeked at the nude bodies closest to me. What a relief! All had hair down there, well, except for me. Well, at a distance none could be seen anyway.

While I was at camp I started my period even though I did not know what that was or ever heard the word before. This blood was coming from my body and I thought I was ill or pregnant. I remember seeing all the blood when Mom delivered her babies. In desperation, I finally confided to Carol and she told me that I had my 'monthly.' She said she would loan me her extra underwear and she recruited the other girls to do the same. When the panties were so wet and soiled, I threw them on a high shelf in the closet. The girls told me I needed to tell Mom about my worry when I got home, so she could tell me what to do. I dreaded to tell Mom anything, but this was one difficult problem I couldn't solve myself. After I told Mom about my dilemma, she turned, left the room without a word. She eventually returned and handed me an old diaper and a sanitary belt. Without another word, she left me to figure out the contraption by myself. First and last 'sex education' talk I had with my mother.

The only attention or compliments I got usually came from people other than my immediate family. My grandma was not affectionate either, and for sure my grandpa wasn't. We kids loved to visit our grandparents as they had a television. We had a problem though. Just as we became engrossed in a program Grandpa would rise from his chair and flip the television off. He had a smirk on his face like he enjoyed taking this small pleasure from us just for plain meanness. Mom asked me a time or two if he turned the television off while we were watching it, and I would nod my head yes. I knew that she knew that was an age-old practice for him.

Grandma was a stern and staunch woman. Her tone seemed to call one "to attention." Usually, her tone softened towards me while we drank tea with cream and sugar. When I was alone with her I felt special to her. One would have to notice her well-endowed bust when you met her. I found out why that was the case one day at the store. Grandma raised chickens and sold eggs to customers. Her crochet handiwork was desired by many of the ladies and she sold those also. When she collected bills from the sales of her wares, she would then pin the bills to the inside of her brassiere with a safety pin. That was her "safe." Grandpa would steal her stash if it was hidden anywhere else beside her brassiere for whiskey.

One memorable evening I was dressed in my cheerleading outfit ready to go to a basketball game. Mom was standing at the ironing board and as I was passing her she reached out her hand to me. She dropped a quarter in my palm—I was flabbergasted. There was not a word spoken, and that's the most affectionate gesture I remember from her during those years. I never did figure out what softened her heart at that particular time.

Buck, an uncle divorced from my aunt, came up the holler to visit once. He asked Mom if he could take me to Madison. He told her he would buy me a winter coat. I was thrilled with his attention and his willingness to buy me a new coat. He bought me a red corduroy coat with a matching cap. Later, he took me to a restaurant. He and the waitress were laughing and flirting with each other, and I was thoroughly amused watching them. He told me he was going to send me an alligator from Florida. I could hardly wait to tell everyone as I was sure no one around those parts had ever seen one before—I sure hadn't. As we headed back over the mountain he stopped the car in a curve. He seemed to be flirting with me like he had with the waitress. Not sure why, but he turned on the motor and he took me home. Whatever his original impulse was, he did not follow through, and I was much relieved. I thought of that alligator many times. It never made its way to the mountains—for that matter neither did Uncle Buck.

Even though I was considered being poor there were many others I knew were poor also. I would watch kids get off the bus without coats, hats, or mittens rushing to get indoors. Going to the doctor was uncalled for in our house. Our cousins went to the doctor but they were Republicans, at least the dad was. I guess they went to the Presbyterian church, too. Mom said the reason that our cousins were sick all the time was that they took baths all the time, took medicine, which they called vitamins, and they went to the doctor all the time. I went to the doctor only once. I was playing with a group of boys, and one of them led us over a tall, rock fence. I scaled that fence just like they did, and I was rather proud of myself. Suddenly one of the boys yelled, "Look at all that blood!" He was pointing down at my foot. When I had jumped down, I had landed on a board which had a rusty nail; that nail had been pointing straight up. After I saw the blood I began to feel dizzy— the boys semi-carried me to their house. Mom had a hard time deciding what to do with me, but someone finally convinced her I needed to go to the doctor. I was given a shot for lockjaw, and I was petrified of shots. A nurse came to our school every year and gave us polio shots. One time my friend Judy got scared, pulled away from the nurse, and she began running around the room with that needle dangling from her arm. What a scary sight! I'm still petrified of needles.

We kids were told we couldn't go swimming until we learned how. That was a joke Gabe told us all the time. I do remember going in the river a couple of times, though. We were told to walk down the riverbanks, clap our hands, stomp our feet, and make as much noise as possible. Snakes would literally fall from the trees and bushes, and we would stare at them as they swam away across the river. Of course, none of us knew how to swim, so we didn't go out that far anyway, so no danger of being bitten by them.

Once my friend Daisy and I decided to go swimming, not in the river but in the water, which had drained from an empty coal mine up on a mountain. A pond of sorts had collected in a flat place, and the water was murky. Even if the water had been clear I doubt either one of us could have judged the depth correctly. We decided we would use only our panties to wear going in the water—we left our clothes on some bushes. I was the first one in the water—I had gone out too far right off. I couldn't reach a solid bottom as it was covered with silt, and it was too slick and slimy to get any traction to push off towards the bank. I went down! I had heard somewhere if you went down three times you were drowned. The second time I went down I was totally comfortable with the calmness that came over me. I just accepted I was dying! I saw the long tunnel with a light at the end, as if beckoning me forward. My life seemed to have been projected from my left as if there were still frames flashing in front of my eyes. I was laughing and crying at the same time as memories were flaring in my brain so fast that I didn't have time to process them. Things I had forgotten came to mind so quickly then leave like it came, as if I was speed reading. The third time I went down, total acceptance of my fate. All of a sudden, something slammed against my head. Daisy had pushed a large log towards me and it hit the side of my head, hard. I grabbed hold of that log and fought for my breath and it came in a rush. I was so ready to stay in this world for a while longer. We left our wet panties on a bush and some boys found them. They teased us all the time about them. They even guessed whose panties belonged to who, and they had guessed right.

Since that experience I have not dreaded death. I have read about many accounts of dying. People call it a near-death experience, and that was what I felt that happened to me that day. I know it will be a welcomed journey that I will take someday, and I will not be afraid. I know some believe in a heaven and a hell but I do not. It is said that some of us have lived in hell already, and we are what they call believing in a spiritual way. The hereafter for me is going to be the knowledge and understanding of the many questions I have had in this lifetime. Fear is not the emotion I have for dealing with death. I will believe this way until someone or something changes my mind.

Mom was coughing a lot. There were slate dumps on the mountains and they smoked all the time. The smoke would hover over the coal camps in the valleys for days at a time. Doctors had told Mom she needed to get to a place with clean air so she could breathe. Tuberculosis was prevalent with people living there and there were sanitariums where people would go when they couldn't breathe anymore and the doctors couldn't help them. Of course, Mom never quit smoking while we lived in WV. She would also take a powder all the time called Standback Headache Powders. A dosage would be in individual paper wrappers. She would tilt her head back and swallow the whole dosage chasing the powder down with a drink of water. She would say she felt a headache coming on and then she would get her a dosage of Standback. We had gotten accustomed to her habit and just accepted it as Mom's medicine. Maybe, it was migraines which were plaguing her.

When we lived by the road there was a white house—actually a mansion by anyone's definition, on the hill located above our little shack by the road. Lucy, the girl who told me I made cheerleader lived there with her two sisters and her mother. There was a dad but I never saw him. Lucy was rich compared to any of us who lived around those parts. But she was sweet to everyone. She invited me to spend the night once and I was beside myself. There were rooms in that house just to play in. We slid down a pole which was like the one in a fire station and it went all the way down to the basement. Lucy had some fancy dresses she used for playing dress up, and we played with them for a long while. I fell in love with a red formal and I asked if I could borrow it to graduate from the eighth-grade class. She gave me permission and I wore it for the ceremony. Lordy, was I overdressed for that event! I would have been overdressed for the academy awards I guess, but I was proud of that dress. The next morning, we had breakfast, and Lucy's sisters fixed it for us. I saw my first banana and they even had a freezer. That big box even had store bought ice cream in it. They poured chocolate syrup over the ingredients, and I had my first banana split! I knew what it was because Mr. Elkins had told us about them in class.

I had several boyfriends back then but I was serious about Billy May. He was a football player and he was known to be rather smart. He would tell me about the exciting things he had learned in high school. Also, he would hold my hand and open the door for me when we hung around the Eastep store. I have joked about him having the same last name as me but saying that was okay. The reason being, was that we were both illegitimate. Both of us were raised in a family named Kindle. His mother was a twin, and she had an affair with her sister's husband and got pregnant with Billy. His grandparents raised him. He was always telling funny stories about them. He said when they got their first television, his grandpa would keep looking in the back of television, so he could see the people who were talking and singing on that contraption. It was always fun being around Billy May.

The sexual abuse I had suffered in the holler lessened, but the beatings continued. One day I overheard my grandpa telling Gabe how he appreciated him taking Sue in and raising her like his own. I was furious! I wanted to march in there and ask grandpa if he knew what that scrounge was doing to me! I didn't though, somehow, I knew it wouldn't do any good. Sixty years later I still know it wouldn't have changed a thing. Some things we didn't bring up, we just suffered through them.

After I graduated from eighth grade I would be riding the bus over the mountains to high school. We had a tour of the school a couple of months before and I fell in love with the library. We didn't have any books laying around our house. Once I chased after the smartest boy in our school to his front door, and I almost fell over! Bookshelves lined the walls, and books were stuffed on every shelf. His mother was a teacher but I gave the credit to all those books he had to read for the reason he was so smart. Mom did buy some encyclopedias once and I devoured them. For some reason, she loved reading about ships. To my knowledge, she had never been on a ship in her life or even had seen one. Those encyclopedias, like many of our other possessions got repossessed also, so no more books.

Many days I watched my mom standing at the coal stove stirring the gravy while at least two of her youngest children were hanging on her dress tail crying constantly. We were hungry a lot, and Mom was aging fast with the domestic abuse and being responsible for five kids with no income to speak of. The coal mines were shutting down constantly—as there was no longer a demand for coal at that time. We went to get commodities. Each month a truck would bring a distribution of food from the government. We got rice, flour, sugar, powdered eggs, and cheese, which we all liked. Mom would hang her head down crying, sitting in the car while I lugged all the boxes to the backseat. Not sure where Mom's sense of pride nor the reason she was so ashamed to take charity came from. That probably was the main reason she stayed with Gabe. At least he worked when he could.

The last winter in WV we had a struggle fighting the elements and having enough to eat. In that small house with two bedrooms, a kitchen, and a living room we survived one harsh winter. There was a fireplace in one of the bedrooms, and by spring we were breaking furniture to feed the flames to catch the coal on fire to keep warm. Thankfully though, we could go a few yards and get coal for the cooking stove and that fireplace. That little house was located at the mouth of an old coal mine. I'm not sure if Mom had planned that far ahead or it was just luck the mine was located close by the house.

When spring arrived, I saw a new resolve in Mom's attitude. She got an area plowed up and she was going to plant her garden and fill the old cellar full of canned goods. She worked constantly in her garden and her spirits seemed to improve.

I used the smokehouse above the cellar for a laboratory. I had read the directions for developing film in one of the encyclopedias we still had at that time. I was using mercurochrome and improvising the rest of the ingredients which mostly I had no idea what the words meant. I knew I had to keep my lab dark and I fought with the younger kids to stay out of my lab. One day a friend came and opened the door. She let out a scream and I was stunned! In the rafters over my head snakes were hanging from the ceiling! They could have been black snakes for all I knew as I didn't look closely as I was hightailin' it out of there.

Snakes to me were interpreted, biblically. Every time I came across a snake in the mountains they seemed to be laughing at me, like the devil if he were real. I would always want them dead. Once, I saw Mom in the chicken-coop yard trying to cut a copperhead's head off. Furiously, with excited cackling the chickens would be helping her by pecking at that reptile's body. Mom and those chickens were on the same team when it benefitted Mom it seemed. But in a week or so, she would catch a fat hen snap or wring its neck, then chop it's head off with an axe. With that done, she would put that thing in a big pot of boiling water. I was made to pull the feathers out of its body and spread the feathers out to dry in the sun. Later, Mom would take a feed sack and stuff it with those feathers and we would have a new pillow. Sometimes the quills from the shaft would poke through the material at night and wake me sometimes.

I hated it, and again was fascinated, when Gabe dug a big snake out of a hole in the ground while shooting it. I'm thinking those snakes must have been poisonous and Mom made him do that. We had black snakes with their babies crawling out of the broken-down Ford Model A every morning in the spring, and no adult ever hurt them.

Norfolk, Virginia

Mom's sister, my Aunt Nina, came for a visit with her husband Gene. He was in the Navy and they lived in Norfolk, Virginia. Mom and her sister were not that close. The reason I thought that, was Mom's descriptive adjectives and nouns she used when she talked of her sister. An "Uppity bitch" and a "!**% Know It All" were used the most, but there were others. Honestly, I think Mom was envious of her. Nina would walk in with her fancy clothes after getting out of her fancy car and Mom felt the sting of her condition which included us five hungry kids. Nina's husband Gene wore Bermuda shorts and Gabe and the other men thought that he was dressed like a 'sissy.' After all, men had to look like men in the hills.

Not sure when my aunt had talked to Mom but she said Mom had consented to let me go back to Norfolk with them for the summer. I knew this would have been beneficial for Mom as we did not know how I would get school clothes the coming year. Nina told Mom she knew a seamstress who would make all my clothes, and I would be ready for ninth grade. Gabe was against this idea and there were fights for a couple of days. He got mad at Mom if she let me cut my hair. He was always looking for a reason to get mad at us, and when he got drunk all that anger would come out at the end of his fists. Mom had dropped out of school in the eighth grade. My aunt told me the reason Mom had dropped out of school was because she didn't have clothes to wear which were nice enough for high school. Maybe, that was the reason she let me go to VA with Nina and Gene.

The big day finally arrived and I was on my way to see what a county and state line looked like. We stopped at a Dairy Queen establishment and I had my second banana split! In Norfolk, they took me to a pier to the ship my uncle sailed on. The only thing I had ever seen larger, was a mountain in the holler. That ship was gigantic and the sailors were whistling and catcalling at all the women within hearing distance walking below on the pier.

On my birthday, I had friends who took me to the Atlantic Ocean. My aunt was always recruiting friends for me. When we drove up I couldn't see anything but a long, tall building. When we went through the back door there lay the Atlantic Ocean! My breath was taken away. It was beautiful and I just couldn't comprehend the vastness of it. We would walk out in the water and a wave would charge at us and toss us back to shore. It was exhilarating! A day I will always remember...

My aunt strongly encouraged me to go out on dates. She told me that being true to Billy May was a waste of time. In the long run, I guess she was right. I went to the movies for the first time and had all the food and treats my heart desired. I had nice clothes for the first time in my life. Back home my friend and I would trade clothes. Since my friend went to high school and I did not, we would trade our school clothes. If anyone noticed our scheme not a word was said for the two years we traded clothes.

One day my aunt and I were just sitting around and I was reading Peyton Place. That was a very sexual book at that time but it was her idea, and I wasn't going to deny the fact that it was fascinating! One morning, out of the blue, she asked me if Gabe was mean to me. I paused for a long time, and she continued by saying a term 'Guy Moses.' I backed her up and asked her what did 'Guy Moses' mean. She said that was my real father's name! I had thought it was a curse word. Gabe called me Guy Moses all the time. If I got mad at one of the other kids and I called them Guy Moses, he would correct me and say I was the only Guy Moses in his house. Not sure why my aunt told me all this information. The most damaging and hurtful thing she told me I figured out was that I was not pure—using her words. She proceeded to tell me a girl had to be a virgin when they married. What a stigma I lived with for so many years! I was deemed not only a bastard, but now I was classified close to being a whore, like my mom, according to Gabe.

I got a letter from Mom and she had a bombshell on that piece of paper. She said we were moving to Mexico in August! "What the hell was she talking about?" I wondered. She had her garden ready to pick and she was going to let all that food go to waste. Besides, we didn't speak Spanish. Not sure if Mom understood the differences between Mexico and New Mexico. As you can tell I didn't either. I never asked her if she knew the difference, all I knew is that I didn't want to go anywhere

Maybe my aunt was genuinely concerned for my welfare but I seriously doubt it. She said she wanted to keep me with her, and I know she was lonely because her husband was away to sea for months at a time. I wrote to my friend and told her my aunt wanted me to stay with her and my friend told Mom. My friend said that Mom went ballistic, and made the comment, "Yeah, she gives her little bastard away, and now she wants mine." Mom and her sister would not speak for years. Once we all were supposed to meet up in WV and my aunt did not show. I felt betrayed and lied to. She died an alcoholic and had moved back to WV at the end of her life; ironically, to a place she had scorned for so many years.

My aunt decided I should have the experience of flying, so I flew from Norfolk, VA to Charleston, WV. I had one of my new outfits on and I thought I was just really uptown. I have written for a magazine about the experience I had on arriving in Charleston that day, and even when I did that, I must have felt guilty. What a shock! I was looking forward to seeing all the kids and Mom, but I wasn't prepared for the image that was in front of me. All the kids were barefoot, with runny noses, and so raggedly dressed. Mom had a faded dress on and she had aged so much in the two months I had been gone. As I was getting in the car I burst out and said, "I don't want to go to New Mexico." She nodded and said, "Just keep your mouth shut." That meant she could not argue with Gabe and me at the same time. Mom was always telling me to keep my mouth shut over those years. We would be getting our ass beat and I had to scream some statement of the injustice that Gabe was doing at the time. Mom would say, "Sue, shut up!" Like that would make him stop or something. Never did find out though, as I had to have my say, even with bruises and black eyes proving I had said something.

Another big problem was that I was angry! I was so mad at my mother for not telling me that her Gabe was not my father. That made a lot of difference on how I was handling the abuse. If I was like all the other kids, I guess I may have accepted the treatment easier, but when I found out I wasn't, then my attitude became defiant and I didn't give a damn about pleasing Mom at all. Her not telling me was just like lying and I was ready to explode at any given moment.

One day a convertible drove up to the house and Mom became visibly upset. It was her oldest boy, Lawrence, who was Karen's brother. The father, Raymond, had gotten custody of them after he divorced Mom. That was the only time Mom saw Lawrence that I am aware of. He had a wife and a baby with him. Mom talked to them for a while and then came back into the house. To my knowledge Mom never spoke of their short visit to me or anyone.

Gabe had an obsession for collecting Model A's. As long as he lived, he never had a driver's license because he couldn't read. He would drive up and down the dirt road in the holler, though. He didn't need a license for that. Mom decided that we could sell the nicer car to her brother-in-law for three hundred dollars. That was the amount of money we had when we left WV. The same relative gave us a gas credit card for our trip to use.

Another deciding factor that helped Mom decide to go to NM was she no longer could get credit. Mom took me to a store in Costa one day. She told me to go in and charge some Bull Durham, the tobacco she used for making cigarettes. After I asked for the tobacco, the man behind the counter shook his head and said my mom could no longer have credit. He went on and explained she hadn't paid her bill in months. I knew Gabe wasn't working much and he got paid by the amount of coal he got from the mine in a day. Sometimes he only made fifty cents a day. He complained about working in water all the time at that. He had water on the knee and had begun limping. Standing by the car I told Mom what the man had said. Between sobs she cursed her/our circumstances. "Get your ass in the car," she ordered. I did and we left.

The Long Trip

We packed our '54 Ford to the hilt. Five kids and two adults. Lonnie, the oldest boy sat in front between Mom and Gabe. Lonnie had speech issues. All he had to do was point and grunt at any object and his dad or Mom got him what he wanted. He didn't have to speak. My spot was right behind Mom so I could help her read the signs. My can-can slips were placed carefully in the back window as they were my prized possessions; and somehow, I think Mom let me use that space so I wouldn't complain so much, aloud, anyway. I shared the back seat with a girl and two boys who were not of school age yet.

All my friends had been left behind, and that was torture for me. Mom and I were destined to have a confrontation, and I had to admit she was one female I was afraid of. I was still brooding in the back seat as we were beginning to cross a bridge. A sign said, "Welcome to Ohio," out of the blue. I shouted, "Mom, turn around we are going the wrong direction!" We needed to go west and we were going north. Gabe's father had said we were going to be stopped and killed by the Russians going that far away! I didn't believe that, but I knew that we were in over our heads doing this trip! Poor Mom had her hands full. She didn't have any experience driving in traffic or towns of any kind but she trudged on for days. We had never seen more than two stop lights in any one town before, and we're practically crossing the whole country according to the map I could barely read.

Mom had packed jars of peanut butter for our meals. One time we saw a sign that said, "Hamburgers, Five for a Dollar." Mom spent three dollars on that meal. My second hamburger in my life. My first hamburger was at a friend's house while visiting her one day. We spent one night in a motel as it was raining so hard that Mom couldn't drive. I had to sleep in a bed with four other kids. Of course, I griped about that. One night we pulled over in a rural area to sleep. I don't recall any buildings being around. We all slept sitting up. However, I remember that Fred would sit on the floor in the back, resting his head on the seat. We were in the big state of Texas and it seemed like that state would never end. I knew New Mexico was supposed to be close by but I was beginning to doubt the map I had been looking at for days.

It seemed that we all woke up at the same time! Things were crawling all over us! We couldn't see what the moving bodies with legs were, because it was too dark. Finally, Mom turned on a flashlight and we could tell they were grasshoppers! They had been feeding in the field where we had parked. Maybe, they were seeing if we would make a square meal. That trip had turned into a nightmare and all of this was Mom's idea. I hated her "big idea" more by the mile.

Elementary school pictures.

*Where I was raised by my grandparents
until four or five.*

*The house in the holler where
most of the abuse took place.*

Cheerleaders.

Mr. Elkins

NEW MEXICO

We finally saw a sign which read "Welcome to New Mexico," the Land of Enchantment. Regrets and disbeliefs were hanging in the air! The landscape was barren, brown, and empty in so many places, and there were no trees at all, just sagebrush. I was so disappointed. This place had vinegaroons, horned toads, tarantulas, and rattlesnakes! The snakes I had been familiar with, but those other creatures were totally foreign to me.

We pulled onto Eighth Street and the Brooks family came out with their five kids to welcome us. We stayed with them for two months in a two-bedroom house. It was hard to find a rental with five kids. Mom found out a place with street lights and paved streets were rather picky about their renters. Every place Mom went to ask about a place they would ask her if she had any kids. Of course, she had to say five, and they would say sorry "no kids". She finally started asking the potential landlords, "What am I supposed to do with them, drown them?" I wondered a time or two, if she was thinking about that.

While we were living with the Brooks, Jean the mother, told me I was to stay away from the Mexicans. No nice girl should talk to them and they are to be ignored. A telephone man came to their house a day or two after that. I was sitting on the couch reading, and the worker asked if I had read a certain book, and a conversation began about books. When he went to his truck, Jean stormed into the room and asked me if I remembered what she told me about Mexicans. I said yes, and she asked me what I was doing talking to that guy. I really didn't think about him being "Mexican" as he was not speaking Spanish, and that is what I associated with a person from Mexico. I'm always struck how strange it is that we, "the hillbillies" look down on others so easily. Maybe, we are doing it just to be spiteful, because we have been put down so many times in the past.

Finally, we moved into the King Apartments. It had two bedrooms and one divided room which was the living room and kitchen combined. The best part was that it had a bathroom with a shower. We never had an indoor bathroom before, and this was a point in favor for New Mexico!

There were six apartments in all in that building, and we were all low-income families, in other words, poor. There were four families who were related, who lived there with the last name of Smith. Our family had five kids and that was about the average for the other apartments except for the one next door, and there were only two kids living there. So, there were twenty-seven kids in that small area. Each place had a small yard with no grass, and a porch that was barely large enough to support one chair and a pathway to get to the door. We sat on the three-foot porch if we wanted to be outside and visit. We lived on a main street of the town which gradually went over a hill to a place called Happy Valley. Mom's favorite description of that place was, "What's so damn happy about it?"

I remember Mom got thirty-seven dollars a week unemployment from the mines in WV. There was an extension of this amount once, and that is all I knew about the income for the seven of us. Thankfully, I had nice clothes to begin school in the ninth grade. I had made several friends who lived close to the apartments and we walked to school. Jean knew a lady who had a little store across from the school and she arranged for me to work for that lady's store during the lunch period. I got a free lunch for working and I was thankful for that.

School was rough! The minute I opened my mouth I was shunned! The Brooks failed to tell Mom that the mines were on strike, and we were now scabs! Jean had sent Mom newspapers that stated that the Carlsbad potash mines needed miners. None of them said that the mines had picket lines. So, the town did not accept anyone from out of state and for the most part we were ostracized. All of us who were recently enrolled in school were not wanted, and we knew it. I had been a cheerleader and the smartest kid in the class in WV and I now found myself totally lost walking down the halls to my classes. I had never seen so many people in my life, and they were all in this school, or though I thought! This building was huge and it was only a junior high school called Alta Vista.

Being shunned by the popular and smart kids threw most of us in with the kids who smoked and drank. The popular and smart kids were doing the same vices as we were, but they never seemed to get caught. My actions had a lot to do with my mother also. I still couldn't handle her betrayal of letting that man claim to be my father.

So, all my self-confidence went down the drain. My classes included journalism, Spanish, physical education, English, and a dreaded math class. Actually, the math teacher was very kind and I passed the class with a "C" but that was with a lot of help from her. I loved the Spanish class and the physical education class. Later, I took algebra and it was as though the teacher was speaking a different language. I shared that classroom with kids I had in other classes, and they struggled in the other classes. In this class I was the one who struggled. Once the teacher wrote a note home, and it read, "Sue must be diligent." Mom asked me what that meant, and I said that I must work harder. She seemed satisfied with that answer but I still didn't get to be "diligent" because I didn't get it.

Mr. Elkins gave me the skills to be athletic. He had taught us to read our opponents' body language and try to figure out what their next move would be and get prepared for their action. I was popular with the PE teachers and at least, and for an hour or so I could hold my own in school in that class anyway.

There were gang fights all the time between the Anglos and the Hispanics during those years. James, a boy who had a Spanish-speaking mother had a real hard time. Both groups would beat him up. One time at lunch break I was leaving the little store where I worked, and it looked like an ocean wave was coming towards me. Every student in that school was coming to see the fight, and I was the only one trying to get away from the fiasco. The Hispanics had chains and so did the Anglo boys, and that boy James was in the middle of the blows being executed. I'm sure the fight was broken up, but I was nowhere around when it did. The girls of both groups would rat or backcomb their hair and hide razor blades in their tresses for the fights. I never did see that for myself, but that was what was said by other students.

One day we were sitting on the benches in the gym. A Hispanic girl sitting on the front bench turned around, looked in my face and hissed, "white trash!" I was totally caught off guard! There was a strange energy in that place that day. A teacher was attempting to give a large Anglo girl swats, but that girl was playing hard to get as she was chased around the gym. The girl kept laughing and telling the teacher she wasn't going to let her give her swats. The teacher was embarrassed and she was losing the battle. We were told to leave and go to our next class and we filed out.

Suddenly, an Anglo girl who had been kicked out of the Catholic school for her behavior grabbed a Hispanic girl's long hair, and literally picked that girl off the ground by the hair which hung down her back. The Anglo girl went around and around with her adversary and never allowed the other girl's feet to touch the ground for the longest time. The Hispanic girl looked as though she were on a carnival ride, a tilt-a-whirl, maybe. Teachers came from exits out of the school and we were broken up. I said "we" but I did not touch anyone nor was I hit. I never did find out what that fight was about but I became very aware when I felt that strange energy I needed to get away quickly!

One time in Spanish class the teacher asked me what I thought of all the fighting at our school. I think he picked me because I was new to the school or maybe because I had a questioning look on my face all the time. I gave a speech how wrong both groups were, and that I felt they should get along. That speech did not earn me any points with either group in that class. I was very naïve on matters like intolerance of different cultural groups but I have noticed those issues haven't been solved fifty-five years later either.

The lady who lived next door to us in the apartments befriended me and she wanted all my friends and me to hang out at her place. Looking back, I'm sure the lady was lonely and unhappy in her marriage. She would encourage us to dance and she wanted to hear about our romances. One day while talking to her she confided to me that she was an epileptic. She told me what to do if she ever had a seizure. The very next day she had one! She fell backwards and began squirming from side to side on the floor. I grabbed a rolled-up magazine and put it into her mouth so she would not bite her tongue. I stayed on the floor with her until she became calm. That was one scary afternoon!

This same lady had a boy about the age of the two younger boys in our clan. One day she caught all the boys playing with matches. She marched into our apartment and told Mom what she had witnessed. She said she took the matches and burned her boy's fingers. She wanted Mom to do the same to her two kids. Mom refused. She said she would whip their asses, but she was not going to burn them with matches as a punishment. Mom would bad-mouth that neighbor every chance she got. Honestly, I think Mom was jealous that I was over there all the time, and I talked about her all the time. Later, I got a job and I rarely had time to visit our lonely neighbor anymore.

A group of us would meet at Marie's house and dance. There were no invitations to meet. We just knew we were welcome any day and anytime of the day. I loved to dance and thoroughly enjoyed doing it every chance I got. None of us had a lot of money or things. I had less than all the other kids. One mother was having an affair with Marie's dad. We all knew about their attraction, and we would watch them flirting and then make fun of the old people behind their backs.

There was a time that a group of us girls had slumber parties. That was a recreation that rarely cost anything. When it was my turn to have the sleepover, I had some money which was a rare thing—I bought some cokes for the girls. Mom pulled up in the car and all the kids were bounding for the door. I didn't want the kids to see the drinks because they would beg for some. I yelled at Joyce, "Put them in the poke!" She just stood there. "Put them in the poke"! I kept pointing at the paper bag. "What the hell is a poke?" she demanded. I folded over with laughter. That's what we called paper bags in West Virginia. During the sleepovers we all had to put up with younger siblings. We talked about boys a lot and one night we discovered why one girl had big boobs. Toilet paper was sticking out of Carol's bra and we all had a good laugh except for Carol. Evelyn told me if I wanted to get more endowed I just should sleep without a bra. We thought we were really wise. Funny, how we figured everything out so young.

We moved from the apartments to a small house on Ninth Street. It had an old-fashioned bathtub which had legs—I loved it. There were windows in every room and we could look outside and see a backyard. The best part though, was that I had a room to myself and a lock on the door. Decorating this little space was a highlight of being a teenager in New Mexico. For my sixteenth birthday Mom bought me a record player and what a thrill that was. One time while living in that house I bought some fish for Mom to cook for us for a celebration. I was so proud watching Mom frying that fish. There was a hint of a smile on her face as she made that dinner that night. A rare occasion, indeed!

We moved to another house on Ninth Street later on. I'm sure it was because the rent was cheaper. I still drive by that place sometimes. I've joked many times about the scene in the kitchen at that house. I would turn the lights on when I got home from work. The roaches would be dragging a loaf of bread across the floor. That's not true; as we always had biscuits or cornbread which Mom baked every day. We never had a loaf of bread. But there were roaches galore in that house and that's the truth!

Billy May was stationed in Albuquerque and he sent me a picture of him dressed in his Navy uniform. I never would see him again. I wonder at times what my life would have been like if I had stayed in WV. Some of my friends married and had several kids while still in their teens. One of my friends confessed she had kissed Billy right after I left for New Mexico. I felt so betrayed! Billy May, later in life I was told, liked the women. He would not have been any different than the man I married in New Mexico. So maybe my life would have not been much different at all.

The first boyfriend I had in New Mexico was Jerry. He made me a ring from a quarter in his shop class. The next beau was older and his name was Jerry also—he worked at a grocery store. He had his own car and he would pick me up and take me to school. In the evenings, we went to the store where I worked. We played the jukebox and danced. Boy, could he dance. As time went on he got involved with a girl who had a baby and worked as a carhop. I couldn't hold a candle to her with her worldly ways and I lost him to her. Later, he would marry the girl he had gone with for years and I guess he had gone with me on the rebound from her...The most I missed about him was his dancing.

The next guy I was involved with was Ronnie. I met him when I went to visit my friend, Marta. He had just come to New Mexico and he had just gotten out of reform school. He was not the nicest guy in the world or even the country for that matter. He drank a lot and so did his whole family. His sister's baby was rolling a beer bottle around for a toy all over the floor at times when I visited Marta. Ronnie began an affair with one of Marta's older married friend, Irene. I got drunk one night and I stood out in her front yard screaming and calling her rather unflattering names. That was not one of my finest moments. Needless to say, Ronnie and I parted. I wouldn't be surprised if he is locked up again somewhere.

Marta's friend Irene, was one slick lady. She taught Marta how to shoplift and they were stealing the stores blind. Once, I went into a Safeway with Marta, and she had lifted steaks! I couldn't believe her expertise. She would steal clothes, make-up, and anything she wanted or any of her friends wanted. She always wore a dress which helped her to hide things but the real trick was her self-confidence! She would be hiding all sorts of merchandise underneath her clothes, and she would start a conversation with the checkout lady. No one seemed suspicious of the attractive teenage dropout that I ever knew or heard of.

Marta was involved with a married man. He had other young girls in his lair. Once Marta had surgery on her ruptured appendix. Before she fully recuperated she wanted to go to a dance, and I joined her. A girl named Judy came into the restroom while we were there. I introduced Marta to Judy and before I finished the introduction, Marta took a swing at Judy. "You bitch, where is he?" Marta screamed at Judy. Marta had her confused with another Judy and this Judy could really fight! By the time, I got Judy off Marta, the floor was covered in blood! Marta's stitches had been ripped out. No more dancing for us.

Another time, and the last time I hung around Marta involved a wreck. Marta's parents took in old men who needed a place to stay and needless to say, they were drunk most of the time. Marta had an idea to go joy riding one night. She told me to go talk or flirt with Ben, one of the men, staying with her family. Marta wanted me to distract him while she stole his keys from a hook on the wall. I did what she told me. Afterwards, I hustled out the door with Marta and we climbed in his old sedan. We drove by the skating rink and picked up a couple of girls we knew. Marta had a plan to go to the next little town about thirty miles away. Of course, we were drinking and talking a blue streak. There were tailights right ahead of us in the highway and BAM! We hit that car which was in our lane and it probably had stalled. When we hit the back of that car it took off! I hit the windshield and Marta slammed into the steering wheel! Needless to say, none of us got treated for any injuries from that escapade.

Ben, the car's owner turned the theft into the police. Marta and I came up with a plan...we would just deny everything! A policeman eventually came to our apartment and asked me questions but I stuck to our plan and denied everything. Well, I decided to sever my friendship with Marta after that. She was out of my league, but it took a long time for me to figure that out. Not sure whatever happened to her but she sure was heading in the wrong direction in my opinion.

The younger kids went to church at the Nazarene church. One Christmas our family was given a couple of baskets of food. I'm guessing the church could surmise by how the kids were dressed that we were rather hard up. Anyway, Mom pulled a giant chicken out of a basket and put it in the biggest pot she had. She said we were going to have some chicken and dumplings! Well, she cooked that bird and cooked it some more. She said it didn't look quite right though. A neighbor came by, looked in the pot, and said she had never seen a turkey cooked that way before. We had never had a turkey before so Mom assumed that bird was a chicken. We were very happy to get the baskets of other foodstuffs too. Mom had swallowed her pride that time, and we all were happy to be feasting for a change.

For some reason, I decided to beat up this girl, Wanda, who lived in the apartments. When you live with a bully you become a bully and I had become one! I had a friend we called Blondie and she was wanting me to get down to business and fight, so she could watch, I guess. I called Wanda outside by the clothesline— I accused her of stealing my lipstick. I didn't even have any lipstick at that time. I knew I had to hit her but I couldn't quite get my nerve up. All of a sudden, Mom slammed the screen door and yelled at me. Not sure what a Smith woman said to Mom but I heard Mom yell, "You want a piece of my ass?" And apparently, she did, because that woman jumped the fence and started for Mom. I was so scared that the younger woman would beat Mom up so I hit Wanda! When I looked over my shoulder, Mom had that woman's head under her arm and Mom was pummeling her! Mom was a much better fighter than me. Of course, she had more practice. Someone called the police and we all scattered. I had no reason to badger Wanda—I just wanted to be a show off.

My friend, Belinda got a job at a drive-in. I decided I should get a job, too. I went to a drive-in across town and the boss was there. He hired me right on the spot. I was to show up the next day. I was so excited—I hurried home to tell Mom. She started shaking her head and she began crying. I thought, "What the hell!" She said if I went to work I would not graduate. I promised if I could work I would graduate. When we lived in the holler in WV I remember Mom saying she wanted me to graduate to her friend, Jean. Perhaps it was because she didn't graduate. Anyway, I would keep my promise, but what a challenge! By working I could buy a Girl's Athletic Association jacket— pay my dollar dues for the year. I remember bragging several times that Mom only furnished me fifty cents for lunch one day during my junior and senior years. I paid my own way in everything I did. I had to.

While I was getting ready for work one day there was a knock on the door. For some reason, I was the only one home. John Brooks was standing in the doorway. He said he came by to see if I remembered when he used to play with us in the yard in WV. I was confused...he continued. He told me crude and vulgar things about myself, supposedly, that he remembered. He said he would put his hand out, and I would crawl onto his hand and he would play with my crotch. Not sure what the terms were that he used to describe the event(s), but I felt so dirty and I guess that was his intention. I slammed the door in his face! What was frustrating is that I doubted my own memory, and the many gaps I had when I was younger. I couldn't deny his claims though not even to myself.

There were not any memory losses in New Mexico for me, and I think the reason was that there was the threat of the police for Gabe. When at work, I would interact with police officers and I let Gabe know it, too. That was a leverage I had as I knew his fear of going to jail. Once in WV he spent a couple of days in jail but I'm not sure for what reason. When Mom and us kids went to pick him up he was crying and I could tell it had been very traumatic for him. When someone would knock on the door he would always run and hide. Not sure if it was from his AWOL days or the time he went to jail. All of us kids just accepted his bizarre behavior, and laughed at him behind his back.

I bought an old '52 Chevy from a boy's mom I knew. It cost me one hundred dollars—I paid ten dollars a week until it was paid for. The young man put a new motor in the car and he kept it going for me for a long time. I couldn't wait to "get it on the road" so Belinda and I took a trip to Roswell, eighty miles away. I had worn glasses since third grade. The day of our trip I decided I wanted to look sexy, so I put on sunglasses instead of my glasses. We're cruising down the highway and thoroughly enjoying ourselves and then Belinda shouted, "Look out for that guy!" "What guy!" I yelled back. There was a man in the center of the road for some reason, and I had to swerve to keep from hitting him! I put my glasses on for the rest of the trip and decided I didn't need to be sexy.

When I got home from that trip Mom was visibly upset and I knew she had been worried about me. We sat on the steps for a while. I told her about Don, one of her friend's husband fondling Raydean, his daughter. Mom didn't say anything—she just listened. For the life of me I can't understand why I didn't tell her then what her Gabe was doing to me. Perhaps, I didn't want to ruin the closeness we had that night. That was the closest I had ever been to her that I remembered up to that point, anyway.

On my way to work one day I was stopped for turning left in front of an oncoming car at a stoplight. The truth was, I didn't see the car. A policeman was a couple of cars back from the vehicle which I ran in front of. I had broken my glasses and I had no defense other than I didn't have my glasses. I was given a ticket. That same night Belinda and I were at a party, and for some reason she had picked up my keys and headed for the door. I chased her outside. She explained she had gotten mad at a guy for entering the restroom without knocking and she was embarrassed, so she was leaving. She gave the keys to me and we decided to go and get a bite to eat. I went off without my purse. Well. I got stopped again. I asked the policeman why he stopped me and he said because I didn't have my license. I said, "You didn't know I didn't have my license until you stopped me!" I still got another ticket but my argument was valid.

Two in one day! I had to go to juvenile court with Mom. The judge started reprimanding Mom. He said, "Mrs. K., why is your daughter out at three o'clock in the morning?" Mom didn't know what to say so she just dropped her head. I jumped in to defend her—I told the judge I could take care of myself. Explaining that I had a job, a vehicle and going to school so I would answer any questions he had. He said he would let me go with a warning, and that I needed more supervision. I thought, "that wasn't happening." Mom told me once that I wouldn't be put in jail instead the jail would be put on top of me! I was heading that way. Even though I lived with many put-downs from Mom, I began to feel she had a higher level of respect towards me.

I began smoking with a group I walked to school with. The boys usually had cigarettes and they would willingly give us girls one. It was almost a rite of passage for the boys to furnish us a cigarette and of course they lighted them for us. They would roll their cigarette packages up in the sleeve of their white T-shirts and we all thought that was cool. One of these boys would become a lifelong friend and a boyfriend off and on. He was my protector in many instances and Gabe couldn't ever run him off. Gabe even accused Mom of having an affair with him. If I was out with someone else he would stay in the living room and wait for me.

I can't remember how Gabe found out that I smoked but he did. He threatened to tell Mom and the name calling began to come out of my mouth full force. Mom smoked for years but I was hesitant about telling her that I did. Gabe chased me into the bathroom one day. As he swung at me I ducked, but my tooth came down on the ridge on top of an apothecary jar. I cracked a tooth. It never occurred to me to go to the dentist. We only went to a dentist when we had a severe abscess. In WV, we would chew tobacco and put the tobacco in the cavity. I had to pay for my own extraction at the dentist when I was forced to go by the pain. The one doctor's appointment I had because I sprained my back; I paid for myself also. Other than that, I had always been rather healthy.

A couple months later I drank several drinks, got my nerve up, and I told Mom I smoked. Heck, I had been buying her cigarettes or the tobacco for her to roll her own. She said she preferred that I didn't smoke. She really didn't have a leg to stand on, so eventually I started smoking in front of her. Case settled.

I would go in a stall in the bathroom at school and smoke. One day I heard an adult female voice yell, "Who's in there?" I came out and I was scared. The rule at school was no student was allowed to smoke on school property. If caught, the student would automatically be kicked out. That sounded a lot like the predicament I was in at the moment. The teacher grabbed my arm and marched me to Mr. Frazier's office. He was the sophomore counselor. Fretting, while waiting for him to see me, I came up with a plan. I did not want to get kicked out of school but I did not want to lie to Mr. Frazier, either.

"Sue, were you smoking in the girl's bathroom?" pressed Mr. Frazier.

"My answer is, I'm not going to say I was and I am not going to say I wasn't," I answered.

Mr. Frazier looked at some papers and then met my eye. "Well, do you smoke?" he asked.

I lowered my head and nodded yes. He took a deep breath and said he would meet me halfway since I met him part way. "I'm going to give you a warning this time, but the next time you'll be suspended three days. Understand?" I just nodded my head and lowered it again. I couldn't get out of that office fast enough. I knew I had gotten a break.

One weekend, Gabe came home from a job he had in Roswell. We came to New Mexico so he could work in the potash mines. He had worked at one potash mine for a month and got laid off. He had trouble with conversations and did not fit in well with people. Sometimes, he would help my friend's dad do odd jobs, but other than that he didn't work until he got the job at the missile sites doing laborer work. Mom took in ironing for people. One night she was standing at the ironing board ironing when Gabe came home. He came in the door, and he was drunk on his ass! He started mouthing off, and all the kids scattered except for me. He said he went to a bar the night before, and he showed some guys my school picture. He said one guy commented, "Oh, I know her, she is a whore in Carlsbad!" Gabe kept ranting and raving. Finally, Mom had all she could take at that time and she said, "You son-of-a- bitch, shut up!" Well, he didn't, so she took off towards him with that hot iron! He backhanded her, and I jumped on his back and started pulling his hair. He bucked me off, and grabbed my hair then threw me towards the couch. The arm in the couch was wooden, and I hit that wood hard with the small of my back. When I got up I headed toward the front door while yelling, "I'm getting the fuck out of here!" First time I ever used that word. Just as I hit the porch I realized I had no shoes on, and the ground was covered with snow and ice. I circled the cars outside and found one which had recently parked; the tires were still warm. I stayed there on the ground as long as I could in the cold. Finally, I went back to the apartment. When I went in the door Mom was crying and Gabe was loading a gun. "I'll kill that little bitch!" he sneered. Mom was begging him not to hurt me. I'm sure he was bluffing, but I didn't know it then. I went in the room where all the kids were sleeping and crawled in the bed with Dora shivering and shaking.

I worked eight-hour shifts, six days a week. Five days a week I went to school half-days when I was a junior and senior. I worked from three thirty in the afternoon until eleven thirty at night. Many nights I went partying after I got off from work. When I entered a classroom the next morning I was exhausted and sleepy. I would look for a large boy and sit behind him. I would lay my head on the desk and sleep that way during most classes. Sometimes, I would tell Mom I was sick and I would stay home to sleep and rest. Mom never questioned me, and she let me. I had a geography teacher, Ms. Garber and she took an interest in me for some reason. When I was a junior, I remember twice when I stayed home and Ms. Garber would come knocking on the door. "Mrs. K., is Sue home? I was wondering why she is missing so much school. You know Sue is a smart student but she needs to attend her classes. Does she need to work so many hours?" Mom would tell her I had the flu or something, to shoo her away. Ms. Garber took my interest to heart. Seems like when I needed someone, an outsider would put in a word on my behalf. I'm very thankful for those people who passed through my life.

Another positive thing happened when I skipped school to rest. One day, Mom's friend Jean came to my door and said, "Sue, you should be reading books!" This was a wonderful prompting. I started reading for pleasure and haven't stopped since. There was a city library in our new town. The first time I walked into that building I thought I was in heaven or at least at the Pearly Gates. So much to know, so little time, and I'm still trying to cram all I can in my head.

The need for alcohol had driven me to only go out with guys who were old enough to buy liquor, which was twenty-one in our state. Sometimes, a customer would come to the place I worked, and he would go buy beer for me, and put it in my car. Once I found myself making out with a guy I barely knew. Suddenly it hit me that I couldn't stand that guy; I had a talk with myself, and I stopped being used by guys I didn't even like anyway. The need for some normalcy in my life, an inkling of control, or someone who cared for me may have prevented my desperate pleadings for attention. I didn't have any of those things, but I kept looking in all the wrong places as the song goes.

A guy asked if I wanted to have a couple when I got off work and I assured him I did. I knew he had a steady girlfriend, but she wasn't with him that night. He also had a patch over his left eye. He got an injury that afternoon at work. He drove us to Werewolf Hill and proceeded to give me another beer. "I hear you just go out with guys who only have booze, Sue. Is that true?" Well, my self-righteousness indignation kicked in. Or I could have said the truth hurt. For whatever the reason, I told him I was walking home. Not a good idea. There was a light in the far distance and I headed across the desert towards it. I could hear that guy calling for me to come back and he was saying his eye was hurting, but I had a point to make. I had a white uniform on, and it got ripped from the cactus and barbed wire fences. Finally, I stopped and decided that light wasn't getting any closer, and I turned around. I was walking away from town! I had been looking at one light while hundreds were behind me! I turned around and headed towards lights instead of a light. Reaching some houses, I chose one that had a light on the porch—I knocked on the door. A man answered the door and he allowed me to use the phone to call Mom. Here she came at three o'clock in the morning with Gabe, and all the kids to pick me up. She never asked me a question about why I was out there. I'm sure she knew.

Another time I went out with a guy named Speedy. You probably have figured out already why they called him that. I had heard he took uppers and I'm sure he took something but I was not too familiar with pills. He was a small guy, but he sure could dance and fight! I saw his fighting skills first hand at a nightclub one night. I was too young to go in. So, some of us sat in the parking-lot enjoying the music and drinking. Speedy and another guy came out the door, and Speedy immediately started kicking the other guy. That fellow couldn't get up fast enough to get in a punch. Speedy had a bad reputation and he had been in reform school for a while. Supposedly, that is where he learned to fight. We enjoyed the entertainment. Anyway, Speedy asked to take me home one night, and I accepted his offer and his beer. When we got to a remote place in the desert, Speedy told me to take off my clothes as soon as the motor stopped. "You have to be kidding," I said emphatically. He said he wasn't, and he had something in the glove compartment that said I would accept his blatant request. "Well, you son-of-a-bitch, if you're going to shoot me it's going to be in my back!"

I opened the door and started walking again! He yelled for me to get back in the car, and I noticed his voice had gotten weaker. Besides, I was not very good at the walking drill in a desert. When I got back to the car, looked in, Speedy had passed out across the seat.

"Get over, Speedy, and I will drive." I said, as I pushed him over and we took off. I drove myself home and yelled at Speedy when we got there. I told him to get up and drive himself home. Well he did, and I stood there laughing because he ran up in every yard on that street as far as I could see his taillights. Thankfully, there were no fences in the yards. He would later go to school and become a college professor. I would have never guessed that ending for Speedy, but I'm glad he turned out okay.

I got a severe crush on a guy who had a mother who was Hispanic. His name was Nick. Of course, he drank a lot, too. He was Catholic and I even looked that religion up in the encyclopedia, that showed how serious I was about him. I didn't know all of this when we started, not dating, but drinking and parking. One of the girls I worked with clued me into some worldly wisdom "You know he's a Mexican, don't you?" she spouted off one day. Well I didn't at that time.

"Well, it's too late, now, thank you," I blurted out. I really didn't see a problem with that. He took me to the black part of town to a nightclub one night and we went inside. He had been there many times by himself, maybe with another female, I'm not sure. Anyway, we danced, talked and enjoyed the place. There were no problems at all. Everyone was polite and they even bought us drinks.

One night, Nick did not show up after my shift. I went with another group and drank too much. I decided I was going to his house and curse him out! Going towards the highway was a road that went up a hill. Not sure what happened, maybe a flat tire, but I went over a cliff. I had a beer in one hand and cigarette in the other one, so there was not much steering going on. When I realized I was going down the cliff I laid down in the floorboard! I used the side of my ankle to slow the car down by pressing on the brake the best I could. Suddenly, I hit an embankment or a big pile of rocks. Some of my party buddies were following me, thankfully. Robert, ran down that hill and got me out of the car. He picked me up and carried me up to their car like I was a sack of potatoes. He wanted to take me to the hospital but I refused that idea. They took me home and I went to sleep dreading what I was going to tell Mom the next morning.

The next morning, I was sick as a dog. "Sue, where's your car?" she asked the first thing out of her mouth before the coffee was done. "I had a flat tire. It went down that embankment by the curve, all the way to the bottom on Eighth Street," I answered.

Still shaking her head, we all piled in Mom's car and headed to the scene of my crime. When Mom saw my car, she started crying. "Sue. you are going to kill yourself, yet," she sobbed.

Every time, I looked down I fought the urge to throw up. So, I just kept quiet for a change, and let her be upset. Well, we couldn't get the car out so I had to depend on Mom to take me to work, and I hated being dependent on her or anyone. There was a guy who kept telling me he knew that car that went over the hill was mine. I denied it. There wasn't any way the police knew who it belonged to! I was never cited, and after a month or so, it was towed away.

I was the only one working in the family at that time. There was a program at school which allowed me to work only one-half a day. Six days a week I worked with Tuesdays off. I ate a baked potato for lunch for over a year. Beans and potatoes were the mainstays for our meals at home. Mom made biscuits or cornbread for every meal. One evening while I was eating, Lonnie kept aggravating me by grabbing my cornbread off my plate. I had a severe headache or as some would call a "hangover" that day. I warned Lonnie several times to leave me alone. When he didn't I stabbed him with my fork. He would show me the prong scars for years later. I told him he finally got the point(s) when I told him not to aggravate me.

On one of my days off, Mom had cooked some fresh pinto beans. I asked her for an onion. "No onion," she said. "How about some mustard?" I demanded. "No mustard," she answered hanging her head, "What the hell do you have?" I smarted off.

"Don't you use that uppity talk to me! I haven't had a broom in over a month to sweep this hellhole," she shouted.

"I'll never live like this!" I retorted.

"You'll be surprised what you'll have to do, someday, young lady!" she argued. She was right!

Well, I took off and went to Charlie's house, who was an older man who was a customer at the place where I worked. He had a convertible and he had taken my friend and me to ballgames a couple times. Sometimes he would let us drive his car. His wife and daughter had been killed in a car wreck years before. He had all of his meals at the café, and we waitresses would fight to wait on him as he was nice and he tipped well. I went up to his door and knocked—he slowly came to the door and I saw that he was holding a book.

"Hello, Sue, come in. I was reading the dictionary so I won't lose my memory," he explained.

"Oh, good, Charlie. Could I borrow twenty dollars?" I stammered. He handed me twenty dollars out of his billfold.

"I'll pay you back two dollars a week, okay, Charlie?" I negotiated. He agreed. Not sure if I ever paid him back, completely. I sure should have, though.

Years later he will fly to northern California to visit me after I married. He was a special friend.

The man who hired me at the drive-in was only there a short time after I was hired as a carhop. But while he was there he asked me to do him a favor. He said if a car drove on the curb with an out-of-state license he wanted me to copy the license number down and give it to him, especially the Texas plates. Being a dumb kid, I did that many times for him. What I was doing was targeting scabs for him! The striking union miners would go and beat the scabs up, drive them off the road, or make their lives miserable any way they could. I never connected the dots. We were scabs! The same thing could have been done to us, but of course we didn't have the money to go to a fast-food place. We were outsiders and not accepted by many, but we were never harmed in that manner.

Working at that eating establishment was difficult to say the least. My lady boss was strict and I was held to the highest standard. I remember being cold during the winter. I wore at least two pairs of socks every day. Under the sink were openings, big cracks in the walls, and the winter cold was hard on my feet during the time I was washing dishes. I had nightmares about washing so many damn dishes even in warm weather. She would constantly lower the thermostat to save money. We would moan aloud when she did that. With the harshness though, there were bright spots. I met people there who became my lifelong friends.

One of my favorite anecdotes was told to me as an adult from a friend. We worked together, at the café. She and I had boyfriends who came in together several times. She ended up marrying the guy who she was going with at that time. Being mouthy and for whatever reason, I asked her one time if she was frigid. I'm sure I did that simply to see the shocked look I saw on her face that day. She asked me what that meant. Playing the drama queen, I sneered, "You don't know what frigid means?" "Go ask our boss, she knows!" I exclaimed. Well, the naïve girl, did go and ask our boss what the word meant.

Unfortunately, our boss was sitting with a group of male coffee drinkers. Of course, Cindy, my co-worker told our boss it was Sue's idea. I was in trouble again, as usual.

After Cindy was married for a while her womanizing husband asked her if she was frigid! She said she thought, "Oh, goodness, Sue knew that I was frigid when we were teenagers!" That was a credit I sure didn't deserve!

Another friend said she remembered a story which happened when I was a carhop. She said I was working as fast as I could one night and a guy yelled at me. She said he was trying to embarrass me in front of all the people parked at the curb. "Hey Sue, your pants are unzipped!" he called out. She said I didn't even look down, and I retorted, "I know, I trained them to do that!" I was always fast on the uptakes, but I had years of verbal abuse, and I had to have a line of strong bull, so everyone would think I was tough!

Not sure why, but I ended up going to a little Baptist church. I remember there were several kids I knew who were going there, so that was probably the reason. We were smokers, drinkers and in general the undesirables in school. We were the undesirables at the church, too, I would soon find out.

There was going to be an outing for the youth at this church and I wanted to go. It was in the desert and I heard there was a little stream there and that itself was an oddity in the desert. I was excited. I hadn't been out in nature but a couple times since coming to New Mexico.

After we crossed the stream in the arroyo we began the climbing up a hill. Of course, I had to be the first one to reach the summit. Just as my eyes could see in the distance, I saw a sight that was totally new to me. A herd of deer were so close I could see the expressions on their faces. They were as surprised to see me as I was to see them! I had never seen any deer in the wild before. I started yelling at the other kids while jumping up and down. They saw deer all the time. Many families would take their kids out of school to go deer hunting. In my antics, I lost my balance and fell backwards on a lechuguilla cactus. I was literally covered with spines and they went through my jeans, but mainly on my hand since I used my right one to keep me from tumbling down the hill. The boy that I had gone with had a pair of tweezers, and he sat for the longest time and picked many of those needles out of me, one by one. The preacher came to look at my hand and decided I should go to the emergency room.

The preacher took me to the emergency room and many more of the cacti were removed. The doctor told me many would work themselves out in time, but one was in there for twenty some years. Sometimes it would fester up and I would pick at it with a sharp object. Finally, I eventually had to go to a doctor to have it cut out. It looked like a piece of petrified wood when it finally came out of my hand after all those years.

When the preacher took me home I was overly excited as I had never had been to a hospital before. I burst in the door.

"Mom, guess where I have been! I went to the hospital!" I exclaimed.

That woman started cursing so bad; I was embarrassed by her language in front of the preacher and all. It took me a while to register what she even was yelling about. Apparently, she had been listening to the radio, and she heard about a wreck with a bunch of teenagers. She thought that was why I had been at the hospital. After the preacher explained why we were at the hospital, she calmed down a bit. He then assured Mom that the church would pay the bill for the cacti removal.

Mom kept getting the bill from the hospital and I dreaded to see that piece of paper in her hand. I knew why she was shaking it at me. "Get your ass over to that preacher's house and tell him to pay this damn bill," she demanded.

Well, I took that bill over there four times. They seemed to see me coming and they would hide and not answer the door. Mom never did pay that bill because she didn't have the money. Not sure why the preacher did not pay it, but I decided I wasn't going to have any more dealings with a church, as they lie and take advantage of poor people just like Mom had said!

The first time I joined Girl's Athletic Association I was a sophomore. It cost one dollar to join for a year. I didn't have a dollar and I never asked Mom, as I knew she didn't have one either. Being in an athletic setting was a joy. I knew the basics of volleyball, basketball and softball. We met every Tuesday and even if I was dog tired I always showed up on time. We took several trips out of town and I felt like I was so privileged. There were several Hispanic girls in GAA and most of them had exceptional athletic ability. We would share stories about boys and school. One girl told us that she went out with Anglo boys, but only to park and make out. One Hispanic girl was chosen to be to be the Rodeo Queen, but she is the only one I remember winning a beauty contest.

There was this girl in GAA who was picked on by all of the girls in the class, including me. Many times, I would go out of my way to knock her books out of her arms or just pester her anyway I could. On one of our trips we were snow sledding down a hill. She was on a sled and as she veered really close to me, I jumped on her back and rode on her all the way down the steep hill pretending to being a cowgirl. I thought of what I had done to her many times and I asked myself, 'why'. Honestly, I think it was just for attention. It was for the same reason I wanted to fight Wanda just for a no-good, made up reason. I just wanted to be seen as being tough and cool.

Once, a girl with special needs came after me with a needle in the showers at school during PE class. I was terrified of needles! Mom had to drag me to the nurse to get a TB test so I could work in a food establishment. Anyway, the girl was large, but my fear made me a worthy adversary. "If you stick me with that needle, I will break every bone in your body!" I threatened. Looking up at her I glared straight into her eyes. She kind of shook her head side to side and turned around and left. I had a lot of practice for dealing with confrontations, and I used all my experiences to stand up for myself with her that day.

One morning Mom yelled, "You better watch those biscuits so they don't burn as she was leaving. Then after a while Gabe told me to get my ass in there and get that bread out of the oven.

"If you want that bread you go get it! Besides, you can't tell me what to do because you're not my daddy, you son-of-a-bitch!" I yelled.

I heard him get out of bed and he charged in the bedroom I shared with all the other kids. He had a board and I thought he was going to swing it at me, but he didn't. He jumped on the bed instead, and he put that board on the side of my jaw! He was straddling me with one knee on either side of my head. I thought he was planning on breaking my neck. I guess the kids crying made him stop, but I'm not sure. When I got up he threw a boot at me, which made my knees buckle.

My friend, Belinda was knocking on the door about that time. I went to answer it, and I was still sniffling. We stepped outside. I told her what Gabe had done and about the sexual abuse I had suffered for years. Again, she was but a teenager and she was overwhelmed with all the information I had laid on her. I felt it changed our friendship. Maybe I didn't know how to handle the situation when someone knew how tarnished and unworthy I was.

Belinda dropped out of school and went to Arizona with two older girls shortly after that day. She came back later, but I really suffered when she left school. She was my best friend and I found myself lonely because I did not have another network of friends to have lunch with, or to chat with. When she left I told her not to tell me where she was going because her mother would come and question me and I wouldn't lie for her. Sure enough, her mom did come and threaten me, but she always blamed me for the times Belinda did something she didn't like. That experience taught me that I needed more than one friend. I have stayed with that policy all through my adult years. Another one of life's lessons for me.

The place where I worked as a carhop was the meeting place for law enforcement of all kinds. City, county, and state officers' cars were in the parking lot continuously. There was a particular sheriff officer who came in the place daily. He would tease me about my cousin chasing me around the ridge and that was why we were called "ridge runners" being from the hills. That got old after a time. When he began making a remark like that one to me I would make a crack right back at him. His eyes would snap as I could tell he didn't allow anyone to usurp his authority. I did. His glare I would return right back at him with one of my own. I was loud and he did not like that at all. The other male customers thought it was funny that I stood up to him and he sure didn't like to be laughed at.

One day he and I were standing at the curb talking. He began telling me about being in court that day. He said that a young girl was in court and she said her dad had molested her. He said anyone could tell the girl was lying. That perked my interest right off. There were many times I wondered what would happen if I turned Gabe in for his abuse. That cocky little guy was staring me right in the face. I was trying to figure out how he knew that girl was lying. I just had the strangest feeling that I needed to remember his words and the smirk he had on his face. A frozen image was made in my mind. Years later, I found out that he was molesting his daughter. Sexual predators get a thrill out of sharing their sordid secrets. I got on his nerves and he probably knew I wouldn't dare tell anyone about that conversation. He was right—this is the first time I've said anything about him. The creep.

Juarez, Mexico was a destination for many teenagers from our town in the 60's, myself included. We could go over there in a couple hours and do the town. We could get served in all the nightclubs and see any kind of show that we wanted to see. We saw hardcore porn movies and even a live bedroom show performed by two females. I can't ever forget that my friend, Belinda, threw a penny on the bed after the girls finished. Belinda was so indignant! Heck, our guys negotiated with their guys on what we wanted to see; the girls did their job. But my friend had the nerve to get upset with them. I never understood her logic in that matter and other ones when we were adults.

I went with two different friends to Juarez. Johnny who worked at Safeway and Robert who delivered milk to the place I worked. Johnny and I also had a standing date to go see Edgar Poe's movies when they were in town. When we went to Mexico we would drive all night and be back home by daybreak. He was a good friend.

Robert had a couple of his friends he took along when we went. Belinda went with us a time or two. There was another girl, Connie who went with us a few trips. Connie was a cowgirl through and through. She smoked Camels and had a crush on a girl. I lost contact with Connie right after we graduated. She had horses and I went with her a lot to feed them, but I never rode them like Connie. I was not a natural cowgirl.

One of Robert's friends, Ken, went with us several times. Somewhere along the way he began asking me out. I was still serious about Nick but he wasn't around all the time. Later, Nick would tell me to go with Ken because he would be better for me. Never knew how he really felt about me. He died at a young age. He was a full-blown diabetic in his thirties and he kept drinking until he died I was told.

As time went on, Ken and I went together quite a bit. Belinda wanted me to go with Ken. She was impressed that Ken had a couple of guns and he could fast draw really well.

There was another guy who really cared for me and he had asked me to marry him. He was the kid who stayed at our house a lot. He was always there for me and never interfered with any of the wild schemes I got myself into. I told him I would not marry him until he had gone into the service, got out, and got a job. He left for the Navy. He hated school, and there wasn't a future for him in our town. I had a lot of conditions for things to be met in my life. I don't remember that plan or any others working out the way I wanted them to, but I kept making conditions.

I was a senior and I felt like things were piling on my shoulders. I had a lot of responsibility within the family. I financed the Christmases my junior and senior year for the younger kids. I bought all the presents, decorated, and did anything else which would help Mom. I took the kids trick-or-treating, bought Easter baskets for Easter, and took them to their first movie.

Any excuse I got I would stay away from the house; especially, when Mom wasn't there. There were always fights. Gabe was always chasing a kid through the house, to beat their ass, usually Fred's! I have seen that kid take so much pummeling, and I would hear his flesh make dull thud sounds when a belt, a board or a fist would land on his body. He never cried much either. Fred just wanted to please everyone. He would make everyone coffee the way they liked it; even carried the cups he made the way we drank it to us. Cleaning my car was considered a big deal for him. Whatever loose change he could find in the car I would let him keep. I introduced him to Elvis, and he stayed obsessed with Elvis his whole life.

Aunt Nina had told me when I graduated, I could live with her. She lived in Florida at the time of my graduation. She said she would pay for my college tuition. I just could not do that! I felt like it would be a betrayal to Mom. So, I was totally in limbo.

Graduation for me was a challenge as I did not have enough credits. I just went to school half-days my junior and senior years. Also, I had failed algebra so I was one credit short. I was advised to take a correspondence course. My choice was Etiquette. I finished the course so I had enough credits to graduate. I was going to make Mom proud because I had kept my promise to her. I was graduating!

The mailman delivered a letter to our address and it was for me. It was from Karen, my older half-sister, the one who came to our school for a short time in WV. She wanted me to tell her all about Mom. She said she had a stepmother and the woman was very mean. One of the saddest stories I ever heard was about what her stepmom did to her. Most houses at that time had sockets in the ceilings. I once stuck my finger in a socket and I became paralyzed by the current—it took forever it seemed, for me to pull away. So, I knew first-hand what she said was true. Karen said she had long hair when she was a kid. For a punishment, the stepmother would put Karen on a chair and tie her hair to a short chain from the socket. If Karen moved, the current would be turned on and it would shoot down her hair and shock her. Of course, there were beatings and verbal abuse which she grew up with also. I'm sure Karen wanted Mom to sound like a nurturing, loving mother. She probably had dreamed that was the way Mom would be. I did the same thing about my own father who I never met.

I was truthful as I could be, and I told Karen that Mom had her dark side. She wasn't affectionate and there was rarely a smile on her face. I didn't want that girl to think I was living in Disneyland. Mom said she did not want to read Karen's letter when I offered to show it to her. Later, I heard that Karen was in jail or prison for forgery. I never heard from her again and neither did Mom.

I was drinking a lot and I had begun taking diet pills. A lot of girls got the pills from a doctor in town. My heavy schedule, drinking, diet pills, and getting married was too much for me. By Sunday night I would be on a crying jag. It was like being on a roller coaster without any brakes.

A lady I worked with lived across the street from Ken's family. She said there was always yelling and slamming of doors. "Sue, that family has a lot of problems and the stepdad is really mean!" she told me. Well, that sounded a lot like my family, so I didn't pay much attention. But I couldn't say I wasn't warned.

There were four kids in Ken's family, one girl and three boys. The girl was illegitimate. Ken and his brother were born in Arkansas and Ken's mom was married to their father. Ken's and his brother's dad had been a judge. There was one story that he had knocked Ken down some stairs when he was real young. Ken's brother was a large guy, unlike Ken. He was said to have Lou Gehrig's disease. I didn't ever believe that story. He never had to work as hard as Ken, and he pretended to be sick a lot. It was said that Ken's mom left her husband in the middle of the night with the three kids. The man she ran off with worked in a sawmill in Cloudcroft and later he went into construction. Ken's mom had a boy by her new man and that boy was spoiled rotten.

Several times I was told how mean Jim, the stepfather, was to those kids except for his spoiled son. He would take a water hose and hose the boys down to make them work faster, or to do a better job. Once the crew was working across the street from our house and Mom said that Jim was mean...if Mom said he was mean, he was mean! The family built a two story out of adobe. It still stands, and in its day, it was quite a showcase.

Jim would take a bunch of us teenagers out on a job site, and we were told to go in and insulate the attics. Like dumb kids we would do it. Ken's Mom would cook us a meal and that was our pay! Jim was lazy, anyone could see that including me. Ken's grandpa lived with the family too. He had lost an eye somehow, and he was pretty scary to look at. He was always working and he had to eat apart from everyone else.

Ken bought me gifts such as a hairdryer and of course candy and flowers during our courtship. He had warned me though, that he would not open a door for me, and I don't recall that he ever pulled a chair out for me at a table. Not sure where he got all his rules or standards, but I wasn't used to anyone treating me with respect, anyway.

Ken's parents had a side business. Ken's mom would write music or lyrics and singers would come and visit them in that big house. The boys were to give up their beds and rooms when company came. They also booked bands for entertainment at bars or nightclubs. Neither one of them drank any liquor that I knew about. Teetotalers all the way. I was really impressed that Elvis had visited them when he first started his career. I was shown a Christmas card which Elvis sent them, and I admired them for knowing a celebrity like Elvis. Another thing that impressed me was that they had meat for every meal, practically. I just knew they had to be well-to-do.

The family belonged to a religion or cult called the Christadelphians. Jim's parents, belonged to that church when they lived in the mountains. They were considered to be conscientious objectors. The stepdad worked under the CCC program during WWII.

Another one of their beliefs was if you pointed a gun at someone you were to kill that person. The boys were never allowed to have play guns when they were young. They were allowed to go hunting and kill deer for food though. Their living room walls were covered with mounted trophies which had been prepared by a taxidermist. Many antlers were casually laid across the furniture. Ken had an obsession for guns, and I have wondered if it was because of the family beliefs from that church.

When Ken was eighteen he rebelled against his family and joined the Marines. He joined the service using his biological father's name. He didn't stay in the service very long, and that was a stigma for him the rest of his life. He got discharged using a hardship discharge. Out of his family and all of his cousins he was the only one who joined the service. Their church affiliation exempted them from being drafted. Ken was released for the reason the family said they needed him home to help with their business.

A man came from a school in Texas and tried to get me to enroll in a school in that state. There was no way I knew anything about college. A dog that I had drug out of the canal, a stray, kept humping his leg the whole time he was there, but it didn't hurry him along. So, I wouldn't go and stay with my aunt, and there was no college in my future so this was one of my cases where I didn't know what to do. I just knew what I didn't want to do.

I had saved three hundred dollars. I decided I would take Mom and the kids on a vacation. It was to be Mom's and the kids first vacation. We went to a place called White Sands. I had been there before on a GAA trip. We played softball there. The kids had a great time and we stopped along the way and had picnics and enjoyed the scenery. Mom had a '57 Ford and it was a beauty, well, it was until I ran up on the divider and hit a light pole a couple weeks before. I had been drinking, but no one was around at three o'clock in the morning, so I did not get a citation or anything. My guardian angel had to work overtime to keep me safe and to keep me from getting in trouble.

Ken did not like me being in GAA. He would pick me up from one of my trips and he would ask me why I wanted to do that "club" thing. He had never been allowed to participate in sports or clubs as he always had to work. He never knew how to have fun. Looking back, his family focused on being critical of most everyone and everything that anyone did. I guess our family did too. I just never paid much attention to anyone but Mom. Still, I did what I wanted to do and when I wanted to do it. So, I didn't have many complaints about my freedom.

I do not remember Ken and I ever discussing getting married. I'm sure we did as there was a date set. We were going to be married at Ken's house by a justice of the peace. I refused to wear the color white. Instead I married in blue. I did not want anyone to think I was something I was not, a virgin. My friend Belinda was my bridesmaid. I thought we would trade that honor, but she had one of her sisters instead for her wedding. I came to her wedding thirteen-hundred miles to be told I had been replaced. I was hurt but looking back on that day I'm glad the sister had been selected. She later committed suicide, and I would not have felt right if I had made a big fuss. To be honest I don't remember if I ever complained, but knowing me I may have.

I never wanted a diamond ring, and I never knew what Ken's plans were for a ring. We ended up going to a jewelry store and getting matching golden bands. A few months after we were married, Ken's ring would prevent him from getting his hand back from under a beam. Ken's hand was injured severely and he did not wear his wedding band ever again.

Thinking back about our wedding day I remember how nervous Ken was. He was pacing and smoking up a storm. I don't remember being especially nervous. I do remember Ken and I talked about the possibility of me getting pregnant. He said that wouldn't be a problem—he said I just could go to his mother and she would take care of me. That would have been a nightmare if that happened! Liz, Ken's mother, was a lovey-dovey type of a woman and I had my guard up around her. I was suspicious of anyone hugging and kissing around me all the time even a female.

When I saw my birth certificate the name for me was Sandra Sue Smith. Mom's maiden name was Smith. I had been raised with the last name of Kindle. But the lady at the courthouse said it didn't matter what my history was, as I was going to change my name when I married anyway. Ken's history was confusing, too. His birth certificate said Johnston and he was raised by a Brazille. When Ken went into the service he went under Johnston. Later, we would get a GI loan so our house was under Johnston and all of our other bills were under Brazille. Our histories were a bonding for us, I guess. Back then adoption was not a common thing for anyone to do, not with our circle of friends and family anyway.

Mom and I never talked about me getting married. I just told her what I was going to do, and she accepted my decisions and she kept quiet. Something that was really important to her was that I have an iron skillet. That was my wedding gift from her. She seemed to like Ken. She thought he was smart. He did read a lot, and we didn't know anyone who read many books if they didn't have to. I guess we all considered him as knowing what he was talking about, most of the time. If I questioned him though, he would get angry, so I learned to keep quiet most of the time.

We went on a honeymoon in Cloudcroft. Ken's step-grandparents had a little cabin in the mountains. The Christadelphian Church was close by and at one time the church was really important to Ken's family. By the time, we were married no one even spoke of the church or their beliefs. I spoke before of the attitude towards guns I thought was odd or unusual. The members of the church were conscientious objectors. The step-grandparents had two boys and they made a living by cutting trees and cutting them into lumber at their sawmill. Ken's step-uncle had five boys and there were rumors flying about them all the time. One son supposedly killed someone. The oldest boy had been married at least three times. Their dad was to have been a millionaire according to a story. He took old army barracks and made them into little houses. He would sell them to the poor Mexican families, and when they got delinquent on their payments, he would repossess the house, and sell it to another poor family. There was a rivalry among the cousins, so one had to decide which story to believe and about who and go from there. Too complicated for me.

For our honeymoon dinner we had hot beef sandwiches at a little hotel in Cloudcroft and I couldn't have been more pleased! Anytime I had meat for a meal, I was a happy diner. While riding around the hills the next day we ran into someone who Ken had known when he was younger. The man invited us to his home for dinner that night. As soon as I entered the door I was disgusted! There were flies literally covering every square inch of the surface of that kitchen! The wife of the man was cooking hamburger patties and the flies would light on the meat before she put the platter on the table. Meat was a delicacy for me but I wasn't eating that meat! I told everyone I wasn't hungry, and Ken glared at me. There was no way I could have eaten. My stomach was churning, but I held my ground and didn't take a bite of that meal. I just watched the flies around everyone's head.

We came back to town and Ken's younger brother's wife was working on an oil painting. Sherry used Ken's hands positioned on his hips as a model for her painting. The title of the painting was the "Lady in Red." She had told Ken if he married before she finished the painting she would give the painting to him for a wedding present. That painting was our second wedding gift right after the iron skillet from Mom. Sherry and Melvin had married when Mel was sixteen. Ken's parents took the couple to Texas and they could marry there if the parents consented even if one was sixteen and he was.

I stayed in Carlsbad until I had my bridal shower. It was the first shower I had been to. As a matter of a fact, my wedding was the first wedding I had attended. Ken and his friends went back to California, or "Heaven," as they called it to work before the rains came in the fall. I was to take a Greyhound bus to Petaluma, a small town in northern California. I was excited about living in California as I used to daydream about the place while I was roaming the mountains in WV.

High school (1960-1963)

CALIFORNIA

It was hard telling everyone goodbye and climbing on that bus to Petaluma. I had no idea what to expect. All the kids were at the bus station with Mom and they saw me off. The trip was uneventful until I got to San Francisco. I was told that Petaluma was only thirty miles from San Francisco, but no one seemed to have heard of Petaluma in San Francisco! I began to get a bit scared at the bus station. The bus station in San Francisco was large. I had to deposit a dime in a slot just to use the restroom. Finally, I saw the town Santa Rosa on an overhead sign and I boarded the bus there because I knew Santa Rosa was north of Petaluma.

As I was seated on the bus, a man who was all hunched over in his back sat by me, and I was afraid to move. He never said a word. We crossed the Golden Gate Bridge and it wasn't even golden! I was rather disappointed as the color looked like a rusty red; but I got over it quickly looking out across the bay—it was breathtaking.

Ken met me at the bus station. He had two cousins living in the small town and they had given him a ride to pick me up. We were taken to the hotel where we lived for a couple of months. There was a housing shortage in the Bay Area so Ken worked long hours. Construction was booming there, but there was a problem. Every job was union, so if Ken's job finished he had to go to the union hall and sit and wait his turn to be called out. It was first come and first served for those jobs. So, there were bad experiences with unions in WV and in California. Mentally, I would recall Mom's logic again; "Churches and unions are great until a poor person needs them."

The night teller at the hotel told us about an apartment that had just become vacant. We didn't have a car so we had to walk the ten blocks there to pay a deposit. Our rent was $89.50 for a one-bedroom apartment and that was a lot of money back then. There was a swimming pool and I taught myself to swim there. There was also a laundry room. Mom had an old wringer washing machine in WV, but she always had to go to the laundromat in NM. I was happy with my new residence.

Ken was not comfortable around strangers so I had to deal with some restrictions. I was not allowed to talk to anyone so I would just nod my head and speak. I could not even open the drapes when Ken was home. He always said he didn't want anyone gawking in the windows at us. I was lonely. I needed to be around people.

Ken and his cousin, Jesse, fought and argued constantly and sometimes Jesse would go to work and leave Ken home. We joined a bowling league due to Jesse's encouragement. Sometimes he would go off and leave us especially, if we were scheduled to bowl his team. Being afoot was challenging for us, especially during the rainy season. Ken had to put cardboard in the bottom of his shoes but his feet still got wet.

We used the bar where Ken had gambled to get a loan to buy a television. That helped us get credit later to buy a car. Ken had to have a brand-new car. When we got furniture, it had to be the best by his standards. I went along with his preferences as I had never bought anything new in my life, other than our wedding bands.

Ken's rules were getting harder to live with as time went on. I couldn't wear sweatshirts because I looked like a lesbian. I couldn't cut my hair and he didn't want to see any rollers in my hair. I had to be home when Ken entered the door. I couldn't do so many things and I was told to do many things. I was not adjusting well at all. Ken wanted to hypnotize me and I thought that was absurd. Ken was mad at me constantly for petty things. I was uncomfortable most of the time in my new environment.

When we began socializing a bit with Ken's co-workers, Ken thought I was having an affair with a guy he worked with. A couple times when the guy left early from work Ken would rush through our door to see if the guy was in our apartment. If I talked to anyone Ken said I was flirting.

Ken bought a Polaroid camera and he was constantly after me to pose in the nude for pictures. I hated doing that. Once I asked him where he kept the pictures and he said he must have thrown them away by accident. I never believed him, and I'm so thankful we did not have the internet back then. I was uncomfortable with his sexual demands. We would have intense fights and then he would want to have sex right afterwards. I never understood that. We were on two different wavelengths about sex our entire marriage.

When I married, I promised myself I would quit drinking. Once, I had been baking some bread which had been frozen. When I woke up the next morning, I didn't remember baking the bread and dough was all over the walls. I told Ken I was not going to drink anymore and he was not happy about that decision. He said I had started him drinking while we were dating—he didn't want me to stop. I wasn't aware that he saw our past that way.

Later in our marriage, a knock on the door led me to open it to a poll taker. The college student was from the Gallup Poll, nonetheless. Ken was so excited as he loved to read and discuss the Gallup Poll. Me, not so much. Ken's face fell immediately when the young man said he wanted to talk to the female of the household.

"She's a teetotaler!" Ken volunteered brashly.

Ken didn't try to hide his aggravation. I answered the best I could with Ken interrupting the interview constantly. I really wanted for Ken to listen and give me a chance to explain my new outlook on drinking for myself. Sadly, that wasn't in the cards that day or any other day for me.

One night we got into an intense argument about race. He was using words and statements which totally offended me. I never had a race issue that I could pinpoint. I guess since I grew up around all white people and I never had to form an opinion when I was at an impressionable age. Ken would always see people as a race first, and then decide if they deserved any merit of being a good person. Anyway, I got so angry with his views I spent the night in the bathtub. The bathroom was the only room which had a lock on the door. I did not know the man I married, and maybe he felt the same way about the woman he married. When we were around each other we were always drinking before we were married. It's hard to get to know anyone under those conditions.

I did not get any birth control until we had been married for several months. Thankfully, I did not get pregnant. Being barely eighteen I knew so little of life. I had no role models so I had to wing things the best I could. I was always at a loss for understanding relationships. I had entered marriage with the thought I could just get a divorce if it didn't work, but somewhere along the way, my thinking changed. I wanted to live without a divorce—have kids who would not have stepdads who could abuse them. I had a lot to learn.

Once after we got a car, Ken and I had another serious fight. Being very angry, I went and got in the car and drove on the freeway for my first time. I was getting more confidence in myself all the time. California, for some reason, was a place where I felt accepted; maybe, because I felt wanted after my experience in New Mexico where I had felt like an outsider all the time. After I cooled off, I went back home. Ken said our landlady had come over and she wanted us to help her manage the sixty-unit apartments. Funny, she thought we were a quiet, reserved couple. She didn't know anything about me being gone for hours while learning to exit on the freeway. We took the job of helping her manage the apartments, we did that for five years.

When we started bowling that was something for me to look forward each week. Ken and his cousin, Jesse would pit his cousin's live-in and me against each other in a competitive match of bowling—the guys would bet on us. Jesse would take his gal to practice three or four times a week. I was a competent bowler, but I was short two things that kept me from bowling practice—transportation and money to rent the lanes and the bowling shoes. One day a lady asked me to bowl in the daytime on her women's league. She said she could pick me up. So that was a thrill for me to bowl with other women and I always had a ride to boot.

Bowling was a good match for me other than it was expensive. I started winning tournaments and I got to travel to many places in California. Once, I won a tournament and got a train ticket, plus the entry fee paid to bowl in San Diego. What a thrill! The first time I saw Disneyland was on a state bowling tournament. I would bowl for thirty-one years. That game gave me so much confidence and many friends along the way.

Eventually, we started a couple's weekly night to play poker and drink with other carpenters and their wives. I never got close to any of the wives, though. One night, Ken came up with the idea to bet on me to arm wrestle the other women, and some of the men. Seems like he was always pitting me against others in athletic matches. Eventually, two wives began having an affair with each other. One of their husbands would take off work and hide in the attic to spy on his wife and the other woman. Later, he confronted his wife. They eventually got a divorce, and right after that the group parted ways.

Ken was a carpenter, and I was told by many that he was a very good one. Over the years, I saw his skills myself. He said many times he was glad he had been forced to do the work for his stepdad, when he was younger, as it made him a good living when he got older. He did make good money in California when it wasn't raining. The whole winter construction was shut down because it rained from October to March. I found it depressing to stay indoors all winter. Ken would read and watch television a lot, and he seemed content to do that for hours at a time.

I was only afraid of two women in my life—my mother and the woman who was my landlady at that time. Mrs. Greves, my landlady, would enter my apartment and tell me how I should rearrange my furniture. She totally intimidated me. She was a tough English woman who thought of herself as being royalty. Maybe, she was. She sure had an uppity attitude.

She told me about her having polio when she was young. She said her toes were twisted under her feet and she had to walk on exposed bones. She limped rather clumsily with a cane and she had to have special made shoes. Her husband Paul was always being reprimanded by her. I didn't care for him. I saw him peering in the windows of the apartments and it reminded me of someone who was a peeping Tom. Maybe, that was one of the reasons Mrs. Greves was on his case all the time.

Mrs. Greves loved to tell me stories. She had two daughters who were usually her topics for the storytelling. Her oldest daughter, Dawn, had married a Las Vegas, Nevada nightclub musician. Dawn shared gossip about the stars and celebrities with her mother; and Mrs. Greves shared them with me. Not sure if they were true or not. The one, I seriously doubted, was that Debbie Reynolds was gay.

But my most memorable story of hers was about Dawn's husband. Dawn and her husband owned a cabin close to Lake Tahoe. One weekend he went to the cabin alone. He picked some wild mushrooms and made some mushroom soup. When Dawn drove up to the cabin a few days later, she saw a dead rabbit, a cat, and her husband's dog lying around the grounds of the cabin. Her husband had picked some poisonous mushrooms! Spellbound by her description of the effects of mushroom poisoning, I listened intently. She said that every pore and opening in his body had bled. He was so bloated that one could not recognize him. To this day, I feel a pang in my gut, perhaps from fear from listening to Mrs. Greves story when I see a mushroom or toadstool in the wild.

One Christmas Mrs. Greves wanted to take me to San Francisco, mainly to see the Christmas tree at Macy's. That was the largest tree I ever saw indoors. We would go up floor after floor in that store's spiral stairs. We could see a different theme and sparkling decorations on every floor. I'm sure Mrs. Greves knew how lonely I was on holidays and she decided that she would give me a special holiday that year, and she hit the mark.

Ken didn't like cats but he finally conceded to my arguments for one. I was always on alert if Mrs. Greves was walking around the court. I could tell if she was by the sound of her cane striking the concrete. We were not allowed to have cats in the apartments but I brought one home anyway. He helped me with some of my loneliness. I taught Silly how to retrieve... well, Pall Mall packages anyway, when they were wadded up like a ball. When he heard that noise he knew the game of fetch was on. He would play hide-and-seek and jump out and swat us when we were close to finding his hiding place. We gave him a bath once a week but Ken quickly resigned from that chore. Silly would yowl and howl but he never scratched me.

When the rules changed and we could have cats at the apartment—I let Silly outside for the first time. When his feet hit the ground, he froze! He seemed to be paralyzed from that experience but not for long. When we moved to the country he became a regular gad about. Once, he disappeared for three days and I was beside myself! He finally limped in and his foot looked like he had been caught in a trap. I cleaned him up and plastered bandages all over the injured. He liked to lay on our gold couch and I was afraid he might bleed on it. Putting band aids on him wasn't that bad of an ordeal, but getting them off was a regular cat fight! Of course, the band aids would yank on his fur so I had to wrap him in a towel and just expose his leg I was uncovering. That wasn't one of the smartest things I had ever done in my life.

When Ken started a new job, he would usually become the foreman in no time. He worked for a fast-growing company for about six years. We went into a partnership with his boss and another foreman and bought a place in the Russian River area. We had a lot of fun when we met on the weekends. The men would usually cook and the women were supposed to watch the kids and relax. Ken and his boss began to have disagreements, not about Ken's work but Ken was always late to work. Looking back, I remember Ken being up late at night and I had a hard time getting him up in the mornings. I would take him coffee while he was in bed. I babied and coddled him for years, because he wouldn't get up in the morning. I think now he was suffering from depression. For whatever the reason he was drinking more too.

I applied for a job at GTI, a diode factory. I didn't tell Ken until after I got the job. He was dead set against me working, and I always felt I needed to pay my own way. I wanted to have my own spending money. I had memories of not being able to afford a spool of thread, and I did not like those circumstances at all. There were machines at the factory, and a flame would melt an "S" inside of a bead, and these were called diodes. They were used for television sets, rocket ships, and other electronics. I worked there for over a year on the hoot owl shift. That was the shift from eleven at night to seven in the morning. I loved it but it eventually closed down.

Ken's brother Mel and his wife Sherry, moved to Petaluma for work in construction. She was the one who had painted the picture of the "Lady in Red." We spent a lot of time together playing cards and watching television. Sherry and I had nothing in common. She was artistic and I was athletic. She loved makeup and girlie things and I was not interested in any of those things. I did like to bake and I did that quite a bit. Sherry would spend an hour or so icing my baked goods. She wanted the icing to go in the same direction, and I could have cared less.

Her washday was always disappointing for her. She always snarled her nose in the air as she hung the whites on the line. She wouldn't use bleach and her whites were a dingy tan and I told her one day why her wash looked that way. Angrily, she told me that my keeping leftover bacon grease on the stove for flavoring was disgusting! We didn't speak for a week. Once she talked me into posing for one of her paintings. The painting was a mother and a little cherub-faced toddler at a waterfall. The mother was practically nude and I agreed to do it. Not sure what happened to that piece of art. Sometimes she would stand over a gas burner with a piece of wax and mold the most lifelike depictions of humans. I thought that was simply amazing that anyone could do that.

Ken and Sherry both wore contacts and I'm sure Ken had the desire for me to wear them and lose twenty pounds. Ken assured me that he would help me with the contacts. I'm sure I would have never worn them without him pressuring me to do so. An appointment was made and I kept it. Back then only the hard contacts were available. They were to be taken out each night—I had watched Ken do that ritual so many nights before. When the optometrist inserted them, I wanted to drive my fist through the wall as the pain was unbearable.

We were told to go and do things to take my mind off the pain. We pulled up to an A&W and we ordered fish baskets. After a while, the pain had gone away, but as I looked in the distance I couldn't see anything. "I ate my contacts!" I yelled at Ken. I visualized they had dropped in my basket and I had simply eaten them. Ken calmed me down and said he would find them when we got home. Lying across the bed with Ken straddling me, he found them and pushed them back over my eye where they needed to be. I was always losing them, and Ken rescued me every time.

The memory that stands out to me was the time I lost one contact in the bathroom. Ken just knew that the contact had went down the drain but I knew it hadn't. With one contact in I took off to a meeting. Ken called me at the meeting and told me he had found my contact! Apparently, Sheba, our dog had been in the bathroom with me at the time I lost it—it got caught in her paw and she had gone outside. Ken took a flashlight outside, held it at an angle, and the contact glistened in the darkness. I've marveled over that found treasure many times.

Mom and I talked about making a trip back to WV, and we were going to drive. I got a job at an egg packing plant where I candled eggs. My friend would pack the eggs depending on their weight and size. That was one stinking job! We had to hold our breath practically the whole time while we worked. There was a light bulb beneath a slot, and I would stand over the eggs as they came down a chute. I was to look inside the egg and see if there were blood spots inside the egg. If spots were found, I would put the egg aside to go to dog food producers. Some eggs had double yolks, and they were put aside so the owner could charge extra from his customers who had requested them.

Petaluma was the egg capital of the world during World War II. There were farms all over that little town raising chickens. When we were there in the sixties there were only a few farms left though, that raised chickens. Hippies began moving in that area and converting those chicken coops into homes. Once, while we were looking at properties that we couldn't afford, it was an eye-opening adventure. We would walk across a beautiful piece of property to a chicken coop, and there laying on wooden slats would be a water bed! Hippies always fascinated me for some reason.

I finally reached my goal of saving money from my job at the chicken farm. I flew back to New Mexico. Mom and I loaded all the kids in her station wagon and headed east. Mom and I both smoked, but I'm not sure who threw a cigarette out the window. A cigarette landed in the back seat and a blanket caught on fire. We stopped and threw everything from the back seat onto the side of the road and began stomping. We saved everything from burning up completely but a couple blankets had holes in them. We only had traveled twenty miles when that happened. We had laughs galore about that near calamity.

Mom read somewhere that women traveling alone should take precautions. So, she wore a man's hat the whole trip while sitting on the passenger side of the car. Going down country roads we would wave and honk at people walking the roads or sitting on their porches. We laughed a lot just watching people watching us with a confused look on their faces. We stopped at parks and ate our sandwiches and it was a very enjoyable time for us all.

My grandma was still alive on that trip and we got to see her but she was bedridden. She shared her secret recipe with me for her coleslaw and fried green tomatoes. Her secret to all her recipes was just to "add sugar". She and Mom could take a can of corn, add sugar and butter, and anyone would swear it was from an ear just picked from the stalk. Those women would grow leaf lettuce and green onions—pour hot bacon grease over it, and it was the best wilted salad in the country, in my opinion.

One afternoon Grandma had me to get her box of doilies out from under the bed and I was excited. I just knew she was going to give me a prized doily! That didn't happen. She had me to put them back in the box and slide them under the bed, again. Mom laughed a lot about that. I guess she knew how possessive Grandma was about her handiwork. I spent a lot of time with Grandma on that trip just listening to her about her life. She became rather independent after Grandpa died. She got her driver's license in her sixties and drove those mountains in Boone County which would be a feat for anyone, at any age.

While visiting the little hollers and the area around where we lived before, people seemed cold and distant towards us. This was typical, I remembered of the way outsiders were treated by the hill folks. One time, I had overheard Gabe and his brother whispering about strangers disappearing and laughing about it when we lived in the holler and it sounded sinister, scary. Mom was not a stranger though. She had lived there until she was in her forties. We did have a New Mexico license on Mom's station wagon and I guess word had traveled. It seemed to forewarn people that strangers were on their way. Once we stopped to take a picture of the school we kids had gone to while we lived back there. I had graduated from the eighth grade from that building. The school had been turned into apartments. People were standing outside of the building, but when we pulled over to take a picture they disappeared, rather ghostlike. They may have thought we were from the welfare office or something, but many knew Mom. We stayed with Mom's sister and her family and didn't venture from there very much. I could tell Mom was hurt by the rejection of her previous friends. She was ready to go back to New Mexico.

However, I did go visit two sisters who I was friends with. I guess they were friendly enough, but I felt a definite distance from them. First of all, they each had three or four kids each and I didn't have any. I wanted to talk about California and bowling. In hind sight, I see we were in two different worlds and each of us had little desire to be happy for each other. They had moved to Chicago for work. At least we got to see each other and got caught up on some gossip but I was never to see them again.

I drove most all the way to WV and back. We did not have air conditioning, so I would wet a washcloth and keep it on the back of my neck. We went to Abraham Lincoln's birthplace, and to the biggest thrill of all for me, Graceland. I had always been a fan of Elvis and that was a dream come true. After seeing the homes that Ken's company built in the San Francisco area, I was a bit disappointed in Graceland. It seemed to be gaudy and not as impressive as I had been hoping for.

Sherry seemed to flirt with Ken all the time. She was always admiring Ken on his looks or his general knowledge on different subjects. Mel and I seemed to be the backdrop for her adoration of Ken. Of course, Ken ate all that attention up. Mel and I always seemed to be left out of their many conversations. I had no idea what they were talking about, and like Mel, I didn't really care what they were talking about most of the time. Of course, Mel and I didn't have much in common either, other than cooking.

Sherry wanted me to learn to do art. She tried to strike a deal with me. She would give me art lessons, and I would teach her to bowl. At that time in my life I did not have enough confidence to learn anything new. She did bowl a year or two, but she really wasn't interested in it. I never became interested in art until I was in my late thirties.

For my birthday, Sherry and Mel got me a puppy, a German Shepherd. She was registered and she had a real fancy name, but I called her Sheba. We had moved outside of town where a river ran in the back of the property where we rented. Later, we would move next door to a nicer house. That house had a big yard and Sheba could have more space to run. That dog was smart. I had her climbing ladders and she lived to please me it seemed. Anything I asked her to do she would try. I could throw a rock in the river, and she would get the exact rock I threw in the water. I would take one of Ken's socks and he would hide in the acreage behind the house, and Sheba would track him down in no time. I went immediately to the library to get a dog obedience book. It was over five hundred pages...she chewed it up eventually, and I had to pay for it. Once a swarm of bees came through the yard and attacked her. Her head and body had become swollen from the stings, and she still chased bees with a vengeance.

When we got a new bedroom set Ken ordered a custom-made bedspread. It was red velvet, quilted, and it weighed a ton. He wanted it taken off the bed and folded neatly every night. About that time was when I discovered I hated to make beds. One time while visiting, Ken's mother, sat on the bed. He had been showing the spread to her, and she just sat down. I thought he was going to push her to the floor, instead he yelled, "Dammit, get your ass off that bed!" That red treasure cost $120.00. Back in the sixties that was about the most extravagant thing we owned which was not made of wood.

Once when I came home from bowling I could tell Sheba had been on that red covered bed as there was an indentation of her body on the fabric. I had to catch her in the act though. That's what I learned in that dog obedience book. Always catch the dog in the act of doing something wrong before you punished them. Leaving for bowling one morning, I shut the front door, waited a minute or two, and then went to the bedroom window. Sure enough, Queen Sheba was sprawled across that sea of red fabric like she was pure royalty or something. I hit the window hard and screamed, "Sheba!" Well, I scared her all right. She peed all over that spread. We had it dry cleaned, but Sheba left her mark or stain on it for as long as I owned that spread. That stain reminded me of her every morning for years when I made the bed.

Sheba came into heat, and of course, she got pregnant. We had Silly Cat still, which we brought from the apartments, and for some reason she scratched Sheba on the neck—and that scratch got infected. I took Sheba to the vet and he said her pregnancy was too close to delivery, so he couldn't lance her neck. We got her a doghouse and she delivered nine puppies!

There was something wrong, though. They had an odd look about them. Their features, especially the head, seemed out of proportion to the body, and they began dying right away. After a couple days Sheba had only one puppy left. I went to get the puppy and it was cold to my touch. I took it into the house and laid it by the heater and wrapped it in a blanket. I made Sheba lie down by her baby. I tried to get her to nurse the puppy. When I squeezed Sheba's breast, blood came out with the milk. I finally told her to take her puppy outside, and she did. Ken was afraid of Sheba as she would growl at him when he got close to her or the puppy. Finally, I brought her in and shut the door, so Ken could get the puppies which all were dead. He threw all of them in the trash dumpster. That night Sheba jumped the fence and took all the puppies under the house. Ken crawled under the house, got the pups, and boarded up the openings, so she couldn't go back under the house. He took them across town and put them in a dumpster there. I still can hear the awful wailing of mourning in my memory of Sheba missing her puppies.

Sheba was always looking for something to eat. I stored a can of Crisco on a shelf under a counter. Somehow, Sheba would push the plastic lid off the can. She would then get a mouthful of Crisco nonchalantly. I had to watch her closely to see what she was doing. She used the same method when walking past a candy dish on the coffee table. With her tongue hanging out on the side of her mouth she would drag her tongue across the candy causing it to stick together. That stickiness was the evidence against her. Guilty!

She also would get in the trash. We did not have a garbage disposal, and there were always goodies that she seemed to like in that tall, plastic trash can in the corner. At my wit's end, I tried to deter her in a rather cruel way from getting the trash. I literally covered the trash with Tabasco and powdered hot sauce, and she still got into that container. Once so frustrated, I picked her up and put her in the trash container head first. She just ducked her head, shut her eyes, and simply endured the punishment. One time she was locked out of the bedroom. She went and got garbage from the container which she didn't like to eat and piled it outside the bedroom door. I'm sure she was thinking I would open the door, come out, and scold her, and her problem would be solved, and she thought right.

On a trip back to New Mexico once she got her fill of Mexican cuisine. Ken's folks had given us two dozen made to order tortillas ready to be filled with taco meat. While eating at a restaurant we watched from a window—we saw Sheba jump from the front seat to the back seat several times. She ate every crumb of those taco shells. She did pay for that escapade though. Her stomach growled and she moaned for miles going down the highway. Served her right.

When I was working at the diode factory, Marilyn, would pick me up for our shift at 11:30 pm. One night I thought I heard a knock at the door. I went and opened the door, and Marilyn was standing there with her arm in the air ready to knock again. Sheba went past me so fast and sunk her teeth in Marilyn's upraised arm... thankfully, she had a heavy coat on so there were no teeth marks on her arm. I was unaware, or ignorant of that dog's power and her protective nature.

One of my fondest memories of her was when we were in the mountains. Ken's boss had his five kids at the cabin. The mother took Sheba with them while they were going swimming in the river. The youngest boy went in the deep part. He went under and began floundering. Sheba went in the river and pulled him to safety right away. Everyone in the group was bragging about the prowess of Sheba that day. For some reason I wasn't there, so sorry I missed that rescue.

We had three bedrooms in our rental house, and I made a television room out of one of rooms. I kept a dish of sunflower seeds on a table in that room. Every morning I would notice the dish, look at the sofa and there would be empty shells lying on the cushions. One night I saw the culprit, a mouse who was helping himself to the sunflowers. He was sashaying down the hall and I caught a glimpse of him passing the doorway. I had been peeling an apple, and I had a sharp knife in my hand. I called Sheba, and we went into the television room—I closed the door. I got the bright idea of throwing the knife I had been using at that mouse. During my tomboy days I could throw a knife but I could never get it to stick in a tree. But past failures didn't cross my mind that night. I threw that knife and it stuck straight up in my coffee table! I missed the mouse though, and he took off under another table. I told Sheba to get him. She hit the floor, crawled on her stomach under another table and brought him up. I immediately took it away from her. It happened so fast I don't think she even knew she had been a crawling mousetrap.

Sheba did not like young boys. After school, young boys would walk by our yard with sticks and they would drag the sticks across the wooden pickets and the noise of that drove Sheba crazy. Not sure if the sticks or the noise made her the most furious. Later, when we moved to a tract house the neighbor wanted to remove a couple of slats in our fence so Sheba could get to her backyard. The neighbor was alone a lot, and Sheba made her feel safer. On Halloween, the woman let Sheba in her house and the doorbell rang. Sure enough, it was two young boys, and Sheba went for one. She got the lad by his pant leg and pulled him down. She never bit him anywhere else, but the skin had been broken and had to be tended to.

A similar instance happened again with me. Sheba and I were in the garage, and a mother walked by with a baby carriage and a young boy walking by the carriage. When Sheba saw the young boy, she charged after him. Again, she got him by the pant leg and pulled him down. She totally disregarded my command. A couple of weeks before she had charged a couple of utility workers in the backyard. She was okay until I went out a side door and stood by one of the men. She ran towards him like a mad bull and I had to throw my body literally in front of her and pull her down.

So, making a hard decision, I had to give her away. My neighbor had a friend who lived in the country and she said Sheba would be happy there. When the lady came to meet Sheba, I called her to come in. I asked Sheba to do every trick she knew, and she performed, beautifully. She focused her gaze on the lady, and it was like she knew that she was the one who was to be pleased in the present and the future. As they drove away I watched Sheba sitting in the back seat, her ears erect, and she did not look back once. That really hurt, but it was what Sheba understood; loyalty to one.

The lady bred Sheba her next cycle and she gave me one of Sheba's pups. Sam, the pup, was the tall gangly type, and she would straddle the electric fence around my flower beds. Ken had put up the fence to keep her from digging in the flower beds but that idea didn't work so well. She also jumped on things to get out of the yard and I decided I did not have enough time to spend with her so we gave her back to Sheba's owner.

Ken decided that we should buy a house and we seriously thought of the one we had rented but it had a well, with no city water. Ken decided to go to look at a housing tract that was near completion. There was a drawback; the houses were located on adobe soil. In the summer the soil would be hard as a rock and a person couldn't break it up with an axe. In the winter during the rains it would be like glue when you walked on it. Native Americans had used it when they built structures in the area. We eventually bought a tract two-story with four bedrooms. My dream home which is going to cause so much dissension between Ken and me brought me so much joy in the beginning. Ken said it was a "bunch of sticks put together" later on. Our value systems would never intersect and so much tension was becoming more apparent all the time.

Around that time Ken became obsessed with flying saucers. He went to a couple meetings somewhere and when he came home he was talking really low, slow with the strangest, eeriest sounding enunciation. I had never heard him talk like that before or anyone else for that matter. He once played a tape and the man speaking on the tape had the same sounding speech as Ken had used. I was critical of the tape and Ken got upset. Ken had a fascination with hypnosis and I sensed that was what the man was trying his best to do to his listeners.

One night, driving on the freeway from a drive-in, something really bright crossed the sky. Ken was excited as he said it was a flying saucer but I said it was a shooting star. Our different slants on reality were worlds apart. I do accept that there may be flying saucers and other life "out there" but I can't make shooting stars become flying saucers.

My Step-Siblings

Ken did approve of me inviting all my step-siblings to visit us. Lonnie, the oldest half-brother went back with us to California after we went to visit New Mexico our first time. Lonnie helped Ken with several small projects but I don't remember them talking much. Lonnie did try to go to college, but he felt it was totally foreign to him. He had been drafted and spent a stint in Korea like his father. Mom worried about him a great deal. He was married by then to Kaye. She and her family were very religious but Lonnie did not attend church much. Kaye managed the finances for Lonnie and her all the years of their marriage. Lonnie worked at the potash mines almost his entire life and had little interactions with people other than Kaye, his wife and Dora, his sister.

Dora, my half-sister spent a Christmas with us. She had red hair and I had memories of her with chickenpox when she was young. Her head was covered in scabs and I was thankful I did not have curly hair like her. Mom was always in a good mood when Dora was around. Dora was fun loving and had an infectious laugh.

The two younger boys were Fred and Randy. Fred was the baby that Gabe swore was not his. Fred would take so many beatings from Gabe growing up that made the rest of us kids feel guilty at times.

Mom called me and asked if I would take Randy, the youngest boy to California with me. He wouldn't go to school and he was put in jail; that was supposed to be used as a deterrent for the other kids who wouldn't attend school. Randy had taken all his clothes off and slid through some pipes and escaped from jail. Randy was hard to handle. When he was in elementary grades the schools wanted to evaluate him for his issues, but Mom would not allow it. She still had the stance that you didn't tell anyone about what happened in the family.

Eventually, I had to throw in the towel as I could not handle his physical abuse either. He never hit me but he would grab my wrists or he would twist my arm behind my back. He considered those actions as "just playing." I called Mom and told her she had to raise him herself as he was too mean for me to deal with.

Later, when he married and had kids, I turned him into social services for child abuse, twice. As an adult I was still afraid of him. Out of us five kids, he will be the first to die. Drugs and alcohol were his coping tools and they eventually let him down.

I had decided I wanted to have a baby...notice, I said I decided. We had been married five years and we were trying to get a loan to buy the house and I thought I had the world and everything in it figured out. Boy, was I ever wrong! The friend who Sheba had bit, Marilyn, and I were around each other quite a bit. She was a Native American and she told me stories about her family and I would tell her about my family. We were always trying to outdo each other. One night, Ken was in bed as he had been drinking all day, and she handed me a note. It said, "Come by tomorrow afternoon because Susie won't be here." I was confused. She said to me, "Sue, Ken handed this to me." I said he must have been joking! I knew she was telling me the truth. I never thought he would be unfaithful, and that was only the beginning!

So, after going off the birth-control pills it still took me about six months to get pregnant. I had morning sickness a lot and I couldn't eat bacon for over a year. I babysat some and worked in a place which made novelty toys. I would go to work feeling sick and come home feeling the same way. We got paid by what we produced which was called piece work. I really didn't piece well, so I didn't make that much money.

Being ignorant and naïve I thought life was to be about my rules and conditions. Rather quickly, I had to face some new facts. Ken was a drinker and apparently, he was wanting to mess around. Later, Ken would say I did not discuss with him on starting a family at that time, but I sure don't remember him verbalizing any objections. Ken had made a pass at Marilyn which was a beginning of a pattern for him. If I did something he didn't like he would seek out someone who would not reject his advances.

I called Mom and asked her to come to California when I was due to deliver. She came a week early and I wanted to impress her with our house, our town, and my domestic skills. But mainly I wanted to give her a gift she wouldn't forget. I planned a trip to the Pacific Ocean! Ken hated the water and rarely would go there. When we did go, he was constantly yelling at me to get back and be careful. I figured out he was terrified of water. Remembering his abuse when he was sprayed down with a high-powered hose may have been the reason for his fear, I'm not sure.

Mom and I went to Bodega Bay which was a beautiful place that wasn't far from where we lived. It was the location for the Alfred Hitchcock movie "The Birds." Mom's eyes were wide with awe when we drove up close enough to see the water and the huge waves. As we were walking on the beach barefoot, I looked down as the tide came in a little further, and I noticed Mom was all wet from the waist down. "Mom, how did you get so wet?" I asked. I knew the water wasn't that deep. She laughed and said, "I peed all over myself, because I was so scared!" We laughed about that day many times during her lifetime.

When my water broke I told Ken and off we went to the hospital. I didn't know how deliveries happened but I was told I would be given gas. I voiced my concern about this to Ken. I knew the nurse, Mae, in the delivery room as I bowled with her. I didn't want to start cursing in front of her. I didn't want her to tell everyone at the bowling alley I "cussed like a sailor."

I got impatient with all the waiting and the pain. The doctor told Mae to call him when I was ready. The pains were getting intense, and I was sucking that gas down. I was supposed to take a deep breath and then inhale one time, but I was taking shallow breaths and inhaling as fast as I could. I yelled at Mae and told her I saw the baby coming. She picked up the phone and said, "Doctor, she says she sees the baby coming!" She said it like she didn't believe me! Truthfully, I had a vision of my baby sliding down the Milky Way. I'm sure it was due to the gas I inhaled, but it was so real and would affect my thinking about God and my new baby. Soon after David's birth I felt the need to go to church because I was so thankful. I had been blessed with a healthy baby, and I began going to a Freewill Baptist Church about two blocks from our house.

Ken had nearly passed out during the delivery and he was rather pale from watching me deliver. When I was put in a room a young woman came in and asked me what I wanted for lunch and she gave me the choices. "How can you eat at a time like this?" Ken remarked. I told him I could, because I was hungry...I had been in labor—simple as that.

Ken shared with me something he had done while I was at the hospital. He had quit his job! I knew things were not going well with Ray, his boss, but I never dreamed Ken would quit with a baby due, but he did. Ken was always late to work and it was a chore for me to get him out of the door many times. He would watch television late every night. No job, no insurance. We ended up paying for Dave's delivery ourselves. Ken would patch things up with Ray, but it was never the same. Ken said he was no longer the "fair haired" boy, and he was more resentful about working for the well-known company.

Mom decided to go home. She said I was so independent and organized and that I didn't need her anymore. So, Ken and I were in charge of a newborn. My guidebook, or reference book, was written by Dr. Spock. I wanted to do everything right, and I tried really hard. That book became my bible. As I recall it was the first self-help book I ever read. Thinking back, I see many flaws in his teachings, but for me it was still better than nothing.

Every day I was in awe watching David see the world for the first time. I would move pictures around on the wall. When I would carry him past the wall, he would point at the blank spot, and then decide which picture or object belonged in that spot. He loved books, and I read to him constantly. When he was around three he had memorized many of his books.

I began noticing plants and other growing things in nature. I needed to touch plants, not sure why. Ken put topsoil over the adobe soil. I bought a package of Four-O'Clock seeds. Those seeds would sprout, and quickly turn into a plant with blooms. They would automatically close their petals in the evening. I thought I was a regular Farmer in the Dell. Fascinating. Having David made me conscious of all living things and how things evolved or changed.

There was an ad put in the paper by a garden club—they were wanting to recruit new members. The youngest member in the club was in her fifties. I was twenty-five. Each time I showed up for a meeting the group would clap—I felt like a celebrity. I learned about spores, favorable conditions, grafting, and fertilizers. I didn't know at the time that northern California was a plant mecca. You could put a stick in the ground in the fall, and have a rosebush by spring in that exact spot.

Another thing I learned was to put tulips and other spring bulbs in the vegetable bin of the refrigerator. Those bulbs needed a cold temperature in winter and where we lived it was too close to the coast—it wasn't cold enough. If one put them in the refrigerator for several weeks the bulbs would think it was winter. In spring when the bulbs sprouted through the earth I would get on my knees and touch the tips of the bulbs ever so lightly—I swear I could feel energy.

Dave's birth, the love of animals, and the amazement of plant life somehow clicked in strongly for my awareness of life and learning. I began making connections with all the insights I was given at that time in my life. That feeling seemed to be very close to being a spiritual gift—there's not another way for me to describe it.

While I was living in California Grandpa died. Mom did not tell me until months later that he had passed away and I was upset with her. She said I couldn't do anything about it anyway. I felt whether I could or not was my decision to make not hers. The memory of her not telling me about my real dad came back to me. She had told me that it didn't make any difference that she hadn't, but she was wrong. Her dad had just died and she knew him all her life. She had been disowned by him for a period but at least she knew she had a dad. She made important decisions for me and I was told to accept them but I never did.

I became very active in the Freewill Baptist Church. It had about one-hundred fifty members. Ken was not interested in going at all. I wanted him to go to church, and a tension developed between us when the subject came up. The preacher said that one was doomed if they were not saved and baptized. Both of those requirements I embraced at the time, but I have no recollection of either one of them causing me any joy or seeking a change in my life. We were taught dancing was a sin. I had an issue with that. Dave was crawling, and when the music was playing he would start swaying back and forth. It seemed to me that the movement was instinctive or innate. How could a baby sin? I was told one thing, but I just couldn't accept that people danced just for sexual reasons or that dancing led to sex like the church taught.

Another issue with the church was that they did not drink. I'm sure that was a factor that kept Ken from that place. I wanted to quit drinking so I used the church's belief for my support. Ken was not happy with my decision, and he continuously made snide remarks about me not drinking.

Smoking was a habit that I had during that time. I felt guilty and not good enough for the good Christians of the church...I always felt guilty. Feeling guilty or unworthy was ingrained in my being or my soul. I will deal with that matter later in my life.

Someone recruited me for Bible School. I was to teach the first and second graders. At the end of the session we were to do a presentation. I had never spoken in front of a group before, and I was nervous to say the least. Standing behind the pulpit I began the introduction of our skit. If I was looking down at my paper I was fine, but when I looked at the audience's faces I began giggling. I checked myself, and sure enough when reading I was under control, but again making eye contact I would start giggling again. Not sure what was happening besides having stage fright, but thankfully it never happened again.

In my twenties, I saw myself as Mrs. Susie Homemaker. I made bread, jellies, pastries, and for sure my cooking skills improved. Then I thought that since I loved the "mother role" I should reach out to other kids and be a foster mom. Ken was dead set against the idea, but I persisted and he finally relented, grudgingly. I was caught up in doing for others, and Ken was not fully on board with that idea.

One night we were driving home from bowling and I was sharing David's accomplishments and rattling along, and Ken said the strangest thing. He said, "I wish you could have been my mother." I thought about that statement many times over the years. There was much about my childhood I was dealing with, and I could see there was a mountain of problems Ken was dealing with, also. Two lost souls so to speak.

Taking birth control pills was my choice for birth control for a few months. I immediately got pregnant again. I was an old pro at having babies, or so I thought. I made sure my hair was up to par every day. I was going to look more glamorous with my second delivery.

Ken finally said he would give being a foster parent a try. Many papers had to be filled out, and several interviews had to be attended by us. We were finally, licensed foster parents in the state of California. We had a four-bedroom home with three bedrooms upstairs and there was only one-bedroom downstairs. California law stated there had to be a fire exit from the upstairs bedrooms. So, we designated that the downstairs bedroom would accommodate the foster kids we would have in our home.

Jackie*

We got a call that the agency had a ten-year-old girl. She had been turned over to the state by the mother. The mother was in a new relationship, and the man did not want the mother's kids. There were two girls and one was sold to a couple and was adopted. Jackie, the other girl, was not a candidate for selling as she had too many issues.

Physically, Jackie appeared to be awkward. She was tall and her posture seemed to be as an adult in the way that she stood, pushing her stomach out with her hand on her hip, usually. She would often be found staring at other kids when in a group. Her teeth protruded and her tongue seemed to be on the side of her mouth.

Jackie had learning issues also. When she saw her mother, she forgot concepts she had mastered before, and she had to relearn them. Jackie had been sexually abused, locked in a closet for punishments, and starved.

I had spent days sewing for Jackie. I made cute dresses with matching purses for her. I decorated the bedroom for a girl, so it would be less formal. I thought I was ready.

Jackie came with the social worker to meet us. I was pregnant with Brian at that time. David was a little over a year old. Jackie gravitated towards David when she had the opportunity. We showed her around, and the social worker left. I had made a cake which we shared, and that was our first meeting.

Jackie had a clothing allowance from the state of California, and we were going shopping for school clothes. We were standing in line at a large JC Penny store at a mall, and Jackie did the strangest thing. She started towards the cashier while pushing people aside while saying, "Excuse me, excuse me!" I was shocked and confused. "Jackie, what does excuse me, mean?" I asked. She looked at me and said matter of factly, "Get out of my way!"

One day Jackie had a doctor's appointment and she didn't want to go. I wasn't sure if she was scared or just wanted to push the limits with me. I tried talking to her and that didn't get any results. That day did not go well. I ended up dragging Jackie down the carpeted stairs on her bottom. I put her in the car and drove slowly. Thankfully, she did not attempt to jump out. When we arrived at the doctor's office she bolted and took off. All I could do was sit in the office with Dave. Eventually, she came back and we met with the doctor.

I would get calls from Jackie's teacher. She would complain that Jackie was helping the janitor empty the trash instead of coming back to the classroom. Her behavior was impulsive, and she would change from one focus to another without warning. Many adults, myself included, were confused with her behavior. She was taking medication for ADHD. One day she said she didn't want to take her pill. I asked her why and she said she wanted to do what she wanted to do. So, she knew the medication was controlling her actions and learning. Jackie taught me a lot.

Due to her being starved Jackie would steal food from the two stores closest to us. I became aware of this when I would vacuum under her bed. There would be wrappers of many kinds of candies, milk and juice boxes, and sweet rolls. Sometimes she would hide her stash in the brick planter in front of the house if she knew it was the day I would vacuum her room. After confronting her about taking things without permission, I took her back to the stores and she apologized—I offered to pay for the items. She never did completely stop taking things, but the habit was lessened somewhat over time or she improved in hiding them better.

Her prized possession was a bicycle with a banana seat that we had bought for her. Truthfully, we used it as a punishment as we would take it away when she broke the rules. That was the only thing she seemed to have an attachment to. She would ride that bike for hours.

There were a set of twins and a girl next door for Jackie to play with. She had difficulty in sharing and getting along for long periods of time though, but she did improve over time. I had parties for her and she was invited to several parties, but truthfully, she always seemed to be an outsider.

One night, Ken and I went out for a party and we got a sitter for Jackie and Dave. When we came home our new drapes had been ripped down from the rods as Jackie had gotten mad at the sitter because she wouldn't let Jackie have some cookies. I thought to myself, "I'll be more prepared the next time." Seems as though her anger was so deep-seated, yet it came to the surface quickly if her wishes were not met—especially if the authority figure wasn't us.

Late one afternoon I felt the familiar lower back pain. I knew I needed to get my friend over to watch Dave and Jackie as my labor had begun. Ken was called and he was on his way. I was walking down the street pulling rollers out of my hair. At the hospital, after being prepped, I told the nurse I had to go to the bathroom. She disagreed, but I won out—I trotted to the restroom. After forcing a thimble's amount of urine, I began looking for the handle to flush the commode. I pushed a button on the wall. Lo, and behold, water shot out of a shower head high up on a wall—I was a drenched! I looked like a wet, bedraggled rat going back to the room. My glamourous self was short-lived.

The gas was within reach on the delivery table and I was glad. Ken was watching from outside the door, and he began pounding on the window. "Take that gas away from her!" he ordered. I had confided in him that I sucked as fast as I could to be pain free for a little while. Now he was telling on me! It was as he thought he considered himself an expert on deliveries without the pain, for him, of course. I remembered he nearly passed out when Dave was delivered.

When we got home from the hospital, Marilyn said she had to talk to me. She said that the night before, Jackie had turned the faucet to the hot water while Doug was in the bathtub. I felt so confused. Once I had observed her by the slide when Dave was sliding down on his stomach. Just as he got to the end of the slide she pressed down on his back. I yelled at her. If I hadn't seen her, Dave may have hit his face into the ground. I had to watch her more closely, I thought. That didn't work so well. I couldn't get the incident that Marilyn told me about off my mind. Ken and I were fighting all the time about Jackie. Once we told, not asked, the social worker that we were going to give Jackie swats. That didn't work, either. Finally, I realized that I could not get through to Jackie. Ken didn't want to tolerate her or her behavior at all. Living in fear of her hurting my boys was taking a toll on me, and I was suffering.

When Jackie got behind in her academics I would try to help her. I had heard of this program called Hooked on Phonics. I did not learn to read by using phonics, rather I learned reading by using sight words is my guess. I ordered the program anyway and used a record player; we began the course. While repeating the sounds, I would hold Dave on my knee bouncing him there. Well, it turned out that Dave learned to read by listening to those records. He loved books and memorized many, so I saw the connection he made when he started reading. His first-grade teacher said he was the first boy he ever had that came to first grade reading. Sadly, Hooked on Phonics did not help Jackie to read.

After a time of mulling it over, I came to the decision that Jackie had to be placed somewhere else. The social worker came after I called her. I was distraught, felt guilty and incompetent. The social worker tried to console me the best she could. She told me that Jackie was better off since she had lived with us, and that was a plus. In my naïveté I thought at one time we could adopt Jackie, but I would not consider it for a minute if I had to risk my boys' safety. I told the social worker that Jackie needed to be in a home without kids as she saw other kids as her rivals. She overstepped her boundaries with us, and she would with anyone who denied her what she wanted. She was placed in a preacher's home with other kids. She was removed from that home in a couple of months. Jackie was stealing things, and she was too much for that family to cope with.

A year later Jackie rang the doorbell and we visited for a while. She wanted to know if she left a bedspread at our house. I think she just wanted to say hello because she never had a bedspread that I remembered. I never saw her again, but I have wondered about her many times over the years.

I signed up for a knitting class right after Jackie left. I drove the twenty miles on the freeway to get to the college. I began singing while driving, and I realized I had not been this light-hearted in a very long time. I had been so anxious about what Jackie was going to do, and it was as though I was a prison guard caring for her, and I was exhausted.

Bob and Brothers*

Soon after Jackie had been placed in a new foster home, we got a call from social services. A teenage boy had to be placed immediately, and the social worker asked us if we would consider taking the boy for a short placement. His mother was in a tuberculosis sanatorium for a short term, and we were told she needed to build up her strength. She worked the graveyard shift at a factory. She had four boys altogether, and two younger boys were staying with an older brother in Wyoming.

Bob, the teenager, came to meet us with a social worker. He had long, greasy hair which was the most noticeable thing about him. He rarely made eye contact and spoke in a soft, monotone voice. There were baggy pants hanging from his hips, and a rope tied around his waist, which kept his pants from falling down. When I asked if he would like to go clothes shopping he immediately said no. He told me that the pants he had on were his older brother's pants and he liked them. We did go shopping a week later, but he only wanted one long sleeve shirt, and definitely not a belt for holding his pants up.

Bob would come home from school and immediately go to his room and stay there. He was not comfortable having dinner with us. He would hurry and eat and excuse himself. He drew many satanic pictures and never mentioned his artwork to me. There was a small box on his dresser—there were pictures of an audience watching a show, but I couldn't tell what they were watching on the box. Their heads were rolled back with mouths wide open laughing.

Ken never did find any common ground with Bob, and Bob kept his distance from Ken as much as possible. Then one day we got a call from social services again. Bob's mom was going to be released in a short time and we were asked if we could take the two younger brothers. They wanted to visit with her and of course, Bob did too. We took a deep breath and said we would.

Now there were three teenage boys to cook for, and I spent hours in the kitchen. I would put a cake on the table, turn around and not even a crumb would be left where a whole cake was before. When we got married I did not know how to cook. Ken wasn't hurt too much by that fact as he would rather have a beer, anyway. Overtime, I had become quite skillful in the kitchen. I made bread and Ken took sandwiches to work to show off the homemade bread which held his sandwich meat. Doughnuts, pies, and cakes were quite tasty and presentable coming from my oven. I picked raspberries and made jams for Christmas gifts. An air of confidence followed me in the kitchen. Cooking for those boys I needed every tool I had learned in the past and the heck with anything fancy.

We met Helen, the mother, of the boys, when she was released to visit. She seemed to be overwhelmed with her sickness and the prospect of taking care of her growing sons. She told me that she was raised Catholic but didn't attend church anymore. I invited her to our Baptist Church. The Sunday morning, we were to attend my church she had dressed in a nice pant suit. When the preacher began his sermon, I was dumbfounded! He talked about how sinful it was for a woman to wear pants, and especially to church. I was embarrassed for Helen and myself, for not being aware of such a dogma of the church I attended. I never invited anyone to our church again.

After the boys were reunited with their mother permanently, they moved to an apartment close to the electronic factory where Helen worked the graveyard shift. It wasn't long after that, we began getting telephone calls all hours of the night. If I answered the phone, the caller would hang up. If Ken answered the phone there would be loud, bizarre laughter like one would hear at a carnival. This went on for weeks, and finally Ken went to the phone company. They told him when there was a call to leave the receiver off the hook. He was then to go to another phone and call a number so they could track the number who called us.

When Ken got back from calling the tracking number he picked up the phone. Someone was pleading for Ken to hang up and they said they wouldn't ever call again. "No way, you son-of-a-bitch! I've got you now!" Ken yelled.

The next day a policeman came to the door and began questioning us. "Do you have any idea who would be harassing you by the phone?" he asked. I told him that I did. I told him about Bob, the foster kid, having that box on the dresser with people sitting in the audience. After a while he told us that I was right. We were asked if we wanted to press charges and we decided not to if the kids would cease doing this practical joke. And there were no more calls after that.

Learning to stretch a penny came naturally for me. Being poor was an accepted fate or the station in my life, and I had no resentment of that fact. Ken was to give me fifty dollars a week for groceries, bowling, gardening or in general, any spending money I was to have. I don't remember how we came to that arrangement but we abided by those terms for several years. But gradually over time, I became uncomfortable with this "doling out" routine. Many times, I would have to remind Ken it was Friday and I needed money for food or another matter. "Is it Friday already?" he would ask in a demeaning way. I had worked for years and had made my own money. His remarks began to get to me and I felt resentful. I had to beg for the allowance I was supposed to have for household matters. I was at the mercy of a "money maker." I didn't like that role at all.

Rarely did we get to eat out, just to put it bluntly, it was too expensive. I read somewhere if this was the case for a couple then eating breakfast out may be a better solution, and so we tried that one morning. There were no distractions for us, but the silence between Ken and me was deafening. We could not enjoy a conversation as neither one of us could put two sentences together and just talk. I suddenly realized that I didn't even know the person sitting across from me. We both bowled, but not together anymore. Ken did projects around the house, but he worked many hours, and usually on the weekends, too.

So, we had drifted apart as the saying goes.

My days were filled with enjoying time with my boys. I would take them bike riding and day trips to the ocean. Ken was not the playing kind, but I was. We would have water gun fights and sometimes Ken did that with us. But he installed a swing set, a sandbox, and an A-frame little house for the boys to play in.

Not only was I proud of my house but our backyard was a beautiful place. Ken let me paint the fence a dark red and my flowers were trying to get every visitor's reaction and attention. Ken extended our family room with a sliding door, laid a patio, and built a barbecue. Inside the house he wallpapered with a beautiful velvet pattern in our bedroom. He paneled walls and installed recessed lighting at the ceiling. His talent always amazed me. He would attempt doing plumbing, painting, and electrical chores in the house. His skills were evident in gardening also. He loved to grow vegetables, especially.

Cake decorating was a class I took for a couple of years. My friend had a business making and decorating cakes for the public and she wanted to retire. She asked me if wanted to take her business over and I decided to do just that. I babysat two kids after school and if I decorated cakes I would then have more spending money I reasoned. I was told to use Duncan Hines cake mix for baking the cakes—that brand seemed to have more resilience for the weight of the icing. I bought themed cake pans and wedding cake stands. The recipe for the icing was practically all Crisco and powdered sugar. I had a source for a white vanilla which came from Mexico. My supplies were in the cupboard and I was in business. Sometimes, I would get a call at two in the afternoon and a customer wanted a Winnie the Pooh cake at five. I had to drop what I was doing and produce a cake. I was constantly wiping up icing from somewhere.

Ken had a drafting table in the downstairs bedroom and I put the cakes in there until I was ready to present them to a customer. My first wedding cake was a stressful endeavor and an exhausting one. Finally, when finished, I put it in the spare bedroom on the drafting table and then I decided to take a nap. While dreaming, I saw the cake with the icing licked off in places, and my cat was sitting on the table purring with icing dripping from its mouth, chin, and whiskers. Being in business for myself seemed rather challenging, and what drove me out of business eventually, was when sugar skyrocketed in price.

Reading became more important to me over time. I learned about history, and I began filling in gaps that my background never seemed to do for me. Anything I wanted to learn about was as near as a book. Petaluma had a library that had been built due to Carnegie's philanthropy, and it was beautiful building with skylights. The boys and I would visit the library countless times while we lived there. I even read War and Peace. I realized that I knew how to discipline myself to conquer a hard goal, and my self-confidence developed at a rapid pace during my late twenties and early thirties. When I began sewing on the machine, I couldn't understand the directions. Ken would read them and sit at the machine and show me what to do, I learned better by seeing it and touching it.

Noticing an ad in the paper one day reconnected my bygone days of participating in sports. A group of women wanted softball players to form a team. That sparked my interest and I asked Ken if he minded if I tried out for a team. His directives were only to take the kids with me, and have dinner ready on time.

The first day of tryouts was exciting and I felt comfortable with the other women players from the beginning. Some of the players were teachers and nurses but most were housewives like me. Annie, the captain, was from Virginia, and her dad started out as our coach. He had a drinking problem though, and sometimes he forgot to show up for our games. Later, Annie's husband began coaching us. Tryouts for pitching started on the first day. The type of pitching we were to do was called "C" class. That meant we could pitch as hard as possible, but without winding up. Nervously, I looked at the pitcher's mound and then at home plate and I tried to decide if I could throw a ball within that exact space, and at that distance. I decided to try out. My turn. I was chosen to be the designated pitcher and I was elated. All the other positions were filled and we were called the Amway Angels. We played together for five years dragging out our balls and bats along with our playpens and diaper bags to the softball fields. We were a happy bunch of women.

We played at night in a women's league but those ladies would slide head first to bases, and some could knock the ball out of the park. Our edge competing against them was we had experience playing with each other, and we knew each other's strengths and weaknesses. A couple of the teams wanted to come in the daytime and compete against us, but we made a rule you had to be a housewife to play in the daytime league. Most of the women at night were lesbians, and truthfully, we had no problem with that, but they were better players than us and we did have a problem with that.

Some of us branched out and played basketball, volleyball, and even formed bowling teams. I found out that I was an aggressive basketball guard. I have memories of being so in tuned to that game that I was the top scorer many times—I surprised myself.

Bowling on a team with women was fun, and my average began creeping upward. I won a tournament called the BVL. Bowling Veterans League was my first win locally, and then I went to the state BVL. I got to go to San Diego by train to compete there. My approach was rather unorthodox, mainly because I took five steps rather quickly, and I would use a lot of body movements to get all the pins down. The women on the leagues for the most part either disliked my style and enthusiasm or they were highly complimentary. I soon developed an attitude of wanting to beat the women who were cold towards me—it usually worked.

For some reason Ken and I went to a yearly awards bowling banquet, my first one. The speaker began talking about the coveted women's Bowler of the Year award for women. She noted that the female who had won the city tournament, increased her average by twenty pins, and had an admirable sportsmanlike character. Thinking to myself; I had won the city tournament in all events and had improved my average so why wasn't I in contention. Then I heard my name announced and I was hit with paralysis! Ken shoved me in an upward posture with my mind swirling as I walked towards the speaker. She put a clock in my arms and with the clock lifted upwards I touched my upper lip as it was quivering so badly. I was sure everyone could see it moving. Up to that time that was the highest honor I had ever received and I'll never forget how happy I was. I would win the same honor again in 1974 but it was decided I wouldn't be in Petaluma to represent the town so I couldn't have it again. A huge disappointment for me as I knew the requirements to earn the honor and I did what was necessary the second time...but I had to accept the denial.

Once when I got on a plane leaving San Diego from another tournament there was the moon right before the plane. It was blood red! I was terrified because of all the hell and damnation preaching I had heard in my life I guess. No one seemed scared but me, and I was afraid to let anyone know how terrified I was. I later found out that the reason for the moon being red and so scary was southern California's air pollution. Mankind has more influence on our "hell" than God sometimes. That was my thought that day, anyway.

Thinking back about our marriage I had clues of Ken's infidelities. I had the note Ken had written to Marilyn when I was pregnant with Dave. Another time which I had pushed back in my memory was a time right after Mel and Sherry had gotten a divorce. Mel had gone to school in Iowa to be a chiropractor. He took Sherry, his wife, his parents, and a baby girl with him. Not too sure why he dropped out months before he graduated but he did. He and Sherry ended up back in Petaluma and they were getting a divorce.

Mel needed money to buy Sherry a car so she could get a job. Mel asked Ken for a loan to "tie the loose ends" of his divorce. The problem was that Ken did not have the money to lend, so he wanted to mortgage the house. I had a big problem with that! That house was my dream home and I did not want to lose it. Ken and I argued for years over whether it was my dream-house or a "bunch of sticks." The argument ended when Ken said he didn't care what I wanted—he was going to do what he wanted as he was the breadwinner.

We only had one car and Mel bought Sherry a sports car with the loan Ken gave him. I was livid. Another problem; Sherry does not know how to drive a stick shift and Ken needs to take her on drives to teach her. Another obstacle; Sherry needs a babysitter for her three-year child and she wants me to babysit. Holly, the little girl was a tyrant! She was so aggressive towards Dave. She would bite, hit, and scratch him every chance she got. Miserable afternoon for us all. Well, not for the driver training couple. Three hours later they arrive, and I was suspicious there had been more than driving going on in that sports car! I ranted and raved at both of them and neither one would meet my eye. That was the end of Sherry's and my friendship.

Our marriage wasn't going well, so I busied myself fulfilling my other roles. I chose not to pay much heed to the signs. I was so naïve that I thought I could control our marriage or maybe I thought I could just ignore it and my problems would just go away. Wrong again. Ken bowled two nights a week on a men's league and that meant more drinking and late nights. One night I happened to be up and I entered the dressing area where Ken was looking at himself in the mirror. A gut feeling, I guess, told me that he was having an affair. "You're messing around with someone aren't you?" His reply was that he was tired, and wanted to go to bed so, that meant the fight was on...only for a short time though, as he passed out immediately.

The next day he asked me what I wanted him to do. Flippantly, I said I wanted him to mow the grass. I had a habit of avoiding subjects in which I was not prepared to discuss. He said the other woman just wanted him to be her, "soul mate'" I knew I was in trouble as there were not too many romantic ideas I had floating around in my head at that time. I did find out her name, Carline. She was from Hawaii and she was working as a cocktail waitress at the bowling alley. I knew her from another place too. She was on a volleyball team in our league and I had competed against her several times. Once, I even walked up to Carline and asked, "Is there anything I have that you want?" She shook her head no, and I thought problem solved! Well, I found it was only the beginning of the end. That problem just kept hanging around.

I decided I was going to leave Ken. I packed up the truck with the kids and my prized sewing machine. There was a show on television about a waitress named Alice and she went to Arizona. That was in the back of my mind at first, but I changed my mind by the time I drew my money out of my Christmas Club. Why not take the kids to Disneyland? So, we headed towards Anaheim. Brian kept asking for his daddy and Dave seemed totally content with just us three riding down the freeway. We pulled into a motel and Brian went to sleep crying for his dad. I had carried my sewing machine into the room so no one could steal it from the back of the truck. The next morning as we were leaving the room I looked in the door and my keys were left dangling in the door. If we had been broken into I guess I would have awaken when they were dragging my sewing machine out the door. I was a mess. "It's a Small World After All" kept playing in my head. Brian was afraid of everything and if I let go of his hand he took off running. I called Ken and told him about Brian crying for him. He pleaded for us to come home so we would all be together and Brian would be where he wanted to be. I took the easy way out and went home to the dogs, my flowers, and Ken in that order which seemed to make sense at that time

So, Ken and Carline had met at the bowling and began an affair. After a couple days Ken and I sat down and discussed our circumstances. Ken assured me that he would end the affair and I wanted to believe him, but things were not that simple I would find out. Things were going on their merry way for a couple weeks and then one day I went to the mailbox. Inside was a bill from a motel from another town close by.. The bill claimed that Ken owed for towels which were taken from the room he had booked one afternoon. I knew that bill was legit and I proceeded to have a talk with myself. Things were not right at all. I recalled a chat with a gal at the bowling alley. She asked me if things were going okay with Ken and me. Being Ms. Positive, I confided to her that Ken and I had some issues but things were "just fine" now. I can still see the expression on her face as she asked, "Are you sure?" I stood and tried to convince her and myself that the words I had just spoken were true. Ken was still seeing Carline.

The very next night I got a call from Ken from his work. "Susie, I am going to spend the night with Carline, and I won't be home tonight." He said it was the last time but I had been down that road before. Woman scorned, called the husband. Carline's husband was a large, young Hawaiian fellow. "Hello. My husband is in Napa at a motel with your wife." I sort of chickened out giving any more information. Truthfully, I don't know if he even went looking for his wife. At that moment in time I wouldn't have cared if the husband had beat the hell out of the lovebirds. Later, of course. I was relieved everyone was in one piece because Ken and Carline came in the front door a couple hours later. "Get your ass upstairs, get your clothes and get out of this house!" I yelled.

Ken turns towards Carline and said to her. "See. I told you she doesn't love me." What the hell he was talking about I had no idea. He did go and get some things and returned with them. Carline sat in a chair the whole time and never said a word. They finally left.

The next day I called a lawyer. The lawyer said since Ken left I could have the kids, house and anything I wanted. I sure was glad about that. I went to a Mervyn's with a charge card and bought uniforms and work shoes. I had worked in an A&W and waitressed at the bowling alley so that was my immediate plan for a job. I also went to talk to our preacher for counseling about my decision about getting a divorce and if it was a sin to do so.

The next afternoon Ken called and said he wanted to come and see the boys. Giving him permission, I left the room when he arrived. He seemed to have trouble talking and his stomach was literally roaring. "Susie, I need to talk to Brother Young," he said. Brother Young was the preacher at the Freewill Baptist Church. Ken had been going to the church and even helped build an addition on to the main building. Ken took passages seriously, and he got into discussions that were heated with the other members sometimes. But I liked that he was going with the boys and me.

I handed Ken the phone and left the room—shortly afterwards Brother Young rang the doorbell. Ken was wailing and crying and I could hear Brother Young's voice low and controlled. After an hour or so Brother Young left. Ken told me he wanted to come home. He said he left Carline at a motel room and she was "crazy." Not sure what he meant by that but he was going to take her back to her husband and everything would be just fine.

Ken seemed to be in a deeper depression after he came back home. We talked and I decided I would never throw the past months in Ken's face, ever. Not sure if Brother Young advised Ken to confess all his past transgressions to me or not but that was what he did. It was like my definition of Pandora's Box. Months into our marriage I went to New Mexico with Jesse and his live-in, Patty. Ken couldn't work so I reasoned I could work and pay our electric bill while in New Mexico. One of the women I spoke of before who had an affair with the carpenter's wife lived in the apartments where we lived. She was married but she was a lesbian or bisexual. Ken confessed that he had sex with her as he thought he could change her sexuality overnight. His brother, Mel, had done the same thing when he was married to Sherry. They had a fantasy I guess that they were such sexual studs that they could change a woman's sexual preference in bed by sleeping with them one time. I guess they read the same Playboy or something.

Ken and I fought about his habit of leaving Playboy magazines around the house. I didn't understand his reason for them. He didn't have a reason other than he wanted to, I thought. He had built an attic of sorts in the garage. One would have to use a ladder to reach the landing. One day, I climbed the ladder to see what was up there. Ken had hung laminated nude pictures in plastic all over the walls. I did tell him that I saw them but I gave up on changing his habits as it was beyond my control I realized. Perhaps he was addicted to pornography. He could have had a sexual addiction. Who knows? Funny in a way as I was the total opposite. Guess opposites do attract; another old saying.

Things were tense and I kept waiting for Ken to have a breakdown. When we went to church together everyone totally ignored Ken. It was as though the whole congregation was ostracizing him. I didn't understand. I was the one who had been wronged and had forgiven him...what the hell did those other people have to do with our marriage. That was the last time I felt comfortable in a church. I still get a knot in my stomach when I think about that day. I saw people siding with me by their actions. I didn't need or want that on my plate.

Ken came up with the idea that we should leave California and things would be alright with our marriage. I totally disagreed with him. I told him we would only be taking our problems with us. He initially talked about going to Arizona as construction was supposed to be on the upswing there. After talking and arguing for days on end I finally relinquished. I did want a compromise though. Instead of going to Arizona, I suggested we go back to New Mexico. If I had to live in a desert again it might as well be a place I was familiar with.

The ladies who I enjoyed softball, basketball, volleyball and bowled with gave us a going away party. We played ping pong and danced all evening. To top it off they gave us a money tree for a going away gift. So many beautiful memories with those gals.

Overcoming Smut

There were some things I was not going to miss about California. One was the memory of the gas shortage. We were living in California when there was a gas shortage due to the embargo in the 70's. One morning, according to my routine I went to the gas station to get fuel for a week. There was a line of cars a block long as I drove towards my usual destination. The attendant who I had known for a couple of years was going car to car and telling them to pull up or get out of line. The deciding factor where the car went was whether the driver was a regular customer at the place or not. People who were asked to leave were yelling and threatening Joe, the attendant. Tires were squealing and horns were blaring as he came to my car. "Go on up, Sue." Boy, was I relieved.

Another threat I was afraid of was a shortage of food. Nightly news would talk of shortages in all kinds of realms of survival. I started hoarding food that was not perishable. I bought can goods and a one-hundred-pound bag of pinto beans. Mass hysteria I fell prey to but it was instinctual for me. We would end up selling all that food real cheap in a garage sale before we moved.

Another loose end I had was that I had signed up for the California State Bowling tournament. I had looked forward to it because it was held in beautiful San Diego. Another reason was that my dear ex-landlady, Mrs. Greves, was going to have surgery at that same date. Ken said I could back to CA for the tournament so I decided to fly back. I met my team in San Diego. What beautiful plants covered that part of California! I got to see the San Diego zoo. For the longest time I watched a boa swallow a rabbit whole, and I was mesmerized by that feat. The first and last time I saw a boa constrictor. What a beautiful day!

Earthquakes I had lived through but that didn't lessen my fear of them. The big one happened one night. First, we heard a noise which sounded like a bus was barreling down our street. Looking out the picture window I swear the glass looked and moved like waves on water. Ken had made fun of my fears but when it hit, he followed my plan. We had a heavy pecan coffee table and I was crawling under it. Ken was passing Dave to me under the table. Our chandelier was whipping back and forth. Ken was walking around as if in a trance and saying "Oh, God!" He didn't seem scared but I sure was.

Later we were upstairs getting ready for bed and the aftershocks began. I was running to Dave's room and the floor was moving like as if on a ship. I would stagger into the wall being off balance, brace myself, and move towards the doorway to Dave's room. Finally, it stopped but not before the seed of fear was planted into my backbone. Terrifying!

My plaguing fear of earthquakes I could discard leaving California. I became obsessed with worrying about those natural disasters. Mom was always fanning my fears also. What if an earthquake occurred and Dave was at school and Ken was miles away? I would fantasize of what I would do going to sleep many nights. An airport was three blocks from our home. I decided I could get a gun and make a pilot take us up in the air. A strange noise of any kind would get my heart racing.

I stayed with a friend in Petaluma. She was a natural athlete and I admired her many skills in sports. She was my doubles partner in the state tournament. When I was going to leave for New Mexico, she went with me to get my ears pierced so I would remember her. While visiting I felt that I was an intrusion for her husband. My visit was not what I was hoping for. Sometimes, it's best not to try to recapture or relive the past. I have to just let some events go and have better memories.

My visit to see Mrs. Greves was a fiasco too. She had a heavy, intensive surgery. I was overwhelmed with all the tubes and hospital procedures—I felt I was going to faint. I let Mrs. Greves down that day. Generally speaking, the highlight of my trip to California was watching a boa swallow a rabbit.

Later, after we moved to New Mexico Mrs. Greves and Paul came for a visit. She and her husband traveled to New Mexico to visit us and that did not go well for her. I had a job and she complained that she had come so far to see me and I was gone all day. Several times she hinted that if I was there for her as she got older she would make it worth my while. There was just no way I could bend to her will and let her boss me around like she did her daughters. When it was time for her to leave I was relieved that she was going. I'll always remember her statement about our marriage though. She said when a man starts messing around on a woman he will always find a way and a reason to do it again. I'm sure she was speaking from experience.

We had to put the house up for sale of course. We bought it for twenty-three thousand dollars with a GI loan. Ken extended the family room and we sold it for seventy-five thousand six years later. The willow tree, the rose bushes, fuchsias and all my beautiful flowers I had to leave. Dave had started a peach tree from a seed. It broke my heart watching him drag a wooden container with his tree across the street to give to his friend. He said he wanted to give it to her so she would remember him.

We had two mongrel dogs, Winnie and Rosie, at the time we left. They rode in a Ranchero which we pulled behind us in a U-Haul. Our cat, Silly, rode with them. He was old and I could not go off and leave him. Someone had pushed a screen out of a front window and he went in and out as he pleased. I knew the new owners of the house would not put up with him doing that.

The bed of the Ranchero was filled with my houseplants including my prized Norfolk tree. I had a state inspector come to the house and label them as being disease free so they wouldn't be taken away from us crossing any state borders. Plants had been taken from me before, so I had the insight to have them inspected.

A banker and his family bought the house but the sale was not finalized before we left. I don't remember crying but there was a sad air over all of us. Our "bunch of sticks" as Ken had called our home belonged to someone else now. It was nothing left to do but leave.

Mom and me.

My boys.

NEW MEXICO AGAIN

Ken's family had built an adobe house when the kids were young. We had married there. Mel, Ken's brother, was living there with some people when we pulled in the driveway. He and Ken negotiated somehow—we were to have the house as Mel owed Ken money from that previous loan we fought about. At one time the house had been a showcase. The wood used for the paneling was a beautiful pine. There were two bedrooms upstairs and a balcony. There were two bedrooms downstairs. The house was not in the best neighborhood but it was right across the street from an elementary school where Brian would begin school and Dave would be in the second grade.

Everyone was in and out of the house all day to welcome us back. I did not want my boys around my family without me being with them. That was the same way I felt about Ken's family too. Mel was with another woman and she had two girls. They moved to a house behind us. I was only in their house once that I remember. I knew they smoked pot and that was a habit which I didn't want to be around. Just watching Mel "high stepping" once while he was pushing a rototiller was a definite clue he was on something.

Ken's sister and mother were the "gushy-gushy, kissy-kissy" type of females and I wanted as little as possible time around them. The sister-in-law was the bad weather-type, instead of the good weather kinfolk. If there was a problem she was at the door trying to interfere and take over the situation—or maybe just to gossip about. She was hard for me to put up with but her husband was liked by everyone.

My mother-in-law was in the process of getting a divorce from Ken's stepdad. She said he was supposed to have picked her up from the hospital after her surgery. He forgot. When she hailed a ride, got home, she walked in on Jim and a gal. They were on the couch in an awkward position, with no clothes. Once, I told Ken that I didn't think our marriage would last a year living by our families. Well, we were past a year, but trouble was coming.

One bright spot at that time in my life was an unexpected surprise. I had bought a dish of cacti at a garage sale in California. I kept it outside for five or six winters through the rain and low temperatures. When we got to New Mexico it was left outside on the porch and forgotten about so to speak. One day as I walked outside bright colors caught the corner of my eye. Masses of colored blooms cascaded down the side of that dish and it was demanding attention. If cacti could talk it would have said, "All right boys, we're home. Bloom!" A couple days before I noticed that "work of nature" I saw there was going to be a flower show at the botanical gardens. I entered my cacti and won the ribbon for "Best of Show!" The only thing I did for that cacti dish was to take it to the desert and it thanked me is the way I see it.

The closing on our house was stalled in California and we were broke. I made a vow to myself that my kids would never be hungry like I had been as a kid. To keep my vow to myself, I decided I needed to get a job. Ken never was in favor of me working and I knew it would be a hard sell but being without food would help my case. "Who will hire you?" he demanded. You haven't worked in years!" Ken had issues with his mom working. I had to beg for him to buy me that sewing machine. His reason was that his mom had a machine and she never used it. I seemed to be trying to do things over obstacles that Ken held about memories of his mother. That seemed unfair to me. She worked by Jim's side in construction on roofs and under houses. I had little desire to do those things, but I could do food service work.

The next morning, I went to a Ramada Inn down the street from our house. I met Lynn, the manager, and I was hired on the spot as a cashier. I made minimum wage and I stayed in that position for several months. Standing behind the cash register all night I figured I could make a lot more money waiting tables. I asked Lynn if I could waitress and a schedule was made for me. I did make more money waiting tables like I thought I would.

There was a woman I worked with who fascinated me. I'll call her Midge. She got married while I worked with her. The groom left her on their wedding night. There were stories that she went to rooms at night to prostitute herself. She spoke of being sexually abused by a family friend. She told me when she told her mother that her mother called her a liar. Midge never got over that. I could feel her pain. I always felt that would have happened to me if I told my mother. Mom wouldn't have believed me either.

While working my shift as a cashier one night another waitress stopped by the desk. She asked me to give Midge a packet of some typewritten papers. I began reading the pages and I was flabbergasted as I read the content. Midge had suffered mental issues due to the sexual trauma she had suffered from her mother's friend. She eventually had been committed to a mental hospital in California. The attendants raped her continuously there. She said she had been diagnosed with a split personality. That would have explained some of the rumors about her that I had heard about her going to the motel rooms at night. She had lost custody of her kids and she came back to her hometown when she was released.

I was beside myself of how I was going to tell Midge that I had read her psychiatric report. When she came to work the next day, I just blurted out to her what I had done. "What did you think about that, Sue? They're going to make a movie of my life," she confided. There was no movie and we eventually lost contact with each other. I did know she remarried and I was told it was a happy marriage. She certainly deserved it.

A young guy leased the coffee shop and he hired me to work for him. He cut back on everything and he was the cook (I use that term loosely) for the place. In his spare time, he chased (literally, the young, cute senior around the place) and went broke in no time.

One morning I went to work at six a.m. and there was a female screaming curse words which could be heard a block away. She was Jim White's daughter-in-law, Marguerite. Jim White was the cowboy who discovered the Carlsbad Caverns. There is a small mall of sorts about twenty miles outside of town called Whites City. It was a coincidence that a family with the last name of White bought the property just before one enters the national park. They do not have anything to do with the Jim White, the discoverer, of the Caverns. Marguerete was married to James White, the only child of Jim White, the discoverer of the caverns. Later in life James White (the son) started going by Jim White after his dad passed away. Jim was with

Marguerete that morning. I soon found out he was always with her if he wasn't driving a bus for the potash miners.

"Who the hell are you?" Marguerete shouted at me as I turned the corner to the kitchen.

"My name is Sue. There is a bus of Japanese tourists in the parking lot. I will show you what we need to do," I ordered.

I got the pancake mix started, told Jim to stir the mixture and I went for the sausages. We needed to make a breakfast dish called "pigs in the blanket" for thirty tourists and a driver. I demonstrated to Marguerete how to cook the pancakes and how to roll the pancake around a sausage. Afterwards, I made coffee and juice. The tourists filed in laughing and waving at all of us, speaking Japanese! The driver spoke English at least. I spent a morning like no other morning I ever had before in my life. Chaos!

As I was walking by some tables I blinked really hard. The batter was oozing out of their pancakes! Thankfully, those customers were not familiar with that American cuisine as I watched them pick up a spoon and push the runny matter onto a spoon and eat away. I just kept topping off their coffee while they talked and laughed. They filed out the same way they came in; happy and waving goodbye to us.

Marguerete, Jim, and I were quite a team. Jim was the cashier, I waitressed and Marguerete would yell at "the lazy son-of-a-bitches," who also worked there. The Whites of White City owned the Ramada Inn at that time. They hired Jim and Marguerete to be the general managers of the whole place. That included a small bar, a ballroom, a formal dining room, and the coffee shop where I met the Whites. After a hard day Marguerete would go to the cash register and hand me a wad of bills. She said I worked hard and she appreciated me. She totally trusted me and I was loyal to her. She came in with a hangover many mornings and she yelled at everyone but me.

Later, one of the owner's sons from White City was my new boss. He was young and totally ignorant of a small town's coffee shop. He would focus on the flower arrangement on the table rather than smile at a customer entering the door. He made a schedule once and I worked three weeks without a day off. When I finally complained, he acted as though I was just wanting a day off so I could throw his schedule off. Thankfully, he just lasted one summer.

White City again leased the coffee shop and dining room to a couple who were well-known by many in town. They had operated eating places for years. Right off, I got negative vibes from the woman manager. Neither one of them were happy that I knew all the railroad guys. The railroaders were our regular customers and they also rented rooms for their layovers. If anyone needed anything they came to me because I was the employee who knew more about that place than anyone. Mr. Zot had a gambling problem and if he lost the night before he was a bear! I asked permission from Ms. Zot if I could get off early the next day to go to Dave's school, as Dave was going to get an award. The next day when I was working Mr. Zot told me to quit talking and go bus a table. I did. When I went to the kitchen he jumped me because he said I didn't do the side work before I left the day before. I looked at the other waitress and she dropped her head. She told that story to him I'm sure. I got my purse and walked out.

Driving up the street the owner of a place I use to work at motioned for me come over and I did. She hired me on the spot. More about that situation later on.

Two days later I got a call from Marguerete and she wanted me to come in and talk to her about being a bartender.

"I don't know anything about being a bartender, Marguerete!"

"I know, that's why I got you a book about bartending." So, then I had two jobs.

I was to work in the little bar. I had guys sitting at the bar drinking and I had to make drinks for the waitresses to take to the dining room. When I got an order for mixed drinks I would hand the book to one of the guys at the bar and I would tell them to read me the directions for making a Manhattan, a martini or some other drink. Those guys would watch as I got the shaker or the blender and they read me each step. They rather enjoyed it. The phone would ring sometimes and a female voice would ask, "Is Bill Thomas there?" I would yell "Bill Thomas!" Of course, Bill would shake his head. I would then tell the woman, "Bill says he's not here." That would usually get the guy over to the phone rather quickly.

Going into a bar on Sunday mornings would turn anyone's stomach. The smell of rancid cigarette butts, spilled alcohol, and Lord knows what else stunk to the high heavens. My shift started at 11:00

am to 6:00 pm on Sundays. Guys came there to watch football games. They reminded me of amoebas in a trance while watching the game, but the second the commercial came on they would start yelling for another beer or something.

Most of the guys I knew, but one night a stranger came in with a gal and her young daughter. He had a knife in his belt and the law said that was not allowed. I went to the table and asked him to take the knife out of the bar. He rose from his chair and went to his car I guess. When he came back he no longer had the knife. Two of my regular customers had an eye on him while I was talking to him just in case he gave me any static. It was like I had a bunch of big brothers who drank a lot and liked to watch football games. But they would look out for me if I needed them.

While working in the bar I met a spunky, stacked, and a beautiful soul. She was a waitress for the couple I had walked out on. She would get behind the bar and ask me for a "little vodka Collins." When I handed it to her she would swallow more than half of the drink down and grab the vodka bottle and pour her glass with total straight vodka. She would call customers honey, asshole, or by their name. I guess it depended on the word she thought of first. She was a barrel of fun. Her name was Misti.

She was living with a guy who had his legs cut off due to an accident while working for the railroad. A settlement was pending, and that was the reason Misti was working. She had a young daughter, Penelope, and her live-in would watch her while Misti worked. I guess I left that place before Misti did, but we will meet again.

Things got really busy for us in our house. Ken got a machete and started cutting down vines which shaded the front porch. His reasoning did little to console my desire to leave them there. I complained constantly that I did not have any planters to plant any flowers and Ken built me some out of concrete and bricks. I spent hours trying to control the weeds in the yard but with little success. I had to learn about growing things in the desert, and those were some hard, back-breaking lessons. Dave grew strawberries in the planters and neighbor kids would be at the door every morning wanting some strawberries. We found out Dave was allergic strawberries. He would complain his ears itched every time he ate them. Dave would share them with the neighbor kids.

The house had been rented out to relatives and to anyone else who had the money. Mom even rented it for several months. Their complaint about the place was that it was haunted. A story I remember was that a knife was moving through the air. It was an old two story with a basement which had hard dirt for the flooring. Anything and everything could crawl right into the house. There were two bathrooms in the place; one upstairs and one downstairs. The upstairs bathroom had plumbing problems so we didn't use it for the longest time. Someone said the sewer was backed up to the ground level and I had nightmares about that problem.

We got an exterminator and he had a job every month at our house because of the "creepy crawlers." One of the freakish sights I had ever seen in my life was in the upstairs bathroom. One day I decided I would scrub the bathroom down using a bucket of water. I raised the commode lid and there were roaches circling the inside rim of the commode! I guess if they went out of that spot the poison the exterminator used would have killed them. They had turned to cannibalism to survive! Body parts were missing from some of them. I have read some insects have survived on earth from the beginning of time. That sight just proved that point for me!

Ken built skylights in the house and my ivy climbed the stair banisters all the way to the upstairs. He devised a pulley and installed large beams in the living room by himself while I was out one evening. Someone had told me Ken was a building genius in California. I marveled while watching him do things which I thought were impossible to do many times. Usually, he had a can of beer close by, a cigarette in his mouth, and a box of cigars in his shirt pocket. His hair was long, but he combed it back and he wore a safari hat while working. There was usually country and western music in the background. This is how he spent many hours of our marriage working alone most of the time.

Ken loved to hunt. I know that was another big reason for him wanting to move back where he grew up. We had made a couple trips back to New Mexico for him to go with some relatives. During the time

I lived in WV I never liked to hunt; the first drawback from that outing was that one had to be quiet and that word was not in my vocabulary of living. The second reason was that I hated to eat wild meat and I definitely didn't want to cook it. So, I guess there were three reasons total. People would give me their recipes and secrets of their preparation. I would grit my teeth, turn my head, and try to refrain from gagging out loud.

We had pecan trees in the backyard. Our neighbors asked if they could pick them up and I said sure. Ken got so angry at me for letting them have them. He was getting angry a lot more it seemed. Dave was still upset that we moved, and Ken would get angry over his sadness. Maybe, Ken doubted his decision for moving us out of California, not sure.

One of Ken's reasons for moving was because the crime rate in California, was so high. He wanted the boys to be safer in New Mexico. That didn't happen. Our boys were outsiders from California and that state wasn't really appreciated much in the ultra-conservative town we now lived in. The boys were picked on and we decided to send them to a karate class. The instructor wasn't the most patient man with kids, and truthfully, I didn't care for him. We went to the school because of fights the boys were involved in and Ken would tell the boys to pick up something or do something violent. I disapproved. Our last name was known all over town and the family had a reputation for being fighters and trouble makers. Ken had issues with bullying too when he was young. I guess he wanted the boys to stick up for themselves. Guess what I'm saying is that they probably would have been as safe or more in California as they were in New Mexico.

The Boys and Girls Club was right around the corner from us. I thought I could get Dave to join and he could make a friend or two. After joining, there was a swimming trip planned for the members of the club at the river. Dave got up early and he climbed in the van with the other kids. I kept waiting for Dave to come home that evening as it was getting late. I finally went to the club and no Dave! I got the name of the driver of the van and called him. I was fuming and scared. I asked him where Dave was and I could tell he couldn't place him. In other words, he didn't know. He said he took ten kids down to the river and he brought ten kids back to the club. "You didn't bring my kid back!" I screamed. I went to the river and I saw Dave right off. What a relief! He was close to the shore just wading in the water. I took him home and there were no more visitations or excursions with the Girls and Boys Club.

When my family had moved to New Mexico from WV we were given food from the Nazarene church. The turkey Mom cooked with dumplings was from that church's basket. The pastor's wife was a teacher across the street. She remembered my family. I was relieved I knew someone at the school. Brian started first grade there and both boys went through to the fifth grade. Dave loved school but Brian didn't like it after first grade. At that time, I was intimidated by schools and the faculty. When I had to go to the school for a teacher's conference I was uncomfortable. Maybe, it was Mom's attitude towards schools was the reason I had that feeling. Put another way I felt incompetent in a school building at that time.

Ken and I continued bowling together but we didn't know anyone who would watch the boys, or who the boys liked. So, we decided all we really wanted was for the boys to be safe, so our German Shepherd was the designated babysitter for a couple years. A policeman lived next door and he said he would keep an eye on them also on Thursday nights for us.

One day, Ken drove in the driveway in a big truck. It was a red, 1975 Ford, and the tires on that thing were as high as my shoulders. It took everything I had to climb in that monster. I had to lift or push the boys up so they could get in. It was definitely not a family vehicle. We needed to haul firewood out of the mountains for the fireplace as that was the only heat for the living room area we had. We had a small floor gas heater in our bedroom and the oven in the kitchen. The first cold spell that hit us I couldn't believe it got that cold in a desert. We needed firewood, and that was Ken's excuses or argument for getting that truck. I didn't fall for that excuse by any means but again what could I do about it.

My vehicle was a Volkswagen. Ken had been drinking with this guy and he had "a deal for him." He had a VW in his backyard and all it needed was a motor. I was not a happy camper when Ken gave me the lowdown on his $300 fantastic deal. He took it to a shop and got a motor and then he took it to an upholsterer and I was kind of excited about it after that, I admit. As I was leaving the shop I had to back up. I could drive a stick shift but I couldn't get that blue contraption in reverse even while looking at the diagram on the gearshift. A guy got in the passenger side, and he told me to "hit it" and it was in reverse. When I got home and we decided to take a spin but I couldn't get it in reverse. I had run up against the fence. Ken was fuming and cussing and I still couldn't get it in reverse. When I tried to shift it gear, it sounded like I ripped every gear away from whatever gears are attached to. Ken went to call the guy while yelling back to me. Somehow, I remembered what he had said, "Hit it!" After it was hit on the top then it would allow you to put it reverse following the diagram. What a relief! I'll never forget the way to put a VW in reverse for the rest of my life.

My dogs and cat would hear me coming a block away in "Old Blue" and they would run out and greet me every time I drove up. That little engine was a regular "animal whisperer." Once while Ken and I were separated he took Sheba, our German Shepherd, to the club with him in his van. I guess she got tired of waiting for Ken to come out so she jumped out the window. Ken called me on the phone and told me that "my damned dog had run away" and he couldn't find her. The next morning as I topped a hill I saw her shepherd's ears rise above some tall grass. She had heard the unique sound of that VW and she knew it was us. Great memories of her in the back seat with Brian and Dave. A carload for sure. Ken had to give her away when I moved out. That is a sad memory for the boys and me.

Ken had gotten work trimming houses out in a tract of homes when he went looking for work. New Mexico was a right-to-work state in construction and he didn't have to deal with the unions. He did piece work for a while but there wasn't much building in this small town. No work, so there was more time to drink. I would come home from work and Ken would be drinking with relatives or drinking buddies who were always at our house. I didn't like Ken's relatives giving their opinions on everything about the house. They all felt they had a say as most of them had lived in the house at one time or another. I never felt like it was really my house or our house at all, ever.

While we were trying to reconcile in California I had told Ken about my abuse that I had suffered all those years. I would not allow him to console me. When he put out his hand or lean in a shoulder I would turn my back towards him and talk to myself silently. I've learned this is a typical response in which young kids do. I've heard the term "self-soothing" but there are different methods of doing that. There was a reluctance on my part to trust Ken. Sometimes his statements would ring in my ears; one of them was "a hard dick has no conscience." I interpreted that phrase as I couldn't hold the adult who abused me responsible because he had a hard dick. Sounds like it would have been an ideal time for therapy for myself but I was at a loss. I didn't know how to go about getting help. I didn't know how to self-talk myself out of all the painful memories even to myself. The whos, and the whys, of my reality in the world were overwhelming at times. I definitely couldn't talk to a stranger or for that matter anyone I knew.

Ken was drinking more. I'm sure he used pot but not sure if there was any other drug he indulged in. Ken and I were at odds constantly and the boys were beginning to take sides in our conflicts. Once, in the kitchen, Dave turned to me and asked, "Mom, are you staying with Dad because of Brian and me?" That statement hit home! I had made a commitment to myself that I did not want my boys coming from a broken home or having a stepdad. I was making judgment calls from my personal experience; that was all the guidance I had. I just never knew it was so obvious to my child.

Ken got where he couldn't sleep. He would be up all hours of the night talking to his brother, James. I heard bits of the conversations at times. Ken was talking about going to Iran with James, a crippled friend, Ralph, and himself and rescuing the American prisoners. No way could I make sense of his world which was invading my reality. If I questioned him about any of those conversations he would get mad at me, and say I never believed him about anything. That was pretty much a fact that I could no longer argue with.

He had begun a job on a Brantley Dam and had made foreman in no time. Several times he would rush home and pull down the shades because someone was going to drive by and shoot at our house. One of the workers came to the place I worked, and said Ken would yell, belittle, and curse the workers on the job site continuously. I never asked him if any of the workers had threatened to drive by our house and shoot at it. In a group of construction workers—I felt that answer was a given.

Another habit Ken got into at that time of his paranoia was to rake the dirt around our bedroom window. He told me if anyone was looking in the window he would see their shoe tracks. At times I would go home from work and I never knew what planet I needed to adapt to for that particular day. He also began collecting guns more, and they were standing or laying all over the house. I tried to make him see how unreasonable that was. He only had two hands and could only shoot two at a time, but he saw no humor or logic in my reasoning.

One day, Ken was especially angry. I didn't know what had set him off that was more extreme than other times. He took off and didn't come back in that big truck. I called in sick from work and waited for Ken to return. I was working in the yard when a police car drove up. A knot was in my gut. A female policewoman got out, and I recognized her right off as I had gone to school with her. She asked me if I was Ken's wife and I nodded my head. She told me that Ken had been in a wreck and he had killed at least five people in another car. My knees buckled as I recalled the many times I had pleaded with Ken not to drive while drinking. She said Ken was in a hospital in another town and he was dying. She asked me about Ken's physical attributes, including his weight. I told her Ken was a slight man with dark hair. "Oh, the "little man syndrome, huh?" I don't remember saying anything to that statement, as I was so shocked that a police person would say such a thing about anyone—especially in front of their spouse.

I loaded the boys up and we headed to the hospital twenty miles away. Dave was crying hysterically and saying his dad was dying and it was all his fault. He kept repeating it over and over. He and his dad argued a lot. There was not much they had in common and Ken had such little patience. Brian, sitting in the backseat, just kept looking out the window. I don't remember him saying a word. When we arrived at the hospital we were allowed to visit Ken. Tubes were in his body and an oxygen mask was over his mouth. Dave did most talking and he was apologizing to Ken for being bad kid. If Ken had died Dave would have had so much self-appointed guilt to overcome. Brian was quiet and just looked around. Myself, I guess I was in shock.

I found out from a policeman outside in the hallway that Ken had not killed anyone. He was in a one vehicle accident! He had lost control of his truck, hit the side of a bridge and rolled the truck over five times down an embankment towards a riverbed which had dried up. He had a rifle standing up by his leg by the door and it was bent in the shape of a snake ready to strike. That gun kept him from being crushed by the cab of the truck. The truck was taken into town and people were allowed to see it and it spoke of an accident that was the result of a DWI.

As I entered the front door the phone was ringing and Mom was on the line. "Sue, Ken was over here and he had a gun. He shot several bullets in the ceiling." I guess Ken had gone there with the intentions of shooting Gabe or at least scaring him really bad. Ken was blaming Gabe for our marriage falling apart. Mom said she told Ken that he was just jealous of a guy I had gone with before. I guess since Ken highly respected Mom or maybe for some other reason he left in the truck and had that wreck. I kept apologizing to Mom for what she had just gone through. Funny, over time Dora and I always tried to protect Mom from any problems she had to deal with. It was as though we were the parent and we had to soothe things over for her.

When I visited Ken, he was usually with a doctor. Ken was improving. Confusing times for me for sure. Everything was on hold. One day, Jim carried Ken through our front door and sat him in a wheelchair. I told Ken when he could walk I was leaving him and taking the kids and that's what I did.

The boys and I took our animals and moved to the country. Ken would call me and some days he pleaded for me to come back to him. Other days he threatened me. After a while he got strong enough to walk to where we lived. His focus was mainly about sex. He said that was the only thing he lived for. One day he said he was going to come and rape me. The only protection I had was a softball bat and a softball. My plan was to hit him between the eyes with the ball and then beat the hell out of him with the bat. No one was going to ever rape me again! When he entered the door, I was holding the ball.

Sizing him up I could tell he couldn't overpower me. He fell over a stool while trying to grab me. In a short while he gave up and left.

For my birthday that year Ken brought me a beautiful cocker spaniel, Goldie. He traded a pistol for her. She was a beautiful animal and brightened my trying days during that period. I let her sleep on the water bed which Ken disapproved. The bed would be wet when we got up in the mornings. Ken said Goldie was wetting the bed and I said that was ridiculous! Finally, mystery solved. The waterbed had a finite hole in it and that was why the bedclothes were wet.

One day Goldie was following the boys across the street and a car must have hit her without the boys being aware of the accident. They saw her lying in the street, and rushed home to tell me. Ken held her as I drove us to the vet but she died on the way. The vet came from the tennis court to his office but it was too late. He never did send me a bill, and I will never forget that kind gesture. We got another cocker spaniel and she got hit by a car too. That was the last cocker spaniel I ever wanted. They're beautiful dogs but surviving in our clan took a knowledge of survival and that breed just didn't have a genetic code strong enough for that.

I moved back with the condition Ken would go to a marriage counselor with me. I found a counselor through a co-worker and I made an appointment. When the session started Ken immediately started telling her what was wrong with me. I did not reply at first as I found anything I said would trigger Ken into a tirade, but finally I had to stand up for myself. I have the strangest allusions of that day. When Ken accused me of things with so much hostility it was as though a sword had been thrown at me and had barely missed my head. When I responded to his accusations I felt as though I was throwing a sword across the room at him. I had been pent up for so long I guess, that there was so much hostile energy going from me and also coming towards me. Strong, hate-filled feelings spoken out loud became animate weapons in that small room. Eerie. Finally, Ken told the counselor I needed help. She turned towards me and asked me if I would consider coming and visiting with her. I told her I would. As a couple she told us she didn't see us ever having a relationship that would or could work. She said, "I wouldn't give you two any more of a chance than a snowball in hell!" Ken said he didn't need any more help.

After talking to her and telling her about my past she did not condemn or ridicule me. When Ken said I was out at night all the time I was taking cooking or sewing classes. Anything or anyone that took my attention from Ken fed his resentment towards me. I had to face the fact that included our sons. Later, he will tell Dave he never wanted him and that was very painful for Dave. Ken told Brian that his mom had a kid, Dave, and so Brian would be his kid. My poor kids had so much to deal with.

I went to the counselor twice. On the last meeting she told me that what I was doing was all I could do. She said I was coping without drugs or any other means of escape in my life. I took her support and words and used them to remind myself that I was doing all that I could. That was the only time I had any therapy. I'm sure I could have used more but somehow, I have blundered through this road of life alive so far.

Supposedly, afterwards the deal was that Ken would quit drinking but we had made those deals before. We had a shed in the backyard which was supposed to have been his shop. He got a call for another job and when he came home that day he had a beer in his hand. He told me he couldn't be an alcoholic because he only drank beer. I had a couple guys who told me Ken was drinking a beer bright and early many times in the mornings. Since the wreck he said he drank because of the pain he had from the wreck, and I could not argue with that. Later, he told me he had always had beer in the shed. The problem was he would be either Dr. Jekyll or Mr. Hyde, and we would not know what role we were supposed to play when he was around. As a matter of a fact he was not very likeable when he was sober. If the boys and I were talking he would interrupt and correct us on the topic we were talking about. If we quit talking he would get mad and say we were talking about him. The truth was we rarely talked about him. In hindsight, maybe we should have been.

The Same Decision, Again

One night I had a talk with myself while looking in a mirror. I was turning into a nag, an enabler, and I was spying on Ken all the time. I decided I had to either leave or accept his ways and keep my mouth shut. I wondered how I could support myself and the kids. Well, I had been working two jobs already so that seemed to be doable. I decided to leave. The place where I worked was close to some apartments down the alley. I could walk a block and cross a bridge—and be at the club the other place where I worked.

While in a wheelchair Ken would go towards the console where the record player was. Sometimes he would take out the gun and clean it and just hold it in his lap. Once he pulled a gun on Dave and me when we went to get in the VW. I sped off while telling Dave to get down and I closed my shoulders anticipating a bullet coming towards my back. Another time Ken drove by Mom's house while we were standing in the yard. I told Mom that Ken had threatened to kill himself. She calmly said, "He won't kill himself because he's a coward." Not sure what she based that statement on, but I was comforted by her words. Maybe that was all she meant for her words to do. Once Ken told me he was going to the club where I worked and he would shoot me and anyone I was around. I told my boss. My boss said if I gave in to Ken's threats I would always be a prisoner of his threats. So, I went on in life looking over my shoulder but I couldn't stop doing what I needed to do. The boys needed at least one parent.

College, You Say

Just before Ken and I separated long term Dave came home with a stack of papers and I started looking through them. Some of the papers were about subjects in history and literature mostly. My interest was piqued.

"Dave, what do you have here?" I asked.

He explained that he had been selected to participate in a regional Knowledge Bowl and he needed to know about the many subjects in the stack.

"Would you like me to help you with some of these?" I asked.

He said he did.

As we were discussing, mainly about the history, he asked, "Mom, how do you know all these things?"

Well, most of the history I had lived through but I read a lot about history. I read about many other subjects also.

One day a couple came in the café where I was working. I bowled with the husband and the wife worked at the junior college on the hill in the library. I was telling them about Dave being selected to be in a Knowledge Bowl. I told them about me getting up during the night and looking things up in encyclopedias so I could help Dave make connections between people, places, and things. Sometimes the Kennedy years were confusing for him. I remember the day Kennedy got assassinated. Ken and I had only been married for few months and the announcement came on the radio. I was looking in the mirror and cutting my hair with a razor blade. I remember my wrist coming down hard and I made a bald spot in the back of my head. Looking in a mirror at the back of my head today, I can still see the spot and that memory comes back fifty-four years later.

Brenda, Bill's wife, made a comment right out of the blue.

"Sue, you need to go to school. I can hear the excitement in your voice. Go to the college and see Chuck Ridenour and he will tell you what to do," she prompted.

Years before I was at that college and they were recruiting students for the coming year. Being curious I got in a line. I told the recruiter for the college I wanted to know what I needed to do to be a physical education teacher. She told me I would need to go to school about two hundred miles away. I said I couldn't do that! She said, "If you really wanted to be a teacher, you would figure out a way to do that." That response of hers haunted me for several years.

"Old Blue" and I went up that hill a couple days later. My marriage was in the gutter, and I could barely scrape up enough money for food and why not go to school as I had nothing to lose. Entering Chuck's office, I was beginning to see my big mistake! Oh well, I would just get more support and that would prove I had bitten off too much. He gave me a reading test and a math test and left me alone. After I finished, I went and sat down in his office. He came back into the room. "I have some good news and some bad news. Which do you want first?"

I chose the good news first. He said I tested on college level in reading. The bad news was that I was on the fifth-grade level in math. All those years I had struggled in math came back to haunt me, I thought. Humiliated, I started towards the door!

"No, wait!" Chuck yelled after me. "I know how you can learn math."

Chuck said there was a lab for remedial subjects and I could try that. He explained that the lab had workbooks and earphones. I could work at my own pace. Five days a week I would enter that lab with my heart beating and a knot of fear in my gut. If I missed a concept I could back up and do it over and over until I sort of understood it. In all, I spent one hundred and twenty clock hours under those earphones. Once I heard a "Yeehaw," from another older woman, and I totally understood her elation.

When I finished my first unit on mixed fractions I reported to Chuck for my test. It had ten problems. He told me to go to a table outside and work the problems. As I focused on the first problem I had no idea what it wanted me to do. Dragging myself back to Chuck I told him I couldn't do the test. He told me to go and have a cigarette and afterwards give it another try. After a while I looked at the second problem. That one sort of made sense. I finished the other eight and went back to the first problem. I did it, but I knew it was wrong.

Watching Chuck grade my test made me a nervous wreck. A red check mark he stroked on the first problem and then he held the pen in the air! I only got that one problem wrong. I couldn't ever remember making a 90% on a math test before. Driving home in "Old Blue" I was singing and entering a state of euphoria. Telling the boys about my proud moment I remember Brian saying, "You were on the fifth-grade level in math and you were helping me with math!" It was true. Brian had a difficult time in math and I tried to help him but he still didn't make any better grades if I did help him.

The first class I was told to take was a Readiness class with Chuck. I was taught to take notes, do writing assignments, and in general, how to distinguish what I needed to know to pass the tests for classes. The second class I took was Psychology. The instructor was a jovial little guy who seemed to see the humor in everything I said. I was the oldest student in the class and the young students seemed to think I was a novelty. Being a blonde, a mouthy bartender at the time I wouldn't argue with them about that matter at all.

One night I was flipping through the class text and I came across the word "hermaphrodite." A memory of when I was twelve or so, at church one night, and the boys had taken Joey Boy outside. That book was explaining what I remembered. I said something to the girl sitting by me and she said, "Tell Mr. Cruz." I did. He went into a lengthy explanation of the subject. For the first time in my life I heard an explanation of a question I had for years and the instructor had an answer, and he could make me understand. "Eureka!" I have decided that is what heaven will be like for me.

There was a lady instructor in my sociology class, a Dr. Siddell. She would say things in that class that totally caught me off guard. She said we treated the Japanese so harshly during World War II. Raising my hand, I told her that we gave their heirs thirty-thousand dollars. (I had no comprehension of thirty-thousand of anything, but in my finances understanding, that was a heck of a lot of money.) "Besides, everything is fair in war and love!" I argued. I thought that would impress her, but it didn't.

Not handling the spoils of war so well, I jumped into the subject of welfare. I did have a personal issue with that! I told of an experience I had at the grocery store the week before. I had to give some background with that subject first. I worked two jobs, going to school and I had to watch every penny. A woman I knew was checking out right before me. She had shrimp and the real expensive ice cream for her kids. My kids had never had shrimp before, and I only bought ice cream for special occasions as it was too expensive. Watching that woman putting those items out of her cart and paying for them with food stamps really ticked me off. I felt I had put forth a good case for the class (most were nodding affirmative) but not the teacher. I'll never forget what she said. "Sue, she didn't know how to budget like you." What the heck! I wanted her to understand my righteous indignation. I felt at the time I was getting the short end of things. Now, I see that I do have the advantage but I wrestled with her statement for a long time. She also said after I completed her class I would never read the newspaper the same way again and she was right about that too.

Sociology gave me a world view of social issues, and I'm thankful for that even until these many years later.

One night several of Chuck's students, including myself, were standing around chatting. Chuck asked a young guy what he was going to do with his education. The boy said he was going to be a teacher. Well, a thought came to me. My grades were

higher than his, why couldn't I become a teacher? A seed was germinating. The next day while I was pitching burger baskets at customers during the lunch hour where I worked a male voice yelled, "Hey Sue, why are you going to school?"

"I'm going to be a teacher!" OMG! I said it out loud and many heard me. A wave of relief and panic came over me at the same time.

I needed money, nothing new, I've needed money most of my life. There was an office called Financial Aid at the college. I entered the door and sitting behind the desk was Betty. She was the wife of a guy I bowled with who we called Indian. I told Betty I needed money to go to college. She said there were loans for women like me. I was now a displaced homemaker, and I was eligible for the Pell Grant and other money if I took a full course load. Why not? Truth be known I had money left over from the grants I was eligible for. Physics, chemistry, algebra, computers, literature were only a few subjects waiting on me. I wasn't sure I was ready for them, but I jumped in head first. "Ignorance is bliss" is an old saying and it has been my stand-in for bravery many times in my life. It's like I'm in so deep I just start faking what I'm supposed to be doing and somehow it works out for me.

Sometimes I would ride my bicycle to class two miles away up a steep hill and sit in a chemistry class and not understand a thing the instructor was talking about. A lot of the time he didn't know what he was talking about either as he drank a lot. Dr. Pike had a cause or an obsession about plastic wrap or cellophane touching luncheon meat. We were told if the plastic wrap touched the meat and we ate the meat we would all die of cancer. Who knows maybe that was true when I think about it, as a lot of people I knew have died and I bet they ate meat which was touched by plastic wrap.

One day during class Dr. Pike announced that he would be taking some time off as he had a drinking problem. Most of us figured that out before he announced it but we didn't know if Dr. Pike knew he had a problem. I guess someone told him. The next class he entered the door and slammed a bottle of Scotch down on the lab table.

He announced, "I don't have a damn drinking problem, a lot of other people do!" Stunned, we dropped our heads and listened to him tell us about those other people. The next night while I was standing, waiting my turn to bowl I caught a glimpse of Dr. Pike standing behind our lanes. When I finished my turn, I went back and spoke to him while I was looking at his bare feet!

"Dr. Pike can I help you find someone?" I questioned him. He grunted, turned and I never saw him again. Rumors said that his wife had left him and he followed her out of state.

One of the basics I needed was an art/humanities class. I took Theatre 101. Dave and Brian were both excellent in plays. I think when we did play acting during their younger years they both found it to be fun. Mimicking commercials and some lines I knew in other dialogues from the television is a thing I've always done. During the eighties, there was a commercial which came out advertising men's underwear. Fruit of the Loom is the oddest name for underwear and that brand name sort of tickled my brain and my tongue. I was selected to be Sarah in a Christmas play. They sprayed my hair silver as the character was supposed to be a ninety-year old woman pregnant with Isaac. Sarah met the Virgin Mary pregnant with Jesus. Sarah was supposed to rush up to Mary and say. "Blessed is the fruit of your womb!" Maybe I have said "womb" ten times in my lifetime. After I said my lines the audience started laughing and clapping and I was confused! Then I was told I said, "Blessed is the Fruit of Your Loom" to the Virgin Mary! Laugh at yourself first is my motto. So, I did.

Another notable class I took because I was told to, was World War II history. How boring, I thought. The class was lecture and interactive. We were told to interview veterans. The place where I worked had a crew of old timers who frequented the place and I enjoyed listening to their stories. There's an old airbase south of town and a few of the fellows were stationed there during the war. When the war was over they just stayed in the desert town because of the women they had met and married here.

Dave wrote of his grandma seeing German POWs playing soccer right over a hill where she lived in an apartment during the 40's. His journalism teacher entered his paper for a competition. Dave was recognized for his paper and we were really proud of him. Funny, before I got an education I thought I knew almost everything about the history of that time period. But the more education I got the more I knew I just didn't know.

To get the rest of my education I had to drive one-hundred sixty miles away four days a week. I wasn't sure "Old Blue" could hold up to that mileage. Lonnie advised me this way on the matter; he told me that motor would be going down the highway for years but the body of that bug would rust away, maybe in the next rainstorm. Dave had bought a Datsun pickup from Lonnie to go to college but he couldn't afford the insurance and upkeep of a vehicle. I bought that little truck and got it painted from a putrid green to a blue and so that matter was taken care of. So, I drove a little blue Datsun truck eighty miles away to school instead of "Old Blue" my beloved VW.

So, the matter of gas for the truck was the next hurdle. I was told I should go to the welfare office and ask for a "gas allowance." Off I went and stood in line for my turn to plead my case I thought. A man sitting behind the window at a desk but not attending to the people in line caught my eye. He came through a door and motioned for me to follow him. I followed him outside into the alley. "Why are you here"? he demanded.

Not sure if he recognized me or not from the places I worked, but I for sure didn't recognize him. I got the feeling he was chastising me for doing something wrong. I told him I was advised to ask for a gas allowance and I told him I needed eighty dollars a week for gas so I could go to school.

"You don't belong here," he said sternly. Once you get in the system many don't ever get out. You're not that type of woman. Go home and figure something else out."

I listened to that stranger and I went to the bank and got an eight-thousand-dollar loan to finish my bachelor's degree.

I did my budget once and everything was fine, for a couple hours until I remembered I didn't have any food money. A couple days later I got a call, and was told I was the recipient of an AAUW scholarship. Things just seemed to get to the point of being a catastrophe and a miracle would just appear from people. I use to try to explain to myself that maybe God was trying to make it up to me because of my abusive childhood. I don't believe that anymore, but again I'm not sure.

I was heartbroken when I found out there were no avenues for me to play softball in this town other than fastpitch. I did join a fastpitch team but I was too old to compete with the young gals. I would tell people our team came in third place but I didn't add that there were only three teams. The men had a slow-pitch league and I'm not sure how I got the idea to form a slow-pitch league for women but I did. I found out that there were a lot of older women who wanted to hit a softball and play fielding positions. Being slower in running and in fielding the ball, didn't seem to matter to us. The first year we had eight teams with ten players on each team for our league.

The coach for our team was a guy who catered to our every whim. Nellie, we called him, and he would carry our water, the first aid kit, and all our equipment without complaint. We teased him unmercifully, as he was not very sharp on women's' cattiness. His wife had recently left him, so maybe, we were his surrogate wives. He knew one gal on the team when he started coaching us and I think he had a crush on her. She was recently divorced but she wasn't really inclined for a man who worked hard, and loved only softball. Later, he turned his attention towards me after I got a divorce, but we were on two different planets in our thinking and lifestyles. Overall, we did give him a source of fun and a sense of belonging for years; which was what he wanted the most.

One night during the warmup before a game Nellie hit a line drive at me and as I scooped up the ball—my index finger got jammed. It hurt. He hit me another line drive and I did the same thing. I had to go to the doctor and he said he would put a "Mexican splint" on it. That medical treatment included two popsicle sticks taped around my finger. The sticks were to keep my finger straight so the bone would heal. That method worked partly as I have a rather crooked index finger.

Once just before a tournament I felt a cold coming on so I took some Dristan and a Contac. Looking in the mirror I literally saw my lips growing and my eyes slitting. Panic-stricken I rushed into the kitchen and demanded that Ken look at me. His drunken buddy was laughing and Ken said he didn't see anything wrong. Not sure if he did or not. He told me to go and take a shower when I told him I had taken Dristan and a Contac. When I finished showering and stepping out I saw my clothes about three feet from me, but I couldn't get that far. I sat on the toilet, my head hit the wall and I began hallucinating. Ken came in the bathroom. He wrapped me in a bathrobe and took me to the ER. They couldn't give me anything as they told me I had an allergic reaction to the cold medicine I took. My entire body broke out in hives. Red splotches covered what the hives didn't. I was told to go home and not take any medication with antihistamines. I went home, put my uniform on, and went to the tournament.

Once we were playing a practice game with a team in softball. Since I was the pitcher I ran in to cover the home plate as a runner was coming to score. Just as she got to me she raised her knee and hit me in the crotch on purpose! I was carrying a full load in school and I didn't have any insurance. I went home, took my mitt and threw it in the garbage bin for pickup. I had to remove my temptation from ever playing softball again.

Karate was a class I had always wanted to take. Brian was involved in karate with a guy we both liked. When I told Brian, I signed up for karate, he told me not to tell anyone I was his mother. Sometimes, I was too loud or outspoken for my sons. Chuck Link was a local artist, a martial arts instructor, an excellent table tennis player, and volleyball player. I loved competing with and against Chuck. He helped Brian train for a marathon, and he was just a person who anyone would want to be around.

One night in karate, Chuck paired us up for a kicking spar drill. I was assigned a young teenage boy. He was the first kicker and he was kicking me so hard that my arms and wrists had turned blue from bruising. As Chuck passed by, I complained that I was being hurt.

He said, "Sue, when it's your turn you can kick him back."

So, I endured, and when I was to begin the drill of kicking I gritted my teeth, and reared my right leg back as far as I could. My focus was so intense I can't recall how my toe got caught in my gee but it did. I couldn't free my toe and I went down hard and broke my toe. I had to miss a day of waitressing and tips due to a haphazard karate kick.

Tennis and bowling were sports I participated in when we first moved to New Mexico. I once asked someone why I didn't play tennis when I was younger and they said tennis was a "rich person's" game. That statement was true years ago for sure. I had taken a summer beginners class in tennis in California. When we moved I took a tennis class in college, so I could meet other tennis players. For some reason in college; when you sign up for a class you need to finish the class even it's just to meet people. I had gotten a job and never gave that class a second thought. When I decided to take classes for a degree that "F" was staring me in the face when I looked at my records. I failed tennis! I used to think I should go back and retake tennis but who cares—I still play in my seventies and it's just not that important anymore.

The person in charge of tennis in our town asked me to play my first tennis tournament. I was playing several times a week and he was trying to recruit more players for a tournament. Off I went in "Old Blue" to my first tennis tournament one Saturday morning. I didn't know what to expect and I didn't know many of the ladies in the tournament. It was called a novice tournament and the rule was that a player couldn't have won a tournament before. That fit me to a tee; I was use to competition, but tennis singles is a very lonely game. In Andre Agassi's book he put his knowledge and experience in a book and I totally understood some of the loneliness he must have felt, especially being a kid.

Sunday was the day for the semi-finals and finals and I had made through to the finals. My opponent was half my age, and her legs were twice as long as my legs. I had to take six steps to cover as much distance as she did in two. I never worked so hard in my life. I won and still have the cup on my shelf.

There was a tennis league that formed and I so wanted to play in that league. I had been playing with a lady I will call Fran. She was a tall, muscular woman and she had power. I was a player who usually could place the ball and we were double partners. There was an older man Mr. Greer, who began calling me to play tennis. He was so loved by all the lady players and I was always happy to play with him. One day, his partner did not show up, and he said he would play Fran and me by himself. We both giggled at that prospect as we walked out on the court. Mr. Greer stood in the middle of the court and I bet he only let three or four balls bounce on his court other than the serves. He volleyed the ball at us blocking Fran's blows, and he anticipated every placement I was going to make. I don't remember the score but he beat us easily! Lessons learned by me; experience can hold its own against power and strategies. Age is not a deciding factor necessarily in competition.

Fran and I joined the league but later we ran into a problem. The league wanted Fran or me to decide who would move up in a different division. I felt that was unfair and honestly, I don't remember if we quit or if Fran went up or if I did. The person who ran the courts was sitting in his office when I barged through his door.

I relayed my reasoning to him and this is what he said; "Sue, you drive up in a VW wearing your cutoffs, well, that's a problem. If you drove up in a Cadillac, wore tennis outfits, and wasn't so loud than the group would see you as one of them."

Ken had bought me six or seven tennis outfits but when that man told me that, I would have played naked before I ever wore one of those outfits! I threw them away. Asking me to be quieter is like asking a river to run upstream. You probably can tell I take issues with what I think of a situation that is discriminatory or unfair.

Many women have told me that I helped and encouraged them with tennis.

One of the members made a statement during play one day "Sue, I love to hear your laugh. By hearing your laugh, one can't tell if you made the best or the worst shot of your life. You find the same amount of joy in either one."

I played a couple other tournaments locally. The last one I played was with a new gal who had just moved to town. She went to turn in her scores and I heard her say to the man who was called a "pro."

"That Sue is sure a lot of fun," she commented.

I heard the "pro" say three courts over, "Sue is too loud!"

I figured he wanted me to hear him and maybe he wanted the new girl to play with a lower tone too, but either way I decided I would never play again in any tournament he ran. That player never played again either that I know of. I don't mean to imply that I'm a great player but I always was accommodating to his schedules and could be counted on to fill in where needed. Tennis has been rewarding for me many times, but the structure and the aloofness of many players in that game and the tournament pros do not fit me well.

I still play with a group of women and have for nine years, twice a week and my age at the age of seventy-two. Once, the lady in charge brought a clipping about the schools of training of young tennis players in regards to grunting/yelling and I figured that clipping was for my benefit when she presented it to the group. I told her right off I had no intentions of checking my guttural sounds and I sure could leave if it bothered anyone. Things may have been said behind my back but nothing has been said directly to me since. It's who I am and by golly, I'm not changing in my golden years for anyone.

The telephone rang as I was going out the door to play tennis with a friend I had graduated with. My sister-in-law was on the phone and she said Mom had just had a heart attack. Mom was in the hospital. I told my sister-in-law I had to go play tennis and I hung up. It was as though I was in shock and I couldn't handle what I had just heard. My previous experiences when I had dissociated or put off the pain until I could handle it, came back to me in that moment.

While I was playing Ken came to the courts and knelt down beside the line. "Susie, Mary had a heart attack and she is in the hospital," he told me in a low tone.

I broke down as I turned into a young girl crying, trembling and thinking I had lost my mother. It was now time to handle the pain. Ken led me to the car and took me to the hospital. A while back I asked the friend I was playing with if she remembered anything strange about me that day as she has never said anything to me. She said she didn't; so, I have no proof of my memories being true or not but that isn't anything new for me.

Mom had not died but she had a rough time surviving. I remember her telling me about the pain shooting up her arm before and during the attack. Later, she told me about them cutting her open and spreading her chest wide so they could work on her. The fear and the pain she went through was the beginning of her losing a grip on many things she had enjoyed before. Doctors would talk to her and she would nod her head. I told a heart doctor to quit using words that a college graduate would know possibly, but she didn't. They told her she had to quit smoking and she did; but she told me when she got out of the hospital that time she still wanted a cigarette longer than a football field.

What I was afraid to face was that if Mom died I had to face some facts for myself. I had always been an outsider in the family Mom had raised me in. I can't recall anyone saying that directly to me except for Gabe. The kids during their teen years had said at different times that I was their sister but life forms different pictures or images as we age. That is my understanding of our dynamics anyway.

One trip while visiting New Mexico from California I told Mom I only wanted one thing and I told her it was the picture with the gold frame. It was a picture of Lonnie and me which hung on the living room wall all the years while I was growing up. I guess I was around five and Lonnie was probably three or four. A traveling photographer would go house to house and take pictures of families back in the hills of WV. When I asked for the picture I could see Mom was conflicted with giving it to me but finally, she said for me to take it and I did.

I took it back to California with me. Well, it seems that act was something that Mom had to answer for. I'm sure Gabe had words for her and maybe caused a bruise or two. Lonnie's wife is the one who made the biggest stink I would guess. She helped Mom a lot. She filled out papers for Mom. She took meals to her and Gabe when Mom was unable to do things for herself. Not sure if Lonnie wanted his wife to demand the picture to be returned to him or not. It doesn't really matter now after all the years. I did return it and I remember writing a scathing note but truthfully, I don't remember what I said.

While Mom was in the hospital Lonnie, Dora, and I had a discussion. I told them when Mom was gone I never wanted anything to do with their dad. Later, Dora told me on the phone that he had taken care of me all those years. I told her he didn't take care of me any better than he did his coon dogs which he had chained and beaten for years. The way I figured it Mom and I had paid for my keep by being beaten and sexually abused all those years.

I got a lot of attention when I bowled and I sure liked that. Ken said my backswing was over my head when I was younger. I took a five-step approach and I didn't waste any time getting to the foul line. Ken thought of himself as my coach. He took me to buy a new bowling ball once. He wanted me to get a sixteen-pound and a fingertip drilled ball. That is the heaviest ball for a man or a woman. The man selling the ball told Ken that weight was too heavy for me. Ken told the man he should see me move furniture! So, Ken's direction in bowling worked for me for many years. Ken had never been involved in any team sports growing up as he had to work. He knew to build up my confidence and that was well-meaning in the beginning but I had a hard time dealing with it later on. Ken once told me when I got a higher average than him he would quit bowling. I tried to tell him that I was competing against women and he competed against men. The number of women especially back in the sixties and seventies, were a lot less in all sports for women so I had the advantage. He never accepted my explanation.

My way of thinking about competition is different from most women. Admittedly, I love to win but I want to laugh and have a good time. I have teased some men about competition and they handle it well. Women not so much. It may be my genetic gender code but I feel that women put the other person down in a catty, female way and I end up thinking there are underlying mean intentions. Some women say they are not competitive but they show the most unsportswoman-like behavior when they win. I guess what Mr. Elkins said to us, a volleyball team, rings in my head sixty years later; "Anyone can be a good loser, but it takes a special person to be a good winner." He was trying to keep us from bragging, getting the big-head, and rubbing our win into everyone's face.

Ken and I bowled on a mixed league when we started bowling. We bowled with a couple who I knew before. One night I got a call from a lady I barely knew who bowled in the daytime.

"Sue, remember you said you would bowl on our team in the fall?" she demanded.

Well, I didn't remember but she was so convincing I heard her out. Muttering to myself, I agreed to give it a try. I didn't like bowling with four other women. Gossip (about things I wasn't interested in) was the main reason women liked to bowl. Gals were never ready for their turn. Once, a woman threw her first ball and went to the bathroom to change blouses. We had to wait on her to come back and shoot for her spare. Women like to criticize the pH factor in someone's hair conditioner and I just don't relate to that female psyche, I guess.

The captain and sponsor of the team was competitive and she was a barrel of fun. Her name was June. The lady who called me was a petite gal who talked about diamonds all the time. There were two other ladies I'll call Carrie and Olive. Carrie was a petite blond and she and I came from two different planets we will find out. Olive was a redhead and owned a car lot. The four of us were the core team. Most of them had Cadillacs, wore diamonds, and liked to have fun. The only criteria I had to offer was that I liked to have fun and I was a decent bowler.

Our sponsor and captain paid for all our entry fees for tournaments, bought us shirts, and furnished us transportation in her Cadillac. We traveled over the weekends to Texas, Arizona, and in New Mexico. We were a team of drama! There were divorces, lovers, and a couple of the ladies were vying for the same guy's attention. Never a dull moment. One of the gals had an ex-husband and two boyfriends with the same first name.

When we needed a new member, we would come to an agreement among ourselves, usually. One new member I knew but I didn't have much in common with her. Getting in the car for a trip the very first time, I heard her talking about masturbation. Sex was an everyday topic for her. No, it was maybe a topic ten times a day for her. Her background and mine did not rhyme at all. She had been raised a spoiled brat, and me, that sure was not the description for my background.

June recruited a new member for us. The prospect was working at a lunch counter at a drugstore. The lady's name was Melba. She looked and acted like Flo on the "Alice" series. A dead ringer for the "Kiss my grits" gal. She wore a scarf around her neck and the reason for that was she had goiters on her neck and her husband hated looking at them. The nearest I can figure out what she was calling goiters were tag moles. Although, I never saw her neck—none of us did.

Melba had only been to the grocery store in our town. Her husband didn't allow her to drive or go anywhere other than to work. We would talk about places and things and Melba just had no idea what we were talking about. She was at our mercy—she had us laughing and shaking our head at the same time. Our first tournament we heard an announcement and it stated that if we got three strikes in a row we would win a margarita. Melba yells, "Pink enchiladas?" Where that came from none of us knew. Maybe, it was because she didn't know what a margarita was. It was just hilarious.

In the room while we were in Lubbock drinking, we were telling tales that would have embarrassed a sailor. We were really trying to outdo each other. We were mostly doing it to shock Melba. "Melba, I bet you don't even know what oral sex is?" I taunted.

"Oh, no! I never talk about sex," she answered. Pause. Laughter!

With that I wanted to go in the pool. Carrie didn't take her suit so I talked her into buying a disposable one at the office of the motel. Carrie bought the universal size and it would have swallowed her three times! She was holding it up with both hands and by the time we got to the pool the man was locking the gate. Just as well I guess, that suit would have turned into a float and covered the entire pool's surface.

When we went to a restaurant to eat Melba would only order a chicken fry steak. We would suggest other foods but she only wanted a chicken fried steak! But Melba did like to dance. Her husband never took her to dance and when she was with us she rarely sat down. She ratted her hair in a tall bouffant and when she came back to the table it would be smashed flat where she had her head close to the guy she was dancing with.

As time went on Melba's husband didn't have an issue with her going out of town bowling with us. As a matter of fact, he would have her suitcase by the door. We suspected he had a girlfriend and we were right. He asked for a divorce and married a younger woman. Melba left for Texas. She came by where I worked once and I never saw her again. None of us will ever forget her.

Later, another lady joined oùr team and she wore a cross around her neck which practically covered her whole chest. She and another team member bumped heads constantly. They were total contradictions of each other. One was a foul mouthed, vulgar woman and the other one wore the cross and reminded me of a nun.

I was a rough teaser and I still am. I told one gal the only reason she was on the team was that I had a larger bra cup than her. Two of the ladies had enormous cups! One of those ladies saw my bra hanging on the door knob of the bathroom once, and she said it had training wheels! What a visual.

We traveled well together. Every time we began a trip June would put on the Willie Nelson tape of "On the Road Again." June took it on herself for us to have fun, especially me. I loved to dance. Carrie and June were usually content sitting and watching us dance. Carrie suffered with her back a lot. One night she got a short dancing partner and she was folded over him for support. He had quite a view from that angle. We teased her for the longest time about that. We would go out to dancing clubs and bars and June would immediately attract an entourage. She was a natural "people magnet" and hearing her laugh once was the draw. Once, a guy quit his job at a club and stayed with us dancing the whole night. When we weren't looking, June would hold a dollar bill over our head, catch a guy's eye and motion for him to dance with the one standing under the dollar bill. June's imagination was always on overdrive.

One night I was dancing with a fellow and he said could read lips. He told me everything we women had been talking about at our table. That was a bit unnerving. Another guy we met kept asking me if I wanted to ride in his airplane. The next day he was at the bowling alley after we finished bowling and ready to take me for a ride. I didn't go but he seemed to be a real nice guy.

Once June had been somewhere and she said she had been bragging to a guy about my bowling—she brought him to the lanes to watch me. It was that time of the month for me plus we were at a higher elevation and my hands had swollen. I took off towards the foul line and when my backswing went up and I couldn't release the ball. By the time I could let go of that ball I literally pitched it fifteen or twenty feet down the lanes with a "crash." June said it was like watching a bronc rider with the saddle stuck to his crotch.

There was an Elvis impersonator in northern New Mexico and we usually looked for him when we were in a tournament. He was a small version of Elvis but large enough to get women excited at the night clubs. The state tournament was in Farmington, NM one year. The impersonator was in town and a hundred women or so were at a club waiting for "Elvis" to appear along with us. First, he went to Olive's chair, he turned the chair around and never missed a beat as he sung, "Let Me Be Your Teddy Bear" to her. The ladies went wild in there. As he passed me he grabbed my arm and pulled me to the middle of the floor. As doing so, he sang "One Night with You." He fell backwards on the floor and he began pulling me down. I locked my knees and he jerked me hard down on top of him to the floor. The women really went wild over that! The next morning women were saying, "there she is" pointing at me. I had instant celebrity status with those gals. I tried to explain to them that he jerked me down—I didn't fall on him on purpose. One lady said, "Honey, if I were you I would have put a leglock on him, and I would still be on the floor with him!"

Once we won a tournament in Albuquerque. I experienced a feeling that morning which I still don't know what to call it. My mind was so focused that I saw myself in the future bowling in that tournament. Talking to myself I saw that I was converting spares which were difficult for me or anyone to make. Plus, I was getting strikes which improved my score a great deal. It was as though I was willing the ball to do something which my shot didn't deserve, but somehow it worked many times that day. I was just in "the groove" so to speak. We won that tournament. After we finished our games I caught June sticking her sore finger in my hot coffee! Who knows maybe that was the reason for me doing so well that day.

Later, we went to celebrate our victory and a guy came to ask me to dance. When the first song was over "Proud Mary" began to play and my partner and I were the only two on the floor. I didn't care. I broke out in a frenzied dance and my partner just stood and watched with his glasses hanging on the end of his nose. Later, when he walked off shaking his head, June teased me about him going somewhere to have a cardiac arrest. Being impulsive like that and laughing about it later has left me with some of my favorite memories in my life.

Olive was driving us home once during a vicious snowstorm. Someone had the idea for us to take a short cut. We're out in the middle of nowhere slipping and sliding. That Cadillac had no traction at all. The driver's diamond rings are clickety-clacking all over the steering wheel. Carrie and I are hugging the front seat from the back as to will the car to go forward hopefully, in a straight line. A Volkswagen passes us going thirty miles per hour! Olive had it in first gear and that was not the right gear for those conditions apparently.

Carrie and I didn't have much in common other than bowling but we were both loud and drama queens. We were closer in age though and she would sometimes say the strangest things which always made me laugh. I was athletic in most sports and Carrie only bowled. She took her first husband to the tennis courts for he and I to play tennis – she would sit in the car and read. Later, she joined the softball team I was on. She never caught a ball in right field but she was a great cheerleader. The most outstanding feat I remember her doing was getting an infield hit. She got a home run because the other team's players kept overthrowing the bases. Unbelievable.

On one tournament it was my birthday. Ken bought me clothes from Frederick's all the time. Frederick's was a mail order place where you could order any revealing apparel and any sex toy you could imagine. Carrie had a small box for me after the game. In it was a pair of purple crotchless panties. Trying to cover my reaction I began a tirade of reading the directions which said for one to iron them on a low setting! I can't remember exactly what I said but I'm sure it was colorful. One of our ballplayers was young and still a virgin. We literally shocked her as much as possible! It's a wonder she ever got married.

Eventually, Carrie was caring for her mother full time and they went to Santa Fe to visit her brother and sister-in-law for the holidays. I was living alone at that time and Carrie was between men and she invited me to go along. Those trips were always exciting, and I always felt welcomed. One special memory was going shopping in Santa Fe on Black Friday. We all got up at four in the morning and drove through snow and ice which covered everything that morning. In the parking lot we were slipping and sliding all over the place and right in front of us were two Hispanic ladies holding in an upright position a young girl around the age of ten or so. One lady heard us giggling, and she turned towards us and said, "Future shopper in training!" I've thought of that young girl many times as I've slept in on every Black Friday since that day.

Belinda, Carrie's sister-in-law, was a professional quilter. From a picture of a landscape in a book, she and Carrie helped me make a quilt and two window shades. Drinking wine, laughing, sewing, and joking around were three days of fun. Belinda introduced me as her artist friend while she was arranging her quilting in a shop in Santa Fe. I was on cloud nine from that compliment.

Traveling back and forth from Santa Fe I told Carrie the story of my past. She was the first one I had told all the painful details. She would ask questions and that would prompt more memories; I would go on for hours. She said I should write a book—she said she would help me. I recorded what I wanted to say and she typed it up. When I listened to the tapes I was overwhelmed with the pain and the trauma of the memories they brought, so eventually I stopped. I guess it was too soon for me to handle the emotional side effects which I had/have to go through sometimes.

Carrie began improving in bowling and her star seemed bright in a lot of areas. My star wasn't as bright around that time, and my bowling wasn't as effective as it had once been. When we bowled a team, it seemed to me that Carrie only cared about one thing; to beat me, and she didn't care if we beat the other team or not. I began taking her digs personally. I even complained to Ken about my issues. He would call Carrie names but that didn't help my mood either. June would come to the bar while I was working and ask me what I was going to do about Carrie. At first, I didn't know what she meant and she finally said that I was a "chicken" for not standing up to Carrie. Even then, I kept brooding, and I was miserable for several months.

We were at a restaurant in Albuquerque. June, Olive, the bowler with the dangling cross, Carrie and me. The wine was flowing for the three of us and Carrie made the boast that she struck out and beat me the last game. June caught my eye and that was all I needed; it was as though a gong went off and I raised my gloves (figuratively speaking) and I tore into Carrie. I had months of put-downs and criticisms stuck in my throat and I needed to spew them out. I caught a glance of the bowler with the cross necklace and she was grinning like an opossum and June slumped down in the booth because she knew she had pushed me to do what I was doing. Carrie apologized and said the reason she goaded me was because I was her idol and to beat me was her goal. She said she never knew I was suffering and she was really sorry. The next day Carrie sent me a live plant and a card of apology. The plant lived for years and our friendship lasted for years too.

Several years later Carrie had to pay someone to stay with her mother when she bowled and that was the only recreation Carrie did at that time. We had been bowling with a guy Carrie had been going with and he was getting harder and harder for me to deal with. We switched nights and he went on another team to the same night we had switched to. He was so self-centered, and a braggart. Bowling wasn't as much fun for me anymore. I had a saying "If I'm not laughing I'm out of here." I told Carrie I needed to take a break from bowling and she was upset. Another thing that was putting an edge on bowling was that Carrie was thinking about running for a political office and she was gallivanting around the lanes all the time and we had to chase her down to let her know it was her turn to bowl. Aggravating.

Carrie took care of her mother for several years and it was really hard for Carrie when her mother passed away. Carrie finally decided to run for that political office and she had a lot of new friends helping her with that endeavor. I likened myself as an observer watching the person I knew become a stranger. She took out a schedule and wrote my name in slots where she wanted me to help her with her campaign. She and other women I knew were taking diet pills, at first from the internet, and then traveling to another town to get the pills and Carrie was on a road I did not want to travel.

Watching the fireworks with Carrie at the club one night seemed to me to be bizarre. She asked me to go and get her a hot dog which I did. She knelt down under the table and ate it in two bites. She asked for another one. Same procedure, and then she asked me to get her an ice cream bar. There was a strange smell coming from Carrie. One of my friends said that when you are starving yourself your body starts feeding on itself. Not sure if that was the case or not but I had never been aware of that odor before.

The next day she wanted to go to the quilting club luncheon with me so she would get more exposure from those ladies via me. Carrie came in late and she tossed her purse across from me to sit to at our table. A quilter came to sit down and she moved Carrie's purse down a place. Two more quilters did the same thing, and by that time Carrie's purse was five chairs down across the table. It never occurred to me to tell the little old ladies that the spot was saved as I didn't know them.

On hindsight I probably should have, but if I remember right, Carrie and I had words the previous day so I'm sure I thought "let her handle the problem herself." I'm not sure what we were discussing in our little group but we were laughing while Carrie was shooting daggers at me with her eyes. Carrie made a comment towards/about me and one little lady said, that Carrie said I was showing off.

"Don't pay any attention to her, Carrie is just hungry!' I cracked.

Everyone laughed, well not Carrie, she was furious. Carrie didn't like my quilting friends and I didn't necessarily like her political friends. Carrie would fabricate stories and I couldn't keep my mouth shut so there was what you called a "bitchy tension" between us. The straw that broke the camel's back was over a wall-hanging of all things. I had made a rainforest with wild animals in a window theme. I had put a type of flannel for the backing and I was rather proud of it. Carrie grabbed it from me and spread the wall-hanging on her lap and started shaking her head. I knew to brace myself.

"This is all wrong Sue, you need a silk backing instead of this!" saying, while she snarled up her nose.

"Hell no! Silk does not go with wild animals," I yelled. We argued our points.

"Who are you?" I demanded. This person before me was a bitch. The old Carrie had been a bitch too but she had been fun.

Carrie bent her head and started sobbing. "If you knew who I was, you would hate me." she said.

Instinctively, I knew I was in quicksand. I turned the subject back to the wall hanging where it was safe to argue, or so I thought. She finally said she only wanted to help me; my answer was that I did not want her help. She jumped from her slouched position and pointed towards the door. "Get out!" she said through clenched teeth and pointing towards the door. It was as though I was watching her mother. Carrie had told me an instance when her mother had ran her brother out of the house. Actually, we were standing in the kitchen where that event had happened. Every motion Carrie made was like an instant replay of what her mother had done.

"You don't want to do this," I muttered. She repeated those two words—I left.

Carrie and I had been friends for twenty years but too many variables were facing us, or me, anyway. But losing a longtime friend I would liken it to getting a divorce.

Carrie won the election and she called me and asked me to come to the celebration. I told her I had golf lessons and tennis lessons that evening, but she insisted and I went. Carrie was on the phone talking to one of her mother's old friends and Carrie always baby-talked when she talked to that lady. I always had a creepy feeling with Carrie and that lady when they did that. But I never had baby-talked even with my kids. When the final results came in Carrie and I hugged but when I went to say "congratulations," I couldn't get that word out, I never did either. Too many emotions were involved I guess.

One day, walking through the library I saw a book called "Forgiveness." It was as though I was given just what I needed at the time. It was a small book. It spoke of when a person can't forgive someone, they are the one who was harmed and that was me. I called Carrie and told her I was sorry that I had hurt her. She said I scared her and that she was afraid of me. I knew that was true. I also told her I had her house keys. She told me never mind that she didn't need them. She said maybe she would die someday and be locked in—her cats would try to eat her and I could save her. We chatted a bit more and she invited me over and I returned the invitation. I knew at that moment I would never go back to her house and I'm sure she knew the same thing about mine. During that period, I think each of us tried to overcome our grievances at different times, but the other one wasn't ready to get past our issues. The timing was just never right. Plus, as the old saying goes, "Too much water under the bridge."

My old team had dissolved for different reasons. A gal, Lottie, was bowling on a night league. She was loud, boisterous, and she used a lot of body language on the lanes. I was naturally drawn to her and so was everyone in the bowling alley. She and I eventually began talking and we made a pact that we would bowl doubles together in tournaments and we did for years. We won many trophies and money. After several years, Lottie hit her prime and since I was older and focused on my education my average was declining. Once I had a 287 game which was the highest game a woman had bowled in town. Lottie bowled a 300 game and another woman did also right after that. My thought was that if someone bowled a higher game than me, I was glad it was Lottie as I liked her so much.

During a city tournament I did not hear from Lottie. One night I saw her at the bowling lanes and she was with her husband. I asked her why she hadn't called about the tournament and she said she had been suffering with a migraine and must have forgotten. I looked deep in her eyes and I knew she was lying to me. I was devastated and assumed that the reason she didn't want to bowl with me was I was not on my game anymore like I used to be. I brooded about her lying and I confronted her outright one night. I reminded her we had made a deal—she hurt me. I thought/knew she was evading me. I told her I would have never treated her like she had me and she spewed, "You are a racist, Sue!" Boy, was I caught off guard. We got in a heated argument as I would not ever have considered myself being a racist. She kept looking back at her husband for support which hit me as being rather strange. Lottie was black and her husband wasn't, and they were a devoted couple as far as anyone could tell. I said something that I have regretted but it was true. Her husband's cousin, a female, was known for racist remarks quite frequently and I told Lottie so. But truthfully, I had told racist jokes many times myself during the time I was a bartender. The man I was going with seemed to tease black workers and Lottie to the point of making me uncomfortable many times with things he said to them. My bowling friends were regularly making jokes about Hispanics, Native Americans and anyone else who were different from us. So maybe I was a racist. Over the years I have had to do some soul-searching. I was a "hillbilly" and I hated that term. I knew what name-calling does to a person thus, the title, "Smut." When there are jokes or put downs of others one needs to let anyone and everyone know that you do not approve of what's being said. If one doesn't, the way I see it is that your silence makes you complicit. I see it as a partner or accessory in a crime just by being in the company of someone who is committing the crime—you're considered guilty.

Lottie and I never bowled together again. I took all the trophies we had won together and threw them in the dumpster. I no longer had any pride in any of them so away I put them, out of sight. So, a dumpster held my softball mitt and over thirty trophies. Later, when I quit bowling I dropped my ball over a bridge into the Pecos River.

June was an abused wife and she had been for years. Her coping skills were mostly in a bottle of Canadian Club. She had a thriving business and she pushed herself to late hours and more drinking. She had adopted a child and she had one of her own. She went to Texas to get her mother from a mental institution and she cared for her the last years of the mother's life. June told of many abuses which she had suffered from her mother. June was promiscuous but I never judged her—I would defend her to my dying day. She was my friend.

June had met a truck driver and they had an affair. Some of the details are rather foggy in my memory. She was friends with a woman who was on the "wild side" in my opinion. That woman bowled with us a few times and she could down a six pack in less than an hour and she never went to the bathroom! One night she left with four German soldiers from a nightclub and she barely made it back in time to bowl. Not one of those soldiers spoke English.

June and the lady above began hanging out together a lot. June's husband recorded the two women's conversations from the phone. He confronted June and then he beat her up really bad. June went to AZ to a battered women's facility. I saw pictures of her when she entered the facility and she was covered in bruises along with black eyes. One day I got a call from the man who June was having an affair. He began asking me all kinds of questions about June. "Aren't you with June?" I yelled at him. He said he was. "Then get your ass in there and ask her those questions!" I yelled at him again.

June and Ben married. June rarely had much to do with Carrie and me after the marriage. Carrie and I walked with Buck and sometimes with the guy Carrie was going with. We would stop by June's house and ask her to join us for a walk but she never did. Sometimes we would stop at their house after we finished the walk. I noticed June was getting forgetful and she was confused about things. She would pull on Ben's shirttail and he would help her out with the conversation. I could sense how embarrassed June was about her forgetfulness.

Ben came into the place where I worked. Then he went home and told June I wasn't nice to him like I was to the other guys. After June told me that I had no use for him and I would barely speak to him.

Something was not ringing true about that guy. One day I ran into him at Walmart. He told me June wouldn't get out of bed and he was her sole caretaker. He said her back had broken by her just lying in the bed! He asked me to drop by and I did. As I entered the bedroom June's eyes were shut. When she opened them her reaction of seeing me startled me. It was a look of terror! She covered her head and she said she didn't want anyone to see her looking the way she did. She had lost so much weight and the June I knew at one time was hardly recognizable.

A few weeks later June was in the hospital. I went to see her and she was joking and cutting up with the nurses the old way she used to do with people. The next morning Carrie called me crying and she said June had passed away. What a shock! I've wondered many times why she put on such a show for me the day before. If I said I knew I would be lying. Maybe she wanted us to laugh together and carry on like we used to one more time. Well, we certainly did that.

On to Hobbs

I spoke before about working to get my math grade from the fifth-grade level to college level so I could enter a college classroom, but lordy—I still struggled with math. The first class I took was algebra. I had a male instructor and he gave that class passion (if algebra can have passion) but I only made a "C." I retook it and made a "B." Algebra II was taught by an instructor who would correct my work by doing it for me. I'm sure she was thinking she was showing the work I should have done. I was passing, so I played table tennis instead of studying a lot of the time (not sure if it would have made a difference or not.) I made a "B" in that class via the teacher and then I hit that old brick wall again. College algebra took me to my knees! I could not retain the multiple steps of doing the problems. I thought I had an edge though. My friend Martha was going with my math teacher. Mike, the teacher, called me into his office. He tried to talk me out of taking his class. He told me my brain was on an "overload" as I had pushed it so far in math in a short period and I needed to take a break. Good advice but I rarely listen to good advice. I flunked the class. I was devastated—I decided I would shadow the class. I did for a couple months, but it was futile. I used to tell people I couldn't pass college algebra even with my friend was sleeping with my teacher. I said Martha must have been doing something wrong—surely it couldn't be my fault.

I drove one-hundred-sixty miles four days a week for three semesters to finish my degree. The least credit hours I took a semester was nineteen. Dave once told me that many of the kids he went to school with would drink six or eight cups of coffee a day and they smoked up a storm. I took two thermoses of coffee and a couple packs of Salems in that little Datsun truck with me every day. I usually left the house in the morning around six. I would hit the road, and many times I wouldn't get home until ten at night.

Truthfully, I don't remember how I got political science as my minor but I did. The first class I took was World Politics. Oh, my goodness, the teacher kept talking about socialism, communism, monarchies, and fascism. The only politics I knew about was Democrats and Republicans. That's a joke as I didn't know anything about them either. The instructor of the class was a retired math teacher and a part-time preacher. Matter of fact, he taught all four of the political classes I took.

The park down the highway was where I would read and do my assignments. I would also eat my lunch there and take a nap. I eventually gave up wearing contacts as it was too much of a bother with all the other things I had to do. I would read my political science text just before class.

That World Politics class was filled with young football players and a couple of us who were older. Every time I put up my hand I would hear groans. One of the players told me one day not to ask any questions because Mr. Goldman talked too long. Well, that's what I wanted but apparently not those guys. One day, Mr. Goldman made the statement, "It is written in England's constitution that a representative has to get a clearance to do that." I sat up straight and he repeated the previous sentence. I reluctantly raised my hand.

"Mr. Goldman, England does not have a written constitution, according to the text I just read," I said.

I heard groans again. "Sue would you please repeat what you just said," he demanded.

Oh, no! I must have misread it, but I had read it three times.

"I guess you were the only one who read the assignment, Sue," he added.

Boy, was I proud even though I had to listen to those groans again.

I took three classes of Constitution history from him. The education classes I took couldn't hold a candle to his classes. One day he asked me why I hadn't started school sooner and I told him of my fear of math. "I wish I had you in my math class earlier Sue, you would have done well," he said. I brushed back a tear hearing that statement.

A tape recorder was my constant companion for a couple years. I recorded all my lecture classes from Mr. Goldman. Dragging myself to my little truck I would insert a tape in the player and begin the eighty miles home listening to Mr. Goldman lecturing and sometimes preaching. I knew when he was going to take a breath and I hung on every word he said. On the way back driving the eighty miles to school the next day I had a recording of my voice. Any material I thought that was going to be on a test I would record and I would have the company of my voice giving me clues on how to remember the material. Not sure where I got the recorder idea, maybe from the books on tape but it worked for me. My truck always had a stack of books on the passenger side a couple feet high. I would lug all those books to the kitchen table in my apartment at night. One time, I looked up at the wall behind the kitchen stove and I saw grease streaks running down to the floor. I stood, got a rag and walked towards the streaks. A thought came to me; 'Sue, you have to set priorities, the grease streaks can wait, but your homework can't.' I used that priorities thought many times—I just had to.

The Old Testament was a class I took, as all the students were required to take a religion class. We were told that we had to do a paper on a subject and turn it in typewritten three different times. There was a problem with that; I didn't know how to type! I took typing for either six or nine weeks in ninth grade and I didn't relate to that class at all. Being a secretary would have been on the lowest rung of the ladder for a job choice for me. So, I decided not to worry about typing. I guess that was one reason I was a carhop and waitress.

The Dead Sea Scrolls was my topic and it cost me sixty dollars to have it typed, which I didn't have. I let the instructor know that fact, and he seemed to be rather befuddled by my complaint. Guess he wasn't aware of us non-secretarial types. I was complaining to a guy I was walking with one day about my dilemma. He told me to get a computer and that would solve all my problems. I took a computer class and the instructor was from India. Bet I could count on one hand all the words I understood him to say that whole semester.

One other class I took was an educational class. I don't remember the topic of the assignment but I had written about Jackie the foster girl we had in California. I got a "D" for that paper and I was upset! I had that instructor in a previous class; a multicultural class and we got along fine. Of course, what I remembered about that class was going to a Chinese restaurant and she gave us a recipe for Green Chile Stew which I use all the time. When I saw that "D" I charged right up to her desk and asked her why. She said I had run-on sentences and no punctuation. She told me that the college where I got my basics did not teach writing and this college was all about writing, so I would be at a loss. I guess the gal who typed my Old Testament paper edited my work as I made a "B" in that class. Not understanding and having a time restraint I just went through the paper about Jackie and peppered it with commas as though I was pitching icicles on a Christmas tree. I'm sure I made at least a "B" in that class. (She probably didn't want to deal with me again).

One night a blizzard blew into southeastern New Mexico and it was a doozy! I usually left the campus around eight at night after my last class. We were told not to drive on the highway as it was treacherous and covered with black ice in many places. I had to go to work the next morning and I needed to travel regardless of the conditions. Another guy who was in the class usually left when I did. I asked if he was going to drive that night and he said he was. I asked if he would mind if I followed his van. He just looked at me without an answer. I rushed to the truck and followed him as close as I could until we got close to the Marathon gas plant, and he ran off and left me. Black ice had covered the highway on that stretch just before, in front, and past that gas plant. I had so little control of my truck but I just kept puttering along as the wind seemed to be blowing me backwards much of the time. Suddenly, a big truck was in front of me. I guess he pulled out from the gas plant. I pulled in behind him and I drove as close to him as I dared, driving in his tracks. He blocked the wind and I kept up with him until we got to the potash mines where another semi had jackknifed turning on to the highway.

I saw every kind of weather that night and I still get an eerie feeling just thinking about it. I was in a thundersnow blizzard the way I recall; I have researched it also. When the lightning struck and the thunder clapped I looked out across that desert and I could have sworn I was on another planet, hell, maybe in another universe and it was a scary place to be.

When I got closer to the accident where the big truck had jackknifed there were several vehicles lined up including that van which had gone and left me. Two men ran towards me and asked if they could manually push me over a hill which lay before us. They said I had the lightest vehicle, and I could go to town and get help. Just between you and me as I passed that van I used my middle finger to bid that deserter farewell! I would have never gone off and left someone on that highway alone. Every time I see his truck around town with an anti-abortion sign as large as a billboard I bid him farewell again and again.

Exhaustion was taking me over as I went over that hill and I told myself I only needed to hang on for a bit longer. Suddenly, there was a scene before my eyes which my mind couldn't interpret. It was as though I was watching a sword fight and the swords were screeching the weirdest sounds; somehow, perhaps from pure exhaustion, my windshield wipers had gotten out of sync and they were tangled, thus, the sword fight about five inches from the windshield. I began laughing with relief when my mind handled that situation. A sheriff's car was across the median and going towards the wreck and stranded cars. I took my first deep breath in hours. I just needed sleep so I could go to work at 6:00 am.

New Mexico history was my most memorable class for all the wrong reasons. The professor who taught the class couldn't teach the class that semester but I forgot why. So, a librarian from the city library was the instructor. For our first class we met at a donut shop for our first discussion and he posed the question: Shouldn't Hollywood be more responsible in sticking to "facts" when they did movies about historical people and events? I disagreed, and I could tell that wasn't what he wanted to hear right off the bat. He kept bringing that subject up about Hollywood's responsibility. It was as though he had a personal vendetta against Hollywood on the matter. He showed the movie "Young Guns" and he wanted us to see how he was correct, I guess. My thought was/is if people wanted "facts" they could watch documentaries. The female characters wearing styles of long ago would not be as pleasing to our eyes of today. Looking at the picture of the real Billy the Kid is not as near as attractive as Emilio Estevez. Hollywood sells to an audience of what the current values are of people who are living today in my opinion.

I don't remember anything I learned about New Mexico from that class. The day came to do the writing assignment and I held the same views so I was comfortable about everything...UNTIL...I got my paper back! I had a "B" and there was not one correction on the paper. I had a friend read it and she assured me it was well written. The librarian wasn't in class to give us our papers back and he had a substitute that day. I drove to the library and he wasn't there either. I drove from Hobbs and my temperature was still rising. The librarian wanted me to change my mind and I felt it was unfair for him to grade us/me on that premise. I wanted to tell him so but lucky for him I couldn't track him down.

When I got into town, I pulled into the parking lot of Albertson's beside a hippie looking van. I got out and a hippie looking guy came around behind me and yelled, "Hey!"

I turned, and he pointed to the door of his van. He told me I had just hit his door with my door.

"I did not! It won't reach that far. Watch!" I exclaimed. I opened my door as far as it would go.

"Oops!" Well, it did open that far.

He had a pencil and paper and he was writing things down. I got a pencil and paper and I circled his van and it was covered with dings and dents. I told him I couldn't understand how he could be upset about another ding.

"I've had a very bad day. I made a "B" on a paper and I deserved an "A." "You call the cops if you want but I have to pick something up for supper. Come and get me or have the policeman to do it, but I'm sick of this circus!" I said. I stalked off. When I left the store he and the van were gone. I think he thought I would hand him some money. He didn't know I barely had enough for a loaf of bread and a tomato.

One of the classes that was required at that private school was Free Enterprise. Money, finances, government restrictions or in other words capitalism which were null and void in my world. I did not relate to finances at all other than being broke. I had a difficult time in that class. Being at the right place at the right time was a lucky break for me one morning. Our teacher walked past me just before the big final test. He was a loud and boisterous fellow and he was talking to a couple guys from the class. I overheard him tell the guys about the test. He said it was a true and false and one-hundred questions on the test. He added it was highly unorthodox. Uh, oh, I thought. While taking the test I thought I would use the strategy of answering the ones I knew for sure first. After I did that I saw that all my answers were true. Why not? I put true on all of them. Eureka! I made a hundred, the only one in the class.

I was told by the office I needed to take another history class, a summer class. I drove six hundred and forty miles times twelve times that summer. I took The French Revolution class. That was a trip I took in over one hundred degrees, without an AC in the truck. It had gone out a week before the class started. I would roll down all the windows, and that hot air would beat me to a frazzle by the time I got home. Then I had to do my homework. Surprisingly, I enjoyed that class.

My education training classes were for the most part useless. One teacher asked us why we wanted to be teachers. She said she would not accept the answer that we liked kids. I thought that was a strange thing to say. My philosophy class gave me theories which were interesting, but totally a waste of time. In one class I was supposed to do a bulletin board using a theme whatever that was. (I didn't know at the time) but I ended up doing Johnny Appleseed as my theme. I had no idea what or how I was supposed to do that. I didn't know anything about scale and my artwork was, well, embarrassing. Johnny was about four inches tall and he was taller than some of the trees I had made. When I walked down the hall where my bulletin board was displayed I would walk as close to the wall on the opposite side of the hallway as I could. I wouldn't even peek at poor Johnny.

Mom's health was failing. She read the Enquirer and the Bible and I think sometimes she got them mixed up. That Enquirer was just like a gospel for her. One day while visiting her she was pointing to an article about education. "Sue, it says here that when you have a college degree you can do anything you want," she explained. All kinds of thoughts ran through my mind of things I couldn't do.

"Not anything, Mom. Some things I can't do," I answered. She gave me her famous dirty look and I knew to back off. "We probably think we can do anything," I added. That seemed to pacify her somewhat. I wasn't going to argue with her education even it was from the Enquirer.

When I had first told Mom about me going to school to be a teacher she was excited. If I needed clothes I would tell her and she would go to garage sales and bring me what I needed. Brian needed a bicycle and there was one standing on the sidewalk a couple days later. She bought me the cutest car coat once. I wore it to work at the club one night and a judge's wife yelled at me as I came in the door. "Sue, come here! Let me see that coat. Turn around. I need to get me one like that one. Where did you get it?"

I didn't want to tell her Mom had gotten it at a second-hand store. But she kept pushing me and I finally told her the truth. She seemed to have been embarrassed then. It seemed to me that she stuck her nose in the air and dismissed me by turning her back towards me.

Buck and I walked with a lady who was from a well-to-do family. She had married once but she didn't have any kids. She did move from an expensive house and area to the street where I lived. She and her brothers watched every dime they spent. She was a dog lover. She had a poodle and when he got tired he just laid down. She would bend over, pick him up and carry him. People would stare and I could tell that bothered her but that didn't keep her from doing it.

Maggy, the lady, I was just talking about and I were discussing Ruidoso one day. Ruidoso is a town located in the cool mountains right next to the Mescalero reservation. The Native Americans have gambling casinos and Ruidoso is prime property. Maggy made the comment that she didn't think it was fair that the "Indians" owned the valuable land in Ruidoso.

"Maggy, that was their land and our government took it away from them," I said. She replied, "If they don't like that they can just get on a boat and leave!" I didn't bother to give her a history lesson.

Maggy belonged to a charismatic church. She was always witnessing to me. One day I was walking by her house and she came out to see the new dog I had. She asked how I was and I told her I had a spot on my retina. Before I knew what was happening she stepped forward, eyes closed and she was going to "lay hands on me!" I jumped back and screamed "No"! That repulsion or whatever it was I was not going to allow. That was a gut instinct or feeling. That was all I needed to know about "the laying on the hands."

My medical needs were handled by the county clinic during that period. One afternoon I awoke from a nap and I was drenched in a cold sweat plus, I felt nauseated. My first thought and fear were that I was pregnant! First, I went to Mom and told her my fears; I was pregnant and I couldn't finish school. She thought for a minute and then she said I could get an abortion. Dave had told me about a debate he had in school about abortions and it started me to think about the controversy involved. So, I decided for myself—I could never have an abortion, but I would never assume that I would have the audacity to decide another woman's fate by deciding what she should do. I really have a problem with hairy-legged men running around with signs on their trucks and condemning women who have decided to do such a serious procedure. I remember the anguish I went through and I'm thankful that I had to make a stand for myself.

When I went to the clinic and shared my problem, one nurse said she wanted to speak to me. Privately, she said that of all the patients who came to the clinic I was the one who stood out to all the workers. She said I was working so hard in so many realms and a pregnancy would have put a stop to all my efforts. I tended to agree with her. Later on, the clinic sent me a check as a scholarship and I will never forget their support and kindness.

Once when Dave was a senior, he asked me about what one had to do to see a psychologist. Caught off guard and being totally ignorant about any process of that kind my first words were, "they cost a lot of money." Later on, I will see a business card of a psychologist high on a shelf while dusting. Dave had the imitative and intelligence to handle his own needs and I always admired him for that. Dave was withdrawn and moody during that time. He was a top student and he let several grades slip but he still ended up being the salutatorian of his class.

Dave was in seventh grade when he first told me about wanting to be a foreign exchange student. I thought that was a lofty idea but he kept bringing the subject up. He had the opportunity to go to New York for a Latin Club competition. He even traveled to Canada and he was excited about the Latin Club, his teacher, and this new venture in his life. I thought all was well and good with him.

There was a man, Chuck, who came into the place where I worked every day. Dave did some yard work for him. Chuck and his wife were sponsors in the American Field Service. Not sure how the subject came up but Chuck started talking to me about Dave being an exchange student. I had told Dave I wanted him to graduate at his home high school first, before he took on academics in a foreign country. Chuck brought me some papers to fill out and I thought that would be the end of that conversation. When I listed my assets the only possession I had was my VW (Old Blue) valued at $600 at the most. I remember the cost for a person to be AFS student was $5,000.00 and there was no way "Old Blue" was going to cover that fee!

A few days later I was in Long John Silver's standing in line to order. One of my coffee customers came up to me and handed me twenty-dollar bill. Chuck had put an article in the paper and he asked the community to help Dave raise money to go to Yugoslavia! I was dumbfounded. The AFS gave Dave a two-thousand-dollar scholarship but he needed more. The money was raised and I still didn't know where Yugoslavia was!

Dave was given a gentleman's name who could teach Dave a language in Yugoslavia, Serbo-Croatian. The man had come to the U.S. during the time of Hitler's brutal treatment of the Jews. Mr. C.'s property had been taken and he and his family fled to our country. Dave would come home from the lessons and be very miserable as Serbo-Croatian was a most difficult language for him to learn.

Dave's grandmother called me and got on my case one day. There was an article about Dave going to Yugoslavia and the paper only listed me as his mother and my address. Ken's mother said the article sounded like Dave was a bastard as his father's name was not listed. I didn't have anything to do with the article but I was sure Chuck had entered the article. Dave was beginning to doubt his decision about being a foreign exchange student. His mother and dad were getting a divorce and he was hearing so many stories and advice from too many people. That was a rough time for all of us.

The day that he was to leave was finally upon us and I drove Dave to Albuquerque to catch the flight to Yugoslavia. Sending my first child away to a foreign country was difficult to say the least. I was emotionally drained. When it was time for him to go down the (tunnel) towards the airplane I literally pushed him in that direction until he was out of sight.

After a couple weeks Dave called me from his Yugoslavia. He told me he was the only "poor" kid in his group. AFS gave him a monthly allowance for his own spending money, thank goodness. He had taken some Levis to sell in that country for extra money. He was told they were high in demand and would sell easily.

Dave took his classes which were spoken in Serbo-Croatian so it was a good that he had graduated locally. A girl was the valedictorian. Only by a fraction was she the top student. Dave was the top male student and the class salutatorian. Apparently, Dave had been given incorrect advice about which classes he needed. He had to give up being the editor of the newspaper his senior year. He had worked so hard for so many years to get where he was academically. I am still pissed at the results that he was credited with in the end. There I said it and I'm glad. For whatever reason other than I thought University of

New Mexico was the best college in the state—I wanted Dave to go there. A couple of his scholarships would be still available a year later so Dave agreed he would go to school there.

While Dave was in Yugoslavia with the host family, their son was in California as a foreign exchange student. Dave used his bedroom. He witnessed the family cutting up a sheep on the kitchen table one day—his appetite for meat would leave him. He became a vegetarian.

. The father took Dave to some beautiful scenic places while he was in Yugoslavia. A little over a year it was time for Dave to return home. He told a story of the day he was to board the plane. Just before boarding the plane two policemen began harassing Dave. Dave was panic-stricken as he thought he would miss his flight home. At the last-minute Dave was no longer any interest for the policemen. A very stressful experience for him. Dave said that rivalry ethnic groups would walk down the street and yell slurs at each other. Dave said there was going to be a civil war in that country and sure enough, there was a short time later.

During the time I was going to school I read a book, "My Own Country." It spoke of a southern town who had a young citizen who had HIV/Aids. That was a subject I didn't know anything about. Without any other education about the subject I based everything about the oncoming shock due to that book and the religious training I had from the Baptist doctrine. Doug had registered at UNM finally, so I thought everything was going to be smooth sailing. Not the case!

One day a call came from a male for Dave. When I answered the voice sounded as if the boy was gay, for some reason. When Dave got home we were sitting in my little Datsun truck and I just blurted out, "Dave, are you gay?" I knew the answer when he dropped his head and slumped his shoulders.

"Why didn't you tell me?" I demanded.

"Because I didn't want to see that look you're using looking at me right now," he said through gritted teeth.

Well, all I had to do was tell him he wasn't gay and things would be okay or so I thought. That period of a week or two I will always consider being the most shameful period of my life. I have spoken of that time always in the same way; I likened myself to an asp attacking my own son! I cursed him, criticized and shamed him until I was beyond being anything but a "mommy dearest" mother. He was going through the most painful trauma of his life. Instead of comforting and trying to understand him I was attacking him with all my might. I just knew I could change him for my sake, I guess. I had dealings with other parents having gay children; I had no problem with them having gay children. But when it came to my child being gay, well that was a different story. I've read that parents know that their kids were gay when they were young. I guess I am such a gifted liar to myself that I still won't accept the fact that I knew when Dave was young. Perhaps he was such an astute actor that he just kept it so well hidden for all those years. Either way, it's no longer important,

My training, if one must call it that, in the Baptist church influenced me in many of my stances in life. Gays, blacks, and the Catholic church were considered to be the "devil's way" of life. I cannot recall a particular sermon of what I just stated but we knew and understood it to be true. Joey Boy, was an example of our prejudice who I wrote about before. During church service a group of five boys took him behind the church and pulled his pants down to prove that he was "different." They laughed, ridiculed, and ostracized Joey Boy for years, his whole life. The Catholic church was the "mother whore" of the world because a woman, the Virgin Mary, was elevated to such a high stature in that church. There were no Blacks where I was raised but we heard of them. I remember them referred to as the "n" word and chocolate drops. Rhymes such as "Eenie meenie, mighty mo, catch a "n" by the toe," was a regular standard verse on the playground and at home. The Brazil nut we ate at Christmas was a "n" toe. My brain just swirls thinking about how religion has hurt so many people I have known and I know.

Dave was gay and he was going to die! I couldn't let that happen and I thought I could change him; I gave my brutal most earnest effort and will always regret the pain I caused for Dave and myself. I was told of books to read in cases where parents had learned and handled this subject in their own way; Stick a Geranium in Your Hat and Find Gregory St. Amand are two. Bettyville was the latest book I read giving me insights of a young man who went through his whole life without being able to confide to his mother that he was gay. What would I have done without books helping me to understand this world of mine; all the beauty and the pain I've dealt with, I turn to a book for the wisdom of others. That type of advice was more trustworthy than from the church-goers around me.

So being of the mind of a fundamentalist church I started throwing stones then boulders at my own son. God created gay birds and mammals of many types according to my readings. I have been known to say that all those animals must've not read the Bible, the Old Testament, or they would've known they were going to hell. Thinking I was saving my son from "hell" was not a good call. The truth was, that Dave was considering hurting himself at that time. If that would have happened, I'm sure that I could not have lived with myself. The author of Find Gregory St. Amand, a nurse, did not see the pain her son was dealing with before he took his own life. Thinking I was saving Dave's soul (who was I to make that call) I was literally pushing Dave towards an action similar to the nurse's son. Thank God, Dave had the strength to turn his back on me for a couple years.

We all have our stories, don't we? An IEP (Individual Education Plan) is what educators follow to give the best outcome for a student's success. I see this world as a large classroom with each of us having our own IEP. Not going to argue the doctrine of any church, but I no longer can accept a religion putting down or rejecting the LGBT community. I was once asked to (well, many times, actually) to come to a Baptist church in town. I told the Sunday School teacher that place wasn't liberal enough for me. She knew I drank wine, I guess she thought that was where I was coming from. Anyway, she said, "Oh, some at the church members drink wine sometimes." I asked her,

"How about gays, does your church welcome gays to your church?" I knew the answer when she dropped her head.

"Well, no, not really," was her answer.

"See, I told you, you weren't liberal enough for me," I said.

While living in this town, Dave was the only one of us who attended church. It's hard for me to understand how he lived such torturous teenage years and being told at church he was unwanted, undeserving, and detested for being born gay. A couple of my friends said that their mothers were gay. I guess it's accepted if people just "don't ask and don't tell." Personally, I know gays who attended the church I was talking about above. Gays in my opinion, seem to be more religious and caring than us self-righteous "straights."

Dave and I have had a tumultuous journey at times but we have come to a place in our road that we are finding a common place. I have had to educate myself and dig deep in my hidden places to live with my truth and dark places. I have to accept that I wounded my own flesh and blood for no other reason than my own twisted judgement of humans who aren't like I think they should be.

Another issue I have is how some just know they are the chosen few who are going to the "promised land." Maybe, I just have a "critical eye." I was once called a "pagan" for not believing as a man did at a party I attended. The virgin birth was what I had an issue with. I see so many flaws of character in the ones who profess the hardest and loudest of their salvation while condemning others.

Another time I was at a party and I've often told the story of a woman I know. I said "that she ran my fat little legs off" getting her more wine during a party. If someone she knew entered the dining room she would push the empty glasses towards me! She told me she wished I went to her church as I was so much fun. She wanted me to go to heaven with her and her friends. The audacity and self-righteousness of some go against my core of being. She drank and gambled and I'm not sure how she justified that to her fundamentalist beliefs. Sorry, I'm throwing boulders myself. Maybe, I shouldn't go to parties with church-goers.

The guy I was going with was Jack, a plumber. He was a regular customer of the place where I worked for years. If anyone needed him they would call that place as he held a schedule practically to the minute. He was a joker and good for laughs all the time. I marveled at how he could innately spot a person's most vulnerable spot of insecurity and bring it to the forefront. He was a master of put-downs. The middle table where I worked was his stage. He usually sat in the same chair and he had his own cup and saucer. Whoever the waitress, was clued in to knowing who all the cups belonged to especially Jack's.

Jack didn't have much of an education but he was a smart business person and very mechanical. He was an alcoholic, and he would tell stories of the many times he tried to get sober and he had a captive audience every time he told his story. I admired the way he would talk about some memories of his painful past but he always laughed—we laughed along with him. Jack was getting a divorce his third, and I was told I was co-respondent. I didn't even know what that term meant. Besides, up to that time I had never had been on a date with Jack.

One day, I was telling a story to Jack about this guy who gave me a ride on a motorcycle to school. Jack said he would give me a ride sometime on his motorcycle, a Goldwing. Jack finally caught me home one Sunday afternoon and we drove to Queen for lunch. He had made me wear a helmet and I got "helmet hair." My hair laid flat to the left side of my head. I bet I spent fifteen minutes pulling, yanking, plus backcombing to make it look normal, but it never did.

While eating we heard another motorcycle drive up and it was Jack's friend, Danny. Jack was from Mississippi and Danny was from Kentucky, and they had been friends for years. I told them about the class I had taken over the weekend and how we had made S'mores. Jack and Danny decided we should do that and we did. We got the stuff needed for S'mores. I bet each S'more cost seven dollars or so as they bought the ingredients at a little mom-and-pop store in the mountains. We stopped, built a fire, and roasted the marshmallows. We all laughed so much that night. Jack and I took a couple trips on his bike and Danny always followed us. It was always an adventure with those two guys.

Jack said we were to make an agreement and we did. Terms: I was always to do my homework before going out with him. We weren't going to get serious as he was too old for me and I needed my education. Looking back at our relationship perhaps I was looking for a "daddy." Not a sugar daddy, as some thought, but he was a stable person in my life and he was the one I called when I needed help. A very dear friend. As a matter of a fact he gave me a ride the first day of school on his motorcycle! My truck was in the shop and his daughter had his car and that was the reason for being on his bike. Later, a couple teachers told me they were a bit worried about my first day "grand entrance" to begin as a third-grade teacher.

Jack's world view was a source of enjoyment for my ears. He would tell of his memories of his previous years and that southern drawl just enhanced his stories. He was an only child and worked many years at his aunt's store. He "ran moonshine" during the prohibition. After he married a girl he moved to Carlsbad and eventually worked as a partner with his wife's brother in a plumbing business. His wife got breast cancer and Jack was the sole caretaker of her. Rarely, could he get anyone to help him with the care of his wife even for a short time. At night he had to rub nitrogen mustard, later called Mustine on his wife's breasts. Jack's face would contort as he spoke of the memories he had of that experience. This was the first licensed chemotherapy agent used (this is my own research). His wife died and he was left with two young girls to raise. His mother-in-law moved in with him to care for the girls but Jack felt she was too controlling. That led to his drinking and looking for another wife, which he found two in a very short time.

He built a bar downtown and alcohol was always handy so he became a full-fledged alcoholic. After three times committing himself, he turned his back on that hard stuff and became a sponsor for others. I only saw him drink one glass of spiked eggnog for all the years I knew him.

Jack decided he needed a hobby to keep his mind busy. He also craved sweets for a while—he sucked on hard candy continuously as his new vice. As for his hobby, he chose to get a motorcycle. He took many a trip with the older boys who called themselves the "Retreads." Many of us envied them while watching them turning onto the street leading out of town. But we always got to hear about their adventures when they returned.

Jack and I went on a couple trips out of town by car. We went to Colorado for my graduation—a gift from Jack. The many shades of green in that state I can recall to mind so easily. It was a beautiful trip visually but that was a period in my life when I didn't know if I would be hired as a teacher. I felt like a dark shadow was hanging over me with all that greenery.

The other trip we took was back to Mississippi where Jack had grown up. We went to a small café and ate catfish. The centerpiece on all the tables were metal gallon cans. Those cans were for putting the bones from the catfish into. Best catfish I ever ate.

We went down the Mississippi River and then we went through the locks. Seeing the moss hanging from the trees in Louisiana was eerie, mysterious, but so beautiful at the same time. We traveled to the Gulf from Alabama after seeing Jefferson Davis's home. I saw my first magnolia tree and was tricked into touching a bloom. That made it turn black for some reason. I got laughed at for that. I saw so much beauty in our country on that trip.

I spoke of Misty before and I need to regress here and include a part of my marriage with Ken to do so. I went to the Elks club to apply for a part-time job. Ken was having a problem at that time getting work. Misty, from my old Ramada days was behind the bar. She was dressed to a tee and looked rather glamorous. As if on cue Misty would go into a skit-like performance behind the bar. She was popular with all the "old farts" who sat at the bar night after night. Just watching her walk from the cold walk-in to get fruit to the cash register, she had an audience of at least eight pairs of eyes. She put in a good word for me and I was hired on the spot. I was to report to the bar in the ballroom on New Year's Eve.

My head was in that beer cooler for eight hours straight; my hands became numb from the cold beer cans. There was a redeeming factor though as I made over one hundred dollars in tips that night.

One evening I burst in the door for work, right after my team had won a ball game. I was excited over a play I had made during the game. Thinking if I had had a dad growing up I could have been so much better at sports, mechanical skills and maybe even math.

"Misty, what if I had a dad to teach me things growing up? Just think what I could have done," I said.

Without taking a breath Misty replied. "You wouldn't have been worth a shit, Sue!"

I bet she was right too. Women like me without a dad have fantasies—about how much better our lives would have been if we had been blessed with a father. But if I had been raised by my biological father and he was abusive, I wouldn't have the argument—at least he's not my real dad which I can use as a way of distancing myself from the pain I had. Perhaps my drive to excel in sports was because I didn't have a father. I just have to be thankful of what I had from outsiders like Mr. Elkins, and go on live my life.

Many times, when I went to work at the club I would tell Misty I needed to make about twenty dollars in tips, then I needed to go home and do my homework. She would laugh and say "sure." I don't remember a time she ever said no. Her support and friendship I was truly grateful for. On Tuesday nights when I worked, Misty and I would do a comedic skit for the "old farts." We would just ad-lib a long-winded skit, and we had a ball entertaining anyone who would listen to us.

Eventually the club got smoke-eaters installed over the bar. One night, Misty told me to flip the smoke eaters off. She meant for me to use the switch on the wall but I used my "middle finger" in the air. We laughed about that at least a million times.

A customer came in one night, sat at the bar, and ordered a Coors. We were really busy and customers were all over the place. When Misty set the Coors in front of him he pulled out a card.

"Young lady you are in deep trouble, as you just served a nonmember," he admonished.

There's a rule, since the club was private, that no one was allowed to be served without a member being with them. The man was from ABC (Alcohol Beverage Control) in Santa Fe. He apparently walked in with a group of members using their cards and he stepped right in the door with them.

Misty's response to his words made me dumbfounded. She threw a money bag across the bar towards him—thankfully, it didn't hit him.

"You dumb son-of-a -bitch do you think I'm crazy? I have a paper which says I'm not crazy! Do you have a paper that says you're not crazy?" she yelled.

The manager came to the bar and quieted things down but he had to go to a hearing in Santa Fe; the club had to pay a fine because of the ABC shakedown.

Misty had three kids. She brought them all to New Mexico in 1976 by a Greyhound bus. She fought with the kids' dad over custody of them for years. Their marriage had always been stormy. The couple would patch things up but separation for them was just only a door, or a couple feet away sometimes. Misty committed herself to an institution. That was the conditions in her divorce for getting her kids back. The paper she was talking about of not being crazy was her release papers from a mental institution. She was artistic and talented in many ways, but her life was challenging for her at times—taking care of her kids, her ailing father, and working full time.

Misty had a couple beaus while she worked at the club. I mentioned before that one of them was my math teacher when I began school. I lost contact with her for a while and one day she called me. We decided to take a walk. Watching her with a cigarette in one hand and a soft drink in the other one was rather comical. She had met this wonderful man, Ed, and she had moved in with him. He had a job as an engineer.

"Sue, people say you think you're too good to go around them anymore since you became a teacher," she said.

Well, I guessed who the "people" were and I told Misty that those two women said that about everyone. Honestly, I think several of my old friends didn't think I would graduate and when I did, they were disappointed that I did. They had to put me down any way they could or anyone else for that matter who had bettered themselves.

Before Misti met Ed, she and I decided to go dancing one night as we were both off work. A couple guys needed a ride. I was driving Old Blue and I told them to get in.

We dropped the guys off, and we went dancing at another club. For some reason, I was on the subject of the sexual abuse I had suffered over the years. Misty listened and then she shared her story. She had been sexually abused by her mother. She said her mom had suffered from a mental illness all her life. Misty said the mom had seduced her brother and her. Women sex abusers are more common in our society now or at least we are hearing about more cases; but Misty was the first person who I knew personally who had suffered by a female and talked about it.

Penelope, Misty's youngest daughter began acting out at school and she got into a lot of fights. Misty was going with a policeman around that time and he would pick Penelope up and bring her home to Misty. Eventually, Penelope told Misty about John, the guy Misty was living with when we worked at the Ramada. He had molested Penelope during her third and fourth grade years. When Penelope had told Martha about the abuse Penelope described the abuse and it was very similar to the sexual abuse Misty had experienced from John. Misty went to their Baptist preacher where she attended church. Penelope ended up protecting John, her abuser. She denied that John had abused her. Penelope will suffer from drug abuse. Her relationship with her mother began to be shaky also.

Penelope had a baby boy who Misty took and raised with her husband Ed, the man who has helped her so much in her life. The boy has graduated by now. Misty still takes medication and goes to therapy which has become a way of life for both her and her grandson.

I lost touch with Misty the second time. More than twenty years passed and out of the blue one day I got a friend request on Facebook. I did not respond at first as I did not recognize the last name. That was because I did not know Ed's last name. Misty messaged me and told me who she was. We have been connected on Facebook for years now. We talk on the phone, share stories and laugh a lot. She reads a lot. She loves her animals and cooks for the homeless. Misty has had a horrendous life the way I see it. But she has the most positive attitude of anyone I know. I have been blessed ever so much for having her for my friend. When she knew I was writing this book she bought me books on the subject of writing and I know we always and forever will be close.

My finals were upon on me and I couldn't believe my goal was within my grasp. I was going to have my diploma. Thoughts were swirling. When I turned onto the Hobbs highway after my last test a dam broke inside me. My body and mind were paralyzed just thinking of what I had been through! Well, done. March on!

Jack drove me to Hobbs for my graduation. My ex-mother-in-law rode with us. Lonnie took Mom over. Dave and Brian were there also. My biggest concern was that Mom would see me cross the stage to get my diploma. I was assured she did. I was a bit taken aback about how much that meant to me for her to see me. I guess we never get over needing approval from our mothers.

If I had any serious depression issues in my life it was right after I graduated. Someone told me, which made sense to me, that I had been going so fast and furious for so long and when things slowed down, my psyche didn't know how to handle it. Right after that time, I went to apply for a teaching position and the HR person almost took me down! I had spent twelve years in school to get my degree and he told me I didn't have anything to offer the school system. Our town required a master's degree within five years of being hired, and I did not have one. He also told me that I didn't have any experience. His question was, "What did I have to offer?"

My knees felt like they had crumbled and a hard knot was in my gut, but I didn't cry. With my head down, I walked out of his office. In a day or two, a local banker, Don Kidd came in for breakfast.

"Sue, did you get a job?" he asked

"No, he told me I didn't have anything to offer since I didn't have my master's degree or any experience," I stuttered.

"What? Give me your resume!" he said

He saw the confused look on my face. (I didn't know what a resume was!)

"Never mind, I'll write you one!" he continued.

Don Kidd was at a meeting in Santa Fe with a friend of mine. She told me that he said I was his hero. He became one of New Mexico's state senators. Several times I have ran that scene through my head. A state senator said that "Me" a snotty nosed, stringy haired, gal called Smut from WV, was his hero. That was the finest compliment I ever remember having from anyone! His reasoning he later explained was that I went through the system and got an education, which he had not. He was grandfathered in, where his position rose to be the president of that bank.

I always wondered about that resume he wrote and on a whim one day I went to the bookkeeper for the schools. I asked her if she would look in my file and see if Don Kidd had written me a resume. I told her she didn't have to tell what it said. I just wanted to know if he kept his word. She said that he kept his word and there was a resume in my file. A politician kept his word! That is a miracle like the parting of the waters nowadays.

June was friends with Don Kidd's wife, Sarah. One night, June and I were at the club where I worked but I was off that night. We ran into Sarah. When I talk I usually wave and gesture with my hands. I was smoking then and while talking to Sarah my hands were flailing. My cigarette somehow touched Sarah's mink coat. I smelled the singe before I realized what I had done. Oh, no! How could I pay for a mink coat? Mom bought my coat at a thrift store.

"I'm so sorry, Sarah," I said.

"Don't be...this is just an old thing I hardly wear," as she consoled me.

Every time I think of that night I think of the many mean things she could have said. Instead, she tried to make me feel like what I had done was no big deal—while

I was counting the dollars I owed her in my head. Lovely woman...

Field Experience was another training class I had to take. I was just scared I was in over my head. I was beginning to get cold feet and things seemed to be moving too quickly for me at times. What if I had wasted all those years and I couldn't do this job? I entered a second-grade classroom at Monterrey my assigned room, at my designated school. The smell of dusty, old yellow chalk filled my nostrils and I was instantly assured that I was where I was supposed to be! Remembering when I was seeking safety in school from my homelife was the connection I made with that chalk smell. That's the way I see it and I just wouldn't believe the story any other way.

Every time I was told to go and make copies for the teacher that bloomin' machine would jam! Papers were stuck every which way in that thing and I was always asking for help from the principal. I was so embarrassed! He was always nice enough, but I made a note mentally never to ask him for a job. I thought he would remember that I was the one who couldn't run a copy machine.

Several years later I ran into him at the senior center. I told him of the memories of him helping me with the copy machine. He didn't seem interested or even cared about those times. All he cared about this point in our lives was if I was a competent table tennis player! I was—we played doubles for years.

Many younger students, mostly women, were vying for a teaching job where I wanted a position. Working at the café in the daytime, and the club at night I knew a man named Myrl, who was a customer of both places. He was sometimes the butt of my sarcastic remarks. The coffee drinkers and I would designate a person that we would goad— that was always a ton of laughs. We would watch for something that was quirky about them, and I was usually the one appointed to be the one who would start the harassing. I had a ball mimicking Flo on the "Alice" TV show. "Kiss my grits!" was my motto for several years just like Melba.

There was one half an acre to park at the place (a bit of an exaggeration but it was a large lot). Myrl would pull in and no matter where he parked he would back up at least ten feet. That drove me crazy! I would start fussing and ridiculing him when he entered the doorway. He never said a word to me. He would just hang his head, then nod and let me tease him unmercifully. Sometimes, I would even feel guilty that I was so harsh. I think he liked the attention because he kept doing the same irritating things.

Seems as though Myrl was the principal of a school, Sunset. I wanted to go and apply for a job there. I had been so disrespectful of Myrl for a long time. Now there was a possibility that I wanted to ask him for a job. What to do? Myrl solved my problem. One night at the club he motioned me to come to his table.

"Sue, I have watched you for years. You have to be the hardest working woman I know. When you get your degree come and see me and I'll hire you," he said.

Someone told me once, that it's not what you know, it's who you know. That saying was certainly true for my life. When I told people that Myrl said he would hire me, almost everyone told me not to believe him. I was on needles and pins for a long time. One day he came in for lunch where I worked with his grandson.

"Sue, you're hired. You can start teaching third grade. There's a problem though, as you have to teach in a portable," he explained.

"Fine!" I thought a minute. What's a portable?" I asked. Technically, I would call a portable a trailer but it will be a setting for many happy hours in my life.

Sunset School as my request to do my student teaching. We were told that we couldn't hold a job outside of student teaching but I had to work. I was honest; I told my counselor that I needed to work. He told me I lived in a different town than he did and he would never see me working—so just do what I needed to do. He also told me with my life experiences I would be an excellent teacher. At forty-six, a first- year teacher, I needed some assurance.

When I entered the second-grade classroom that I requested, my mentor teacher was behind her desk and spoke these words "You know I didn't want you in here. The only reason I said yes is because you are an older woman," she informed me.

That was pretty much my welcome. I told her how much I admired her teaching style; she was high energy and that was exactly the way I wanted to teach or so I thought. It took me a long time to gain her trust. She had been a teacher a long time and she had been grandfathered in her position. I think she was afraid or insecure about what she didn't know. She was rather secretive about the gradebook or any writing she had to do.

There was a girl in the class who was hard of hearing. There was a sparkle in her eye when I presented a lesson and the reason for that was that she could hear me. My voice tends to be louder and in her case that was welcomed. There was a boy who would take straight pins off the bulletin board and try to stick other kids with them. He had to be monitored constantly due to his behavior. Classroom management classes were required and I took them all to get my degree. But there are some students who do not fit into any mold you have been taught about. The way I learned and I'm sure I speak for most teachers you have to be in the trenches (classroom) with kids. Once, I listened to a beginning teacher doing a presentation about having animals in the classroom. I could just see a kid popping a goldfish in his mouth or sticking a mollusk in his ear. Not sure I would be brave enough to start a year off with some of the classes I have had in the past with animals.

Well, maybe under lock and key (just kidding.) No, I guess I'm not kidding.

Living in the apartments, we were not allowed to have animals, well, I wasn't anyway. Finally, I just didn't ask; I just got a kitten. I wanted/needed a dog, so I moved outside of the city limits eventually. The house was ready to fall down and before I moved away a couple years later, the back room's roof had caved in. I asked around to see if anyone knew of anyone who had a dog to give away. I wanted a golden one. I had been to the shelter and had put one on a leash and taken it outside but its stools told me it had parvo. The lady told me I could get it treated but I told her the reason I came to the shelter was because I couldn't afford to pay for a dog so, that meant I couldn't afford vet bills.

Finally, one of my customers said he knew where there was a golden dog. I hesitated getting in the truck with him as he usually reeked of alcohol, but I did. He drove down the canal road like a "bat out of hell" as Mom used to say. I just knew we were going to end up in the canal which had water in it at the time. I pressed myself against the passenger door and just held my breath. We ended up behind his cousin's house. My benefactor started climbing a wire fence, got stuck at the top, and fell flat on his back over to the other side. Dogs came from somewhere, I didn't see where, as I was laughing so hard at the man staggering to get up.

There was a golden dog and his mother had the bluest eyes. A man came and let my chauffeur out a gate, thank goodness. Carrying the dog to the truck I felt ticks all over his body. While riding in the truck the dog threw up in the brand-new truck. It was a him. I never requested a particular gender. I'll always remember to do that with the dogs I get in the future. After I cleaned him up I named him Buck. I always had a love for the Buck in Jack London's book, "Call of the Wild."

I did not have a fenced-in yard, a big problem! Later, I got a fenced-in area, as I learned rather quickly, Buck was a busybody and he did like the females. If I was home he would stick around, but the minute I left he would go visiting the girls. One guy, who walked down the road in front of the house and Buck were enemies. I bet the guy kicked Buck or something because Buck sure hated him. Once a lady brought Buck home with a rope around his neck. She had seen him in my yard so she knew where he belonged. I tried to tie him to the clothesline with a rope a couple times—I watched that dog out the window patiently chewing the thickest ropes I had. He was loose in an hour. I thought of Buck as a pleaser, if he got what he wanted first.

Buck loved my little truck. If I said "okay" he would start running towards the truck, literally sail over the side and land in the bed. Once I backed the truck up where I usually parked—he went sailing, ending up on the hood of the truck. I could tell he was embarrassed from the befuddled look on his face. That male dog just had a sense of pride about himself that I've never seen in another dog.

I took him everywhere with me and only twice did he leave the back of the truck. Once it was so hot in Tucson and I was shopping in a mall too long: he got under the vehicle for shade. Another time he was dognapped! Coming out from a Kmart once, I immediately saw that Buck was gone and I called the police. The policeman tried to tell me Buck ran off but I wasn't buying his predictable story. Buck wouldn't leave that truck for a cat or even two cats. I just knew someone had taken him. A report was turned in—I was told by the policeman. So, then all I had to do was wait.

Two days later I got a call from the little Stop n' Shop where I stopped all the time. All the employees knew me there. The cashier asked me if I was missing my dog. I told her yes, and she said he was sitting outside the store's door. I was on my way to school in Hobbs and I asked Jack if he would drive my truck for the day and I would drive his car. I gave Jack the directions for getting Buck, "Just drive up and honk the horn—he will get in."

Jack said he drove up and Buck had a rope around his neck; he was sitting in front of the door like the cashier had said. Jack said he talked to him and pleaded for him to get in the truck, but Buck wouldn't budge. Finally, Jack walked over and honked the horn and Buck sailed into the back of the truck. Someone did steal him but he chewed that rope in two, and went where he recognized that store. I sure wish I could have told that policeman that Buck had been stolen!

I got Buck neutered so he would stay home more. That helped some, but he would hit the back door every morning, put his nose in the air and try to catch a scent of a female in the breeze. He still went through his old routine at first. I saw confusion on his face though. Reading his canine mind, he seemed to be thinking, "I know there is a reason I do this, but I can't remember why."

Once, I took a photography class and I thought that Jack and I should go to Black River, so I could get some pictures out there. While walking, Jack held back talking to a man. I walked through a brushy path and a kid ran by—he said a porcupine was treed up the path. When I hear the word "treed" it is supposed to mean to be in a tree, or so I thought. I entered an overhang, a cave-like place, and we barely could see a porcupine, three feet or so, high on a ledge. Buck saw him at the same time I did. He jumped for him! I yelled at Buck but it was too late. That varmint switched his weight and filled Buck's face full of quills. Buck moaned. I drug him out into the light. Sure enough, he looked like a pin cushion! A man came up behind me and said he had some pliers and he would pull the quills out of Buck for me. The man opened Buck's mouth and his tongue and mouth were covered inside with quills that resembled stalagmites and stalactites. I watched as the man proceeded to pull the quills out, individually. Afterwards, he said I could take Buck to the vet when we got to town. Well, I didn't take Buck to the vet over that catastrophe. I threw him some steak and it was gone in no time, so I considered him healed.

One hot day I decided to cut Buck's fur around his neck, as I wanted him to be cooler. I was squatting behind him, using new sharp scissors. I was reaching around him and it was impossible for me to see what I was doing. I felt Buck shudder. Like an idiot, I had cut a gash out of Buck's neck. He never offered to bite me. I took him to the vet that time, so he could get stitches. The vet put a cone around Buck's neck, as I told him Buck wouldn't leave the wound alone.

I asked a friend and her boyfriend to watch Buck for me, as I had to go out of town for a class. My friend had to change Buck's bandages. Buck didn't like that too much, so he bit the man on his side. She had to take Buck to the vet once. The man hid in the garage from Buck. My friend honked the horn, Buck jumped in, then the man got in and off they went.

I got a female dog for company for Buck. Her name was Sam. The day after I got her I threw a couple bones in the back of the truck. Sam went for Buck's bone and Buck bit her. Her eye was lying by her nose. I had just been to the vet and I turned around and went back to him. I was beside myself with shame and hysteria. The vet was an old horse doctor, and as calm as a cucumber he pushed that eye back where it came from with his finger. He said she would be fine and she was.

When I worked in the portable at the school I took Buck and Sam with me. Buck spent hours chasing gophers who resided in, and on the playground. One day a lady across from the school yelled at me. She had a rodent looking animal, and she asked me what it was. I guessed it was a gopher as there were so many across the street on the playground. I told her I would take it to the place on the hill which had animals from the area. I would let them decide what to do with it. Buck and Sam were in the back with the critter who was in a tall barrel. When I arrived at my destination the barrel was tipped over. I hadn't heard it and I'm not sure how it had tipped over. The animal was dead. Buck did not make eye contact, so I knew what happened. Buck had made friends with an older couple and the man had taught Buck to kill gophers on the man's property. Their holes were dangerous for the man's horses because they might trip and become crippled. When I moved into town that old couple would sometimes be by my fence petting and talking to Buck. They sure did like Buck and he liked them right back.

I had bought a little house in town with a fenced yard. I could leave the gate open all day and Buck nor Sam would leave. When I drove by the place where we had lived outside of town I would watch Buck as we drove by that place. He would look towards the cab at me, make eye contact as if to say, "I know that place. We use to live there. See it?" That was one special dog.

Male dogs would seem to sense how vulnerable Buck was as he aged. A couple times we were charged by dogs, and I would have to fight his battles for him. I would scream, kick, and sling the leash at the attackers. One morning Buck was gone and a neighbor came by and said Buck was at the store down the street sitting in the snow. That was unusual for my aging dog as he had become rather paranoid about going out the gate even for walks. He used to live to go for walks but it was as though he was suffering from dementia. He got confused a lot. I went and picked him up, wrapped him in a blanket, and took him home to the heater.

Buck struggled to get up many days. I would help him and I was hurting thinking about the inevitable. He never messed on the floor once. He was fifteen years old—he and I had a special connection. Tears are falling down my cheeks now as I am telling his story. I came home one day, and he couldn't get up. I carried him to the truck and sat him in the front seat. I kept touching him and talking to him; he would hold my gaze, and I knew he understood. When I got to the vet I went and told them Buck needed to rest outside for a while. The receptionist started for the door but I stopped her. I told her I would go get him and I did. I picked him up and his body relaxed completely. I carried him into the examining room. We held that precious gaze and I talked to him until he closed his eyes.

Sam was lost without her old buddy. She didn't live but about month after Buck was gone. Her life had revolved around Buck and me, but mainly Buck. I had to go through the same pain with losing my loyal Sam who was always willing to play second fiddle to Buck.

Mom told me that she wanted to help me get a house before she passed away. She didn't last long enough for that to happen. That was a goal of mine for a long time and she knew it. I just wanted a small place where I could work in the yard and putter around. The house I rented was going to be sold so I started looking for a place close to the school where I was working. If need be I could walk to work. I called a real estate office, and I found a house.

I found a small two-bedroom place. It was locked up but when I went into the backyard—it just felt right for Buck and me. Not sure why I felt that way because when I look at it now it is rather nondescript. It was just a gut feeling, and I usually follow that type of directive. Another selling point was that it was close to the senior center. There were so many activities to do there, and I was planning for years down the road. Then I bought my only brand-new Toyota truck I wanted running boards (I call them) installed. I told the installer the reason being was that little old ladies would be climbing up to the seat, and I would be one of them!

Over a few years, my relationship with my half-sister and brothers had eroded away. The only glue we had was Mom. She was gone. Dora had only visited me a couple times in over twenty years. She shared resentments that she held against me when we were younger. I truly feel that her resentments are still raw and she can't get over them. I've tired of listening to her resentments and complaints. I can't make them go away for her.

Once, I invited her to take a weekend trip with me; we discussed our experiences within the family, even about her father and brother. But when we met again a couple months later the wall was back up. The way I see our issues is that I tried to belong but we don't have anything in common. I have to admit they helped and supported me when I was getting an education. My political views are a sore point with them also. Getting an education alienated me from them and some others in my life, I'm afraid.

When I was going to school, Dora's then husband called and tried to chew me out for not helping with Mom when she needed care. I hung up on him. I wasn't going to allow a person who I had little or no respect for tell me what to do. Mom doted on Dora. I was working two jobs and going to school. Jack tried to get me to understand their accusations were unreasonable. I guess I finally understood what he was saying.

Another reason for our friction is I won't/haven't kept my mouth shut. A memory of mine is of a short time after Mom got out of the hospital. She was staggering up the sidewalk and Gabe called to her, "You doin' okay, hon?"

Dora said to Lonnie, "How cute!"

I saw red! Mom was covered in bruises and she was living alone with Gabe. I couldn't prove it but I would bet Gabe was beating the hell out of her! That was a lifelong pattern with him; why would he change. My thoughts were voiced and it was received with a cold silence. He's their father.

One day while I was going to school Mom handed me a twenty-dollar bill. She told me that it was from Gabe and he wanted me to have it. I screamed like a banshee! "That bastard can stick that right up his ass!" With all the abuse I suffered from him, a twenty-dollar bill was not going to soften my stance against him at all. He thought that money would somehow earn him forgiveness.

While having lunch with Dora one day she said that I wasn't like them. I was confused at first but then I understood her meaning. It was in the back of my mind but I had never verbalized the thought out loud. Gabe had only a third-grade education but there were other weaknesses in his thought process. He couldn't read nor write and he couldn't pronounce words like Christmas. I remember times when we taunted him with his pronunciations. We would laugh at him and then run like hell! It was true that I was different. I owed him nothing. Not sure when or where I heard stories about him being made fun of in the mines. There was a story of feces being put on his buggy by other miners. I had to feel sorry for him, but again I had been treated so cruelly by him. But I didn't have to forgive him! I never felt safe living in the same town where he was living until he died. So, I have to deal with this plight, forgiveness. I have memories of waking up so many nights in a cold sweat. I was at his mercy and torture for years. Later, an aunt will tell me that Mom locked him out of her bedroom for years. I was an easy prey. That's why I slept with a butcher knife. I guess I have forgiven him for my sake. I never spoke to him since Mom was taken to the hospital. I never acknowledged his presence when I was around him. Some memories bring that little girl out in me—I guess she will be a part of me until I go to another classroom of life.

When Mom passed away Dora and Lonnie came to me and asked if I would sign some papers at the lawyer's office. Seems as though Mom had left me the house she and Gabe had lived in for many years. They reminded me that I said I didn't want anything after Mom was gone. I did remember I wanted that old golden frame picture of Lonnie and me of long ago. I did remember also that such a stink was made that I gave it back. I marched right down and signed the papers that they requested me to sign. The lawyer asked me if I knew what I was doing and my reply was "yes." I was only keeping my word.

I've wondered many times why Mom left me her house. True, she had told me she would help me get a house when she was ill. What I really think the reason was she knew and remembered what I went through growing up by Gabe's and her hands. I helped her for years financially when we came to New Mexico. I kept my word and graduated from high school. Over the years I had gained her respect, and perhaps she was compensating for her guilt feelings. I don't know for sure though, as she took all of her story with her when she died.

Frank is still living in Mom's house. He suffered so many beatings and abuse and it should be his to live in. Dora and Lonnie told me when their dad died they would sell the place and we would split the money of the sale three ways. One day out of the blue, Dora said the property was going to go to her daughter. I'm sure there are no plans for them keeping their word and splitting with me. Once at a get-together, Dora went around the room and told everyone in the room how much she loved them. The sister-in-law who Dora always bad-mouthed was bestowed with flattery and love by Dora. She saved her words for me last. It was just a gesture because I was in the room with the others, or so I felt.

When their dad died Dora and Lonnie came and asked me if I wanted to be listed in his obituary. I said, "Hell, no!" That family is no longer mine. It never was. The way I see it they just couldn't muster the nerve to tell me. They have bad-mouthed my kids and me for years. When that happens, I feel that Dora wants to hurt me. I've asked myself why I am around a person who wants to hurt me. So, I made the decision to never darken her door again, and I've stuck to this resolution for the last three years. She called and wished me birthday wishes last year but I did not reciprocate and have no intentions of doing so. She loves me she tells me, but the words are superficial and empty. I'll find acceptance elsewhere.

While I was looking at the newspaper one day I took a deep breath! There was a notice that Mom and Gabe had applied for a marriage license. Not only was I a bastard but all the half-siblings I was raised with were bastards also. Not sure they know that fact and I sadly don't care. I guess the reason for a marriage license was so Mom could draw Gabe's social security. When Mom called them little bastards while we were growing up—she really meant it.

A trip was planned for a history class I took during a summer and there were six credits to be had. It was to be followed by a road trip following the Gold Rush Trail. I asked if I could take my dogs on the road trip and I was granted permission. Another teacher I knew asked if she could ride with me so she could get six credits. I was caught off guard. I couldn't/didn't say no. We were supposed to leave early one morning and when I called she wasn't even up. When I went by her house she wasn't even ready; my pulse began to race. I forgot to get a lantern, so I rushed back home to get it. After I got it, I raced back to pick the lady up. In racing around trying to get caught up with the group and all, I had lost Sam, my dog, somewhere!

When my traveling buddy got all of her stuff in, we had enough supplies to last a year. I backtracked to find Sam but she was nowhere in sight. The rest of the class was already gone and I was pissed. I called Jack and asked if he would keep an eye out for Sam. A friend put an ad in the paper and even offered a reward...

In tears, I drove towards our campground. We had to pitch a tent. My traveling buddy had assured me she knew how to do that chore. NOT! We finally got it up and settled down. Buck was sleeping by me and all of a sudden snoring was so loud that I kicked at Buck to get him to be quiet. Well, to my surprise it wasn't Buck—it was my traveling buddy. She had sleep apnea and it was to be a challenge the whole bloomin' trip. She also told me she knew how to read a map. NOT! We were always lost and I would get up cussin' and I went to bed cussin.'

We went through Petaluma where I had lived in the sixties. That place had really changed and there wasn't an empty square foot in the whole town. I could not decipher any landmarks and no one I asked knew where Eastside Circle was. I finally spotted the drawbridge which crossed the Petaluma River. Finally, I found my bearings. I spotted my old street and the two-story where my boys were brought home from the hospital after their birth. I went across the street and found my old neighbor, Dick, home. We waited on his wife Betty to come home and we all went out to eat. We ate octopus, my first time; not much to my liking. Betty had become a devout Christian—she told me about her missionary trip to China. I sat in awe listening to her story about the way the women stuffed Bibles under their dresses and took them into China. Which was totally illegal! I would have never thought that meek and docile woman would have had that much bravery.

Jack called with good news five days later. He said while watering my garden Sam just showed up! When I got her at eight weeks I would put her in a cloth laundry bag and carry her by the canal while I was walking with Buck. The water in the canal must have been a clue for her to find her way to the house. When I saw her the skin underneath her chin was gone. She probably hit the pavement so hard that it left an open wound for quite a while. Anyway, she was home and safe and I didn't have to worry about her anymore.

We caught a ferry and went to Fisherman's Wharf from San Rafael. A couple travelers came and told me that my traveling buddy was asleep and snoring. What could I do? She spent hours riding along with me in the truck doing the same thing,

When we got off at the docks there were vendors selling fresh fruit grown locally. The strawberries were the size of small apples and they cost one dollar each. I didn't want to pay that much for one strawberry but my resolve broke, and I handed my dollar to a lady. My goodness! If I focus I can recall that sweet taste, my memory will bring it to me. My mouth still waters thinking about that strawberry.

One of my fantasies that I took on that trip was eating a great dinner on Fisherman's Wharf! My traveling buddy had a difficult time walking the streets of San Francisco but there was another younger traveler who was in the group and she tagged along with us. I took off walking and I decided they could be a team. If I had waited on my traveling buddy I would still be in San Francisco the way I reasoned it. (My reasoning is always in my favor). We reconnected in Fisherman's Wharf. We sat in a patio area of one of the restaurants. My traveling buddy ordered and drank (no exaggeration) five glasses of ice tea! Then she said the menu was too expensive for her. The younger traveler told her she would split a meal with her, but my traveling buddy wouldn't even entertain that idea!

We got up to leave and I paid the tab for the tea. As a matter of a fact I had been paying for everything! That had been in my craw for days. My traveling buddy had left on the trip without any money. She said she didn't believe in credit cards (but she believed in mine). Her son was supposed to send her a money gram but she kept putting off stopping anywhere to pick it up, thus, I kept paying. So, no wonderful dinner for me.

At Alcatraz, my traveling buddy asked me how we were supposed to get up that rock. I told her "by climbing' and I took off. She finally made it. That is the same way we visited Yosemite, too. I would be so irritated with her; then she confided that she was having more fun than she ever had in her life. I would talk to myself, and tell myself to be more patient with her. Lordy, I tried but my resolve didn't usually last very long.

When we washed our clothes, she would stand over the machine, and watch each cycle. I informed her rather strongly, she could multitask and do things which needed to be done instead of doing "observation" at the washing machine. I had stopped in Nevada and bought a propane cooking stove. I only had a hibachi and a propane coffee-maker; we needed a stove. My traveling buddy had brought spaghetti in the package to cook! My goodness! I eventually threw it away. With the elevation in those mountains we would still be waiting for the water to boil!

One night at a campground in southern California I found myself eating peanut butter on molded bread.

"Why am I eating moldy bread?" I yelled.

"Because we don't have any money," she replied.

"Wrong! You have no money. I have money," I replied.

I drove to the nearest store and bought anything and everything my heart desired. I took it back to camp and left it out so she could have some decent chow. I still shake my head at the way I took her conditions as my own. Not sure what that was about.

We spent the night in a motel in Lake Havasu. Our first night out of a tent. I couldn't arouse her after her nap. She watched television in a zombie state. When she woke up she was crying. She said she lost her money, and she didn't have enough for dinner. Day in and day out I watched her drop a ten-dollar bill at stores and gas stations for snacks. I did not offer her any money. When she saw the rest of the group she began her story of not having any money. Someone gave her some.

The next morning when I got up I told her she had better be ready when I got back from getting gas, because I was heading home. She was. We drove hundreds of miles without a word being said. We stopped for lunch and I paid again. I told her that she needed to stay awake and help me to stay awake and alert as I was driving through Albuquerque. Large trucks in that city scared me. She did stay awake after my warning.

A few days after I got home my ex-traveling buddy came over to my house. She had a wad of bills and handed them to me. I had some mechanical problems by Sacramento and she went halves with me on that bill. We never traveled together again. Could I have been more pleasant on another trip? Yes, I suppose so, but I don't wish for a rerun to find out.

When I got a divorce from Ken I paid for it. I had been told about a divorce lawyer who only charged three hundred dollars. I took an empty coffee can and put it in the freezer. I stuffed that can with bills of all denominations until I got the three hundred dollars I needed. You might say the lawyer was paid in cold cash. In the divorce decree Ken was supposed to pay four hundred dollars a month in child support. He handed me six hundred dollars once and that was the total payment he ever made. I knew he couldn't work and I felt it would be a waste of time going to court. He had to let his family's home be repossessed. There was a break-in before the repossession, and all of his guns were stolen.

Having six hundred dollars kind of went to my head I guess, because I decided the boys and I needed a trip. We hadn't been anywhere, other than Six Flags in Texas in years. My boss let me use her Cadillac for that trip if I promised not to smoke in it while I was driving. I saw it as a perk for working for her during a surgery, and she wanted me to stay working for her. The boys and I had a great time for two days and nights. Collecting coke cans and selling them was one way the boys made money for that trip. I had stashed every extra dollar I could get in a coffee can and put it in the freezer.

On the trip back from Six Flags was the first time I noticed that Brian was extremely talkative and he just wouldn't or couldn't shut up. He kept Dave and I in stitches as he was so funny. We laughed and laughed. That was a clue for me about my youngest son but I didn't know about manic episodes then.

The boys and I decided to make a trip to Cloudcroft so we could go snowmobiling. I had the six hundred dollars which Ken had given me. As usual, when one least expects it a blizzard hits the route that one would be traveling. I had sent a deposit for a room for us for two nights, and that was a chunk of money for me. If we cancelled the trip we would have lost all that money so, I was hell-bent on going. The highway patrol message had advised all travelers to stay off the roads. I can't say I didn't know. My ex-mother-in-law called me and told me we were all going to be killed. She had designated herself as the "soothsayer" of the desert. I always disregarded anything she said about her predictions. The boys and I took off.

About sixty miles into our trip I had noticed the heater in the VW wasn't warming up. I stopped, and a young inexperienced attendant at the station couldn't find anything wrong. Sitting around was wasting my deposit the way I reasoned it, so we took off again. Traffic was really sparse even for the long highway stretch we were on. Cars were in ditches stranded on the side of the road along the way. Dave was sitting in the front with me, and Brian was in the back seat plucking on an old guitar. Brian kept admonishing me for going too fast. Later, he told me he could feel the back end of the VW skidding on the road. My focus was straight ahead. Going in a straight pattern down a patch of the highway I still lost control of the steering! I guess I hit black ice. We went over the embankment as Brian was yelling, "I told you you were going too fast."

We got out and I threw a blanket under the wheels for traction. I was wishing for a helicopter to hover us with those big claws and lift us out. No helicopter was in sight! But a crusader in a big truck with a big chain yelled from the highway and asked if we needed help. I thought that was obvious. He hooked us up and pulled us out in no time. I did slow down after that but the heater still was not working.

Dave was using my Bealls credit card to scrape off the ice...from the inside! We were freezing and it was dark. Ten hours later we pull into a Stop and Shop to get something to eat and a hot drink. I had a can of that spray, De-Icer. I decided to spray the inside of the windshield. Just as I hit the button I realized I had the nozzle turned towards my face. I screamed! I wasn't hurt but that had scared me into a panic mode. We were in the coldest storm for that area in two decades. We had been in the cold inside and outside of our Volkswagen so we knew it was true. Not the best timing for sure.

The hotel where we were to stay was dark and it looked as though it was closed. When Dave went to the door and there was a note—it was addressed to me. It said that the room was open and warmed for us. When we entered the room, I crawled into the bed with my clothes on, my teeth kept chattering for the longest time before I went to sleep.

The next morning my eyes went to Old Blue and it looked as if it just had arrived from Siberia. Ice was hanging from the frame and the ice even touched the snow on the ground. Other guests of the hotel were walking by our blue mode of transportation pointing and laughing. They didn't even know about the non-working heater. I took money that I didn't want to spend to a clothing shop and bought more layers of covering and socks for all of us. My feet seemed to have been two blocks of ice for so long. When I walked out of that shop my feet immediately turned into two blocks of ice, again!

We had planned our trip around snowmobiling so we drove a short way to our destination. Just as we drove up a woman was driving by on one of those snowmobiles; her husband (I guess) was on another machine. The woman headed towards a patch of ground where there was no snow for some reason. She immediately tipped over! The man rushed up to her and stuck his finger in her face. I'm sure he was berating her for being incompetent or stupid. My thought; I will never have to listen to Ken ever again do that to me! It was a freeing moment for me just watching that scene.

I guess I was riding high on my new sense of freedom and that feeling led me to do a rather brazen or a foolish action. My gaze went up a hill which was covered with virgin snow; on impulse I took off up that steep incline—laughing to myself. Short lived euphoria though. My machine stopped and I sunk down in the snow. Looking down the hill, I saw the rest of the group with the guide coming towards me; the guide was shaking his finger at me! Guess the shaking of the finger is a male thing. I didn't have to listen his words and I didn't. He took me back on his vehicle to the group.

"Mom, are you okay?" Dave asked.

I wasn't. My hands wouldn't work and they were numb. The guide took off his large mittens and put them on top of my gloves. He started rubbing my hands and he decided to take me to heat. So, I spent hours in a hut with a heater while the boys finished their ride. Then they went inner-tubing on the snow. I had no desire to do that either!

While taking Old Blue to get gas before the trip home the next day a thought came to me. Once, I remembered someone saying that a hose from the motor heated up a VW. I told the young mechanic what I had remembered. He reached down real low—sure enough he pulled up a hose! He attached it to the motor (I guess). I got in that snow-covered VW which still looked like a snow-covered sled. Heat was warming and defrosting just like it should have done a couple days ago. We were comfortable going home; now all we had to do was remember the trip and of course, we all remember different details. But we all agree it was the coldest trip that we had ever been on.

One day at Sunset School I walked in on a discussion about an Alaskan cruise. The visitor was talking about dog sledding in Alaska! It was as though a vision of sorts was in my face and I was excited about the prospect of doing that someday. A couple months later Carrie called me about a group she worked with who were going on an Alaskan cruise. Carrie and I had a spat over something but I can't remember about what. I had taken an educational trip with a group of teachers to Mexico with a friend who had lost her husband. Carrie suggested that I ask that friend to go on the Alaskan cruise with me and the numbers would work for a group discount. At first the friend said yes, but later changed her mind which I will explain next.

Later in the week Carrie and I went to an art show. Carrie and I went off in different directions. While still in sight of one another I heard Carrie yelling at me and she was pointing at a younger woman. The younger woman was a gal who used to be the rover on our softball team. Mary, the young woman, and Carrie were reminiscing about our "softball days." Mary turns to me and asks me what I was doing these days; I told her I was a teacher. She thought for a moment and then she asked me if I knew a teacher name Cindy. That was the teacher I had gone to Mexico with! Cindy was also the young gal whose husband called her frigid.

"I sure do. She's marrying an older man and I told her she should try on the shoes before she bought them," I added. (I meant she should sleep with him before she married him.)

"Sue, that older man is my dad!" Mary said.

What a small world is all I had to say. Cindy and I discussed marrying an older man. At that time, I had been dating Jack for eight years. Jack and I were stuck in a routine. I was changing too fast I guess and gradually we were developing a distance. I attributed it mostly to our age difference. Jack's health was failing and I was a nag about him going to the doctor. Finally, I told him that decision was up to him and I wasn't going to hound him about it anymore. He complained that I didn't laugh at his jokes and I guess in his way he was telling me I was a "know it all" with all that book learning. He had made a few comments about me being too old to be playing tennis and admittedly, that irked me. Anyway, I knew our relationship was in was having some rough spots. I needed to handle it when I finished school. Giving Cindy those feelings I was experiencing, I advised her not to marry the older man.

She didn't listen and she married. Cindy was a domestic type of a woman. She liked pleasing a husband. She was soft-spoken and non-confrontational, unlike me. They're still married and as far as I know things are well for them.

Carrie came back to town after her divorce. Carrie and I decided to take the cruise to Alaska, my dream! While talking to a travel agent I told Carrie I would not fly to Vancouver under any conditions! She was upset with me but I told her I would take Amtrak to Seattle. That's what I did. I had the summer off but she didn't, as she had to work. Friends took me to El Paso and I caught the train. It was great. I met two teenage boys and we visited a lot and they carried my luggage. Seems as though the older boy had gotten the younger boy's sister pregnant and he was on his way to Washington to marry her. For some reason he was traveling with his future brother-in-law.

Traveling up the west coast was a unique experience just as the travel agent told me it would be. Going through small communities and towns the train would stop and a guide of the place would get aboard and tell us about the features of the place especially the fauna and flora. I thought of Steinbeck while traveling through the Salinas Valley and it was a very special trip for me. I only ate a skimpy breakfast and then dinner as it was rather expensive in the dining car. I slept on my seat and the seat next to it. I couldn't afford a sleeping berth. That idea worked fine going to Canada but an attendant gave me a hard time about my sleeping arrangements coming back. She had to wake me up a few times so she could remind me what I was doing was not allowed. I ignored her and went back to sleep.

When we got to Seattle I had to board a bus to cross into Canada. I was the only one in the group who was searched before crossing into that country. I was real late getting into Vancouver and Carrie was waiting in the bus station with many of the homeless in the area—she was a bit miffed. The next day we saw Beluga whales at the zoo and they were amazing. We also went to an Imax theater my first one, and then to the Botanical Gardens.

We boarded the cruise ship in Vancouver. While waiting for things to be readied I sat down by a lady who was crying. Seems as though she had recently lost her husband and she was now alone taking an Alaskan trip. After listening to her story, I invited her to stay with us on the excursions we were taking. I did warn her however, that Carrie and I were loud and we used strong language; that meant a lot of cursing. Carrie was off buying a case of wine for us as I was trying to warn the widow from Australia, our new-found friend, that we were not the passive type of women. She never complained once.

We signed up for a seaweed massage and I got my first professional pedicure. I was awestruck with that scene. I was tended to by a beautiful girl from South Africa, while gazing across the water looking for whales! It was as though I was in a fantasyland which I couldn't even have imagined in any of my dreams.

Looking at our ship's agenda the daily activities reminded me of being at camp and I was excited! There were table tennis schedules plus Trivial Pursuit tournaments which were my first choices for each day on the ship. I met a guy who enjoyed ping pong as much as I did—we played every day. He asked me to play in a tournament with him that the ship was sponsoring. I told him my traveling companion would probably be upset with me and I needed to invite her to play. Carrie came to watch but there wasn't another person around to be her partner. After a while a priest came by, and he stopped to watch us; he leaned against a pole and got comfortable.

"Hey, do you want to join us? We need another player." I yelled at him.

In a lickety-split that priest tore off his collar and the cuffs around his wrists. He then grabbed a paddle and joined Carrie on her side of the court. We had a match and I hadn't laughed so hard in my all my living days. Carrie said it took a priest with God on his side to beat me at table tennis. I had played the game before and I decided I needed to play it more in the future—as it made me laugh so much.

I had another role for the priest. We played Trivial Pursuit every afternoon. We named our team the Internationals. That was due to the fact that we had a couple from England, the Australian widow, and Carrie and me. We had a hard time with the religious questions so I tried to recruit the priest to be on our team. He wasn't an easy recruit! He kept telling us he didn't know anything about the Bible. The first question came up and I told Carrie to go and get the priest. The question was: What is the shortest verse in the Bible? That priest jerked his arm from Carrie and said, "I told you I don't know anything about the Bible!" He was right—he didn't. The answer was, "Jesus wept." When we got home, Carrie asked her mother that question and she knew. I don't think she even went to a church.

The big day for me was when we got to go dogsledding. That was the reason I wanted to go on an Alaskan cruise! We picked up another single lady from Santa Rosa, CA. That was twenty miles or so from where I had lived in CA. We had to board a helicopter and I was a nervous wreck. We got in and we flew across glaciers which were beautiful and breathtaking. The pilot saw some wild goats and he swerved down towards them. Looking deep in the crevasses there were the color blues I likened to Paul Newman's eyes! I had never seen those colors blue in nature before. The helicopter took a serious, quick turn. I was sitting in the middle and the pilot yelled at me not to touch his stick! I yelled back, "You're the first man who had ever told me that before!" We were still laughing when we landed on a pallet.

The dogs were waiting! They were chained and laying on top of their houses so they wouldn't be in the snow, I guess. When we walked up with the attendant, those canines began barking, jumping up and down on their houses, and pulling as hard as they possibly could on the chains which held them. The young man in charge chose six dogs for the lady from Australia and my sled. He then chose six dogs for Carrie and the lady's from Santa Rosa sled. I was the musher on our sled and I did that by standing up. It was a surreal setting for sure. The temperature was comfortable; we were in a hollow place between mountains glaciers and the total scene was awe-inspiring for me. For the first time in my life I yelled "mush" to a team of sled dogs! What a fantasy which had come true for me.

Tiny specks of ice (is the best I can describe it) met my face head on which had been cut from the new trail made from our sled's runners. If I shut my eyes then bring up my memory bank, I can bring back that image right before me, with all the amazing sensations I experienced that day. The dogs were going at their top speed gladly. with my urging. I want to call that moment in time a connection of two living beings, human and canine on the same dimension. I did get carried away though. We made a sharp turn and I felt the sled tilting over towards the icy ground. I could barely see with all the white in my face. I just knew I had to get the sled back to an upright position. With all the strength I could muster I arm-wrestled that sled the right-way up. My passenger yelled with a sound of relief. I had totally forgotten about her, during my Jack London moments. Unforgettable day!

We were assigned tables for dinner. We dined with the English couple and a mother and son duo from Seattle, who were rather stuffy. That case of wine was dwindling quickly. One evening the mother said, in a condescending tone that since we were from New Mexico that we must be gun advocates. From her tone which kind of irked me, I began a Wild West scenario and lied through my teeth! I started a tale about carrying a gun everywhere. I went on and bragged what fine markswomen we had to be. We regularly had to shoot rattlesnakes and all kinds varmints where we lived. I saw their reluctance in believing me at first but I saw that I had pulled them into my Wild West show. The mother's eyebrows arched as high as her hairline in the beginning but gradually they returned to their designated makeup markings. What fun.

We had a chocolate themed presentation at midnight one night. There were chocolate fountains with running chocolate and chocolate mermaids sitting nude on the buffet. One of our guys walked up and said, "I'll have a breast, please." I still laugh to myself about that comment.

We did a show for the ship towards the end of the cruise. The young director kept getting Carrie and my name mixed up. I thought I was the main character as he kept saying Sue but it turned out that it was Carrie he meant. We mimed the hit song "It's My Party." I have to confess, I was a bit miffed. No, actually, I was pissed about not being the chosen character who walked across the stage with a diamond ring. I was in the line for the back-up singers and we had to do a dance routine. I did make a mistake in the dance steps while rehearsing.

Chaos. An idea formed. When we did the finale, I did the same mistake on purpose, and it was chaos with an audience. The other dancers did the routine with questioning looks on their faces but I just kept dancing in the wrong direction—they followed. When we watched the video, I saw that same questioning look on Carrie's face. I turned my head and giggled to myself. I don't know if she figured out my devilish scheme or not. It doesn't matter to me anymore about that incident; I am just glad I can be honest with myself. I guess I was oppositional defiant in my forties too.

I have no desire to do any cruises anywhere other than the one to Alaska. I remember going to bed and talking to myself about the beauty of Alaska. Colorado had so many shades of green in her landscape, but Alaska's beauty took my breath away over and over throughout each day I was there. I would get out of bed every morning expecting to see that some beauty of that place would have faded overnight, but it never did. Looking in any direction from the ship or anywhere on land, I was overwhelmed with the rawness in the beauty which surrounded me. That scene literally touched my soul.

My plans on visiting the Butchart Gardens in Vancouver were not to be. By the time I got to my hotel the last tour had just left. I decided I would see Vancouver on foot. I spent an hour or so chatting with a small store's owner about Vancouver. She had lived in southern California and she spoke of the discrimination that she had observed while living there. She said there was always a tenseness in the air when she met any dark-skinned or a black person on the street. She said she had never experienced that uncomfortable feeling in Vancouver. The people in Canada were accepting of all cultures, religion, and ethnicity and she was so happy she moved there. I pondered many times about our conversation that day. Her contentment of her decision to live in Canada shone brightly in her eyes and her smile—she seemed to be true to herself and me.

I came upon a library in Vancouver and it was a sight! It covered a whole block; it boasted nine stories and it was called the Downtown Library. Entering that building, I remembered the first time I had been given the opportunity of seeing the public library in New Mexico. I again felt awestruck. The only difference, I finally decided was the size of the building. But a library is a library after I pick up a book and it speaks to me no matter the size of the building.

Overcoming Smut

The bus took me to Seattle and I boarded the train again. I had fresh caught salmon in the dining car as we crossed the Columbia River. One of the best meals I ever had. There was a group of Spanish speaking women on the train and we shared our life's stories for miles. While sleeping, close to entering Tucson, AZ, the train stopped. That had happened before in CA, due to the fact someone had snuck on the train without paying. But this stop was because the engineers had worked an eight-hour shift and they just stopped the train out in the middle of nowhere! They waited for hours for a van to come and pick them up with the two engineers to relieve them. Of course, we waited too. I was four hours late getting into El Paso and that was a bit scary. Seems as though the driver knew a shortcut and we were out in the desert somewhere, going to the nearest hotel. When I got to my room I put a chair under the door handle. I got a bit spooked that night, probably due to my exhaustion.

Brian was always content with the world even as a baby, or so I thought. He was never demanding for extra attention and entertained himself for the longest time. When he was around three, his dad was mainly his focus during the day and night. He would ask for Ken's safari-style work hat; then he would look for a cigarette butt on the ground, stick it in the side of his mouth and walk around the yard. On occasion, Brian would sit in a green chair with his legs crossed and then Ken would hand him a pistol. Without moving a muscle, Brian would sit, and he never tried to touch the gun in any way. I never saw anything wrong with this ritualistic game Ken did with Brian. I did make my issues known with Ken giving Brian sips of beer from his can. I felt Brian was strongly identifying with his dad at that time. I remember Brian being upset that he didn't want to go to school as he didn't know how to read. He didn't want to take required Spanish as he didn't know how to speak it. His anxiety was intense. I was at a loss on how to console him. I didn't understand any of the cues Brian was putting out—I was just hoping things would get better somehow. I so wish that I had the training I have now as a retired teacher. Perhaps, I could have lessened or saved Brian from his years of misery in school.

After first grade Brian's years in school were difficult for him, and me. He did learn to read and the books he really loved to read were comic books. He would take them to school and read them every chance he got. Once he was caught reading them by a teacher and she asked him to bring all his comics to school the next day. He took his prized possessions to school and she put him in the hall and she told Brian, "You want to read these, well, you just stay outside in the hall all day and read them!" That was a terrible day for my son, actually, it would have been a terrible day for any student. Dave said that Brian had the worst teachers (at least for Brian) anyway, and they influenced his attitude towards school. Mom always told me if I got in trouble at school she would give me worse than the teacher when I got home. So, I guess that was my stance with Brian's schooling. I always took the teacher's side. I wouldn't do that now. Not sure that would have been the right answer either.

I remember I needed to get Brian for a doctor's appointment one day. I stood outside the door and observed Brian for a long time. He reminded me of a prisoner of being locked up; his mouth was in a tight grimace for the total time I watched him. As a teenager he commented to me, "Mom, if you would have been my teacher I would have done better in school. You make school fun!" Not sure if that would have been the case, but I know that he was still being haunted by the school experience he had. At the time my help with his homework didn't help him, especially in math. Many nights we would struggle to do his assignments and then he would forget to turn them in.

When Brian was in the seventh grade I told him if he made any failing grades I was going to "whip his ass!" The day he handed me his report card, I told him to go to my bedroom and lay across the bed. "Mom, you know this is not going to do any good," he said. "I know it, but I said I would whip you and I keep my word. I will never do it again." It didn't do any good and it was the last time I whipped him with a belt. Another time I slapped him. He came home from drinking, we argued, and he made the comment, "You think you're so tough!" My hand went up and I let it go across his face. He repeated his comment and I slapped him again. I saw a small tear in the corner of his eye. I turned and walked away. I made myself a promise I would never do that again either.

One Thanksgiving Day we were invited to dinner by Ken's stepdad. Brian didn't want to go. Ken insisted. Ken eventually pulled off his belt and started striking Brian. I felt worse for allowing that action, then doing it myself. I didn't understand the anxiety Brian was suffering. I had said many times I didn't want my boys to have a stepdad as I didn't want them to suffer under a stepdad's hand. But I allowed Brian's father to whip him with a belt in front of me. Guess I will never get that image out of my head. I shouldn't have allowed that.

Brian had a friend who was his accomplice in skipping school and heaven knows what else. One morning one of my customers told me they saw Brian playing hooky and I barged into a house and I found Brian hiding in a closet. I took him to school cursing, threatening, and as a last resort reasoning with him.

But there were worse days. I got a call from the school that Brian was being suspended and as I pulled up to the school I watched as a policeman put handcuffs on my son. That day he bought pot from a kid in the bathroom and the kid ratted on Brian. He was ordered to go to a drug counselor and that was a nightmare. Brian said that the counselor just kept telling him how not to get caught. Those sessions ended up with Brian and I yelling at each other. I had lost him, and I didn't know what to do about it.

When I left Ken, Dave stayed at the house and Brian lived in an apartment with me. One day, I don't remember why Brian and I were at it again. Brian was so angry with me his nose started bleeding. He went to the house with his dad and Dave came and stayed with me. When I went to the house for something Brian had broken or allowed someone else to break all the furniture in his room. What was happening to my smiling little boy who was always cracking a joke.

Brian went to Colorado in his twenties. He talked of him running down a street in a snowstorm. I could tell that he was scared, confused and he didn't understand what was going on. I only listened to his stories he chose to tell me. I knew there were many more.

He lost a girlfriend as she passed away and he asked me to come and see him in Washington. He had never asked me to do that before and I went. Brian would cry and then he would laugh. He would assure me that he was okay. We had a beautiful visit and we decided the key to everything in life is "moderation." Brian filled out papers for himself to get medical treatment for a hernia. His tolerance for pain was always a mystery for me, even when he was a toddler. Ironically, he could handle severe physical pain but emotional pain would tear him up.

I couldn't give Brian much direction in his life. I knew he held a lot of pent-up resentment towards me. Much of that, I gave his father credit for. In Ken's way of thinking I was the reason for all of us having issues and misery in my opinion.

As hunting was a big deal in New Mexico. Brian became obsessed with the idea of deer hunting. There is a requirement that young hunters must take a hunter safety training. We signed up Dave and Brian for the course. Since Brian was having issues in school we thought Dave taking the class would be helpful. On hindsight, I have found that Brian can do very well in the classroom if he's interested in the subject. They both were issued deer hunting license.

I went to work one stormy morning and then reports started buzzing around about a blizzard going through the hunting location where Ken and the boys were. I kept calling the house and there weren't any answers and I was in a tizzy by the time I got home. I noticed the van in the driveway right away and I knew at least Ken was okay. I burst through the front door and I saw that everyone was accounted for. Then I got mad! I began scolding them for making me worry. Finally, when I calmed down a bit,

Brian asked me, "Mom did you see it?

"What?" I asked angrily. He told me to go to the front porch and look. I had no idea what he was talking about. There hanging from a rafter was a buck. Brian posed for a picture; to my knowledge he never picked up a gun again, and never killed anything else.

Brian went to a therapist for a year or two. He was diagnosed as schizoaffective. He takes medication and he usually avoids people. I read mental illness is usually inherited. When Ken passed away his sister gave my boys all the small possessions he owned. They took most of the items with them when they left; but they left his wrist band from the hospital in the ashtray in the back seat of the truck. Written on the band was the word 'bipolar'. I had only heard of that word before, but I've had classes sf training about the subject. Thinking back, that word would have explained so much for my understanding of Ken's behavior. Would I have done anything differently? No, I couldn't have, I've decided I was ill-equipped to deal with a person who was self-medicating with alcohol and who had such issues with anger. I did what I had to do and left. But with a son it's a different decision. I had no idea why Brian was so miserable in a structured environment such as a classroom. I said before I wish I had my educational training back during those turbulent years. I may have helped Brian. But I will never know, so I will just have to wonder about it.

My years of teaching were an exciting and insightful time for me. I loved walking through the teachers' lounge or having lunch there. I would hear teachers talking about so many subjects I had never heard of before, and I loved it. I began teaching third grade my first year, and memories of my third-grade experience were instrumental for me staying in that grade for eighteen years. That year for me was when I dressed as a gypsy, stole money from Mom's purse, but I was beginning to be happy, as I was accepted from a teacher. I later learned that a professional person in education could spot a potential dropout in third grade, and I felt I was important in that grade level so I wanted to stay.

I had to begin my master's classes and lordy, what an ordeal. The first class I entered I swear it sounded as though the professor was speaking a foreign language. He kept talking about manipulatives and hands-on activities, and I knew I was in over my head. I struggled with so many concepts and theories my head seemed to be under water most of the time. One class I thought would be a breeze was physical education class for elementary students. I considered myself to be athletic but when that instructor finished his lectures I couldn't have told him, or anyone, for that matter, which side of a ball was up (just kidding.) He explained the elements of kicking a ball and I couldn't have done that feat, with my feet, if my life depended on it. I made a "C" in that class, my lowest mark in the master's program.

I took many classes in special education. Those classes helped me in many ways. Child Psychology classes were helpful also. Perhaps I could have learned so much more if I wasn't so terrified of failing the program. Truth to be known, I would have never taken any masters classes if I hadn't required to do so. Thankfully, I was forced to by the threat of losing my job if I didn't do it.

Theories and philosophy of education were nightmares for me. They could have been theories and philosophy of outer space gardening for all I knew. I had to write papers and that overwhelmed me but somehow, I finished the program and then I had "the orals." I would walk Buck by the canal with a cassette player and listen to subjects I didn't have a handle on or a clue about. I was in a state of panic when the big day arrived. Jack drove me to Las Cruces for the dreaded day. We stopped for a sandwich and a cold sweat broke out on my body beginning at my head. I was drenched. A feeling of calmness came over me though. I had done everything I could—I accepted what would be would be.

I entered a room where four guys were sitting with stacks of papers in front of them. Two of the instructors were Hispanic, and they taught multicultural classes which I thoroughly enjoyed. One was a psychology professor and the fourth one I didn't even remember. For some reason I took the offensive stand instead of a defensive one. Maybe, because it was from being a smart-ass bartender for so long. "The last time I was in a room with four guys, they were all drunk and playing poker," I began.

I heard them laughing and that was all I need "Sue, what is Dewey's theory of education?" one asked. Uh-oh "I went blank on his theories but I will give you mine," I stammered.

Tapping his pencil, he then said, "Okay, give me your theory or theories of education. They were all listening so I blundered on. "There's not a third grader who enters my classroom each day who doesn't want to please me. I have to decide how I can help him or her to learn to love learning, in a non-threatening environment "Please you, that's what they are supposed to do, Sue, please you?" he asked.

"Hey, I didn't make up those rules. They were made before I got here. But isn't that what I have been doing, I am doing right now, pleasing you?" I demanded.

For some reason they didn't have an answer. They excused themselves, and I heard laughter in the hallway. When they came back to the "interrogation" room they were all smiling. Truthfully, I don't remember a word anyone of them said other than the words, "You passed your orals, Sue!" I was elated! That cloud over my head dissipated and I could take a deep breath—the first in a couple of years.

I kept taking classes, though. I have bragged yes, bragged, that I have ninety hours over my masters. I just was allowed to take classes in subjects I wanted to take. When I was taking masters classes I didn't get to read any books I wanted to read. So, I had a lot of words to catch up with.

There had been another obstacle in my mentor's classroom I had to work with, her assistant. The assistant had her daughter in that second-grade class. She had been Ms. T's right-hand person for most of the year. Three adult women in the same classroom took some maneuvering by all three of us. They had had their routine and I had put a kink in their usual procedures. Ms. T. would not eat in the lounge with the other teachers. She sent the assistant down to lounge to get the gossip and then she would report back to Ms. T. with what she had found out. One day the assistant and I were eating lunch in the lounge. She turned to me and said, "I don't like you being here, Sue."

I replied, "I know you don't, but you can't run me off. I've been through hell getting here, and no one is going to run me off!" She nodded her head. Actually, I felt that cleared the air some, well, for me anyway. Later on, she began school, got her degree, and became a teacher.

At first, I was overwhelmed with my new job. The first time I took up permission slips from twenty-two kids I panicked when they rushed to my desk. Simple, right? My mentor teacher had a hard time letting go of her classroom and that was the first time I took up papers. She never allowed me to see her grade book so that was a lesson for me to learn also. Simple tasks—but I was used to making margaritas and I couldn't transfer what I had learned in the bar to the classroom. Once I was asked by one of the customers how the kids in the classroom were different than the guys in the bar. I said the kids in the classroom used more curse words then the men in the bar did—but other than that I could not tell any difference. He got a kick out of that.

When my mentor teacher finally let me begin teaching lessons I taught reading. I used a recorder and I would let the second graders listen to themselves read. I would tell them to judge for themselves how well they read—and decide how could they improve. My first solo lesson where the teacher left the room was enjoyable. She later told me that she looked in the window at me and my arms were waving and flailing all over the place. I explained that was normal for me. Later, I would see students mimicking me out of the corner of my eye waving their arms. I took that as a sign they were listening.

The year after I had her students she came to my third-grade classroom one day. She had her test scores in her hand. She said she wanted me to know that those papers she held were the highest scores she ever had before. She then told me it was because of my instruction! I was flattered to the nth degree.

As the saying goes, there were never two days the same in teaching. Right off I knew I wanted to use art a great deal in teaching. Not sure where I got the idea. I went to the college to sign up for an oil painting class. The instructor was a well-known artist in the area. While I was telling her that I felt art was important to students she asked me if I knew how to draw. Well, no, I didn't—but I always wanted to know. She suggested that I take drawing lessons along with the painting classes she taught. Oh, my goodness, she opened a whole new world to me. I began looking up at clouds all the time. Before that class I only saw white globs. I began seeing shapes, colors, and how nature displayed everything for anyone who wanted to see it; I was constantly awestruck. She taught me to see!

Another idea I had, was to use paper-mache in my classroom—maybe because it was the cheapest resource for art projects. In science we researched birds from encyclopedias and made them in paper-mache using the exact scale for them. I hung them from the ceiling and they were beautiful. One girl did a peacock and she worked every recess on her project for months. I entered her piece in the state fair and it never came back. Someone must have stolen it, sorry to say, as it was a beautiful piece of artwork.

Another project we did in social studies was man-made structures of the world. They did their reports, read it aloud to the class, and constructed the structure in paper-mache. The Eiffel Tower, the Taj Mahal, Machu-Picchu, along with Promontory, Utah's golden spike, were some examples of that unit.

I had a Native American boy in my class who had moved from a reservation in AZ. He was below grade level in all subjects but math was especially difficult for him. I worked many of my lunch periods with him in math. When we began the man-made structures, he was befuddled by the assignment. I decided to have him to do the railroad at Promontory with the golden spike. He knew what a railroad was and he turned his project into a masterpiece. As a matter of a fact it was so good another student stole it. I let him take some class time to do another one. I had two Native American students in my class that boy and a girl. She could use crayons and create the most beautiful pictures—I was amazed at her creations. Not sure if I could make a blanket statement and say their artistic ability was as though it was innate but it seemed to be. They just went inside of themselves and produced art which was amazing.

Another theme we used in paper-mache was famous Americans. Again, they chose the person, did a report, read it aloud to the class and proceeded to make a life-like American. One boy did Billy the Kid and it was so lifelike—down to his boots. I let him work on it for a long time mainly because he wanted his caricature to stand upright. We usually put hooks on the back of the work and I would hang them from a bulletin board. The art work those third graders turned out made me stop in my tracks many times.

Another way I taught social studies was presenting plays for the whole school. We did Rosa Parks, Jackie Robinson and Famous Women. We also did the OK Corral and a play called Bookworm. There was a high achieving girl in the class and I asked her to do the Rosa Parks part. She memorized all her lines over Christmas break. When I watched her perform—the hair on the back of my neck stood up. Two students chose me as their favorite teacher to be recognized at graduation. She was one of those who chose me and the boy who played her husband chose me also. They both were in the top twenty of their graduating class. I felt their involvement in the plays from our class were the reason I was chosen by them.

One day a principal observed me during the early hour of our class time. I must have read somewhere about putting students in cooperative groups because I did that. The students were assigned tasks such as a homework collector and noise control. Out of a hat they would draw a piece of paper. On the paper was a Native American tribe's name, and that was the name for their group. We did studies of

Native Americans throughout the year and the third graders loved it. We would also do Trivial Pursuit skills and on Friday, whichever group had the most points would get out of the treasure box. They chose prizes which I bought for the box and they enjoyed that.

After the observation my principal called me to her office. She wanted me to explain how I did my groups. She told me to write a paper on the method and give it to her. I balked at the idea then she said she would write an article with my permission. So, I agreed. A few weeks later I went to the copy machine and on the bulletin-board was a publication from "Better Teaching" which had in bright red the words 'One of us is famous!' The article Ms. Owre had written for me was selected for publication. The article was published in the United States, Mexico, and Canada. I was so pleased she did that for me.

There was a write-up about the article with a picture of the group who got out of the treasure box that week in the local paper. A television reporter came from Roswell and spent an afternoon in our classroom. He interviewed some of the students. He told me that the story would be broadcasted the next day. It wasn't aired. I called to check on the problem and seems as though he got fired for some reason. Our fame was short-lived but it was totally unexpected anyway.

Classroom Learning the Hard Way*

My first year of teaching I had a boy in my class with Tourette's syndrome. My mentor teacher placed him in my class. She explained that she sat him away from the other students as he was distracting. I was told that he would make grunting sounds which sounded like a pig, just before he began an assignment. He was a very intelligent boy, and he could speak of facts especially facts about planets which amazed me. I placed him in a group with mostly boys and they really enjoyed his company. He was known to string a barrage of curse words together at times—that could have been one reason for his popularity.

As the year was winding up, TJ's parents decided to put him on medication. I asked the parents to come to our class and explain to the class about TJ's quirks and they did. That class of kids were so considerate and tolerant of TJ, which I marveled at many times.

Overcoming Smut

Field day was on the schedule and I did not know what to expect since it was my first-year teaching. Jumping rope while running, was the first event and TJ was on a squad with three athletic boys. TJ struggled with simple motor skills, and I knew he would struggle with running. I could tell right off he had never jumped rope with any mastery before. He picked up the rope and he froze! I rushed out on the field and began coaching him before he could start his colorful words. I told him to look in my face and follow my directions. I saw raw fear, confusion, and frustration in his eyes. Nose running, tears falling, and feet stumbling TJ kept moving even dragging the rope at times. Somehow, we ended at his relay partner's line dead last. TJ passed the rope to the next runner after I told him to. The other three boys excelled and TJ's team came in first place! I know it was only field day and I was totally unorthodox but I couldn't just stand by and watch TJ fail. His team could have gotten upset with him. Besides, I didn't want TJ to be a loser. I'm rather proud of my decision to be unconventional that day—if nothing else it made a beautiful memory for me.

One day I was walking down the sidewalk to get to the office for some reason. A woman got out of a car holding a boy's hand. The boy made a sound and the woman began swearing. I looked back and the boy had just begun urinating on the sidewalk. I wondered which teacher would get him. The next day I got Jeremiah! He was from Arkansas and he hadn't been tested for any Special Education classes in New Mexico. He needed to stay in my classroom all periods. He quickly learned that he needed to follow his group's procedures. In a couple of days, I saw a backwards boy turn into a smiling third grader. He was later placed in the classes he needed to be in. Jeremiah was chosen to ride our school's float in the Fire Prevention parade. His face was beaming as he went by me and his class waving him on.

Another special student I had was Cliff, a boy, who had Asperger Syndrome. He was hard to handle at first. He liked to roam the room. I eventually began telling him his group would lose points if he didn't sit down. If he didn't obey right away I went to get the eraser and would move towards the board where the groups' points were recorded. I would erase a point, wait a second then erase another one. After a while he got the idea and his behavior improved greatly. I was told he didn't show affection. But one day his classmate gave him a sucker and Cliff gave Brent a bear hug that lasted longer than Brent wanted it to. Cliff began missing school a lot and I called the Indiana school where Cliff had attended before. The person I was talking to said that Cliff's dad was under suspicion of beating Cliff. When our principal called the father about Cliff's absences they up and moved. So many kids are in a situation like this, unfortunately.

Artistic kids amazed me and I had many. I remember being in an assembly one day and I heard a voice which I will use the cliché, "sounded like an angel." I'm not trained in music at all but when I hear a gifted voice I recognize it. There was a girl who had some behavior issues assigned to my class. She was also an artist with skills above the third- grade level. We were to do the Fire Prevention Poster for the city. I gave all the rules and I told the class I would not accept any posters which did not follow the rules. The girl I just spoke about brought her poster to my desk and she was proud of it. "Sorry, not acceptable," I told her. She had her name sprawled all over the front of the poster. She pleaded her case and I rejected her pleas. "Do it again," I demanded. She stomped off. We went through that routine again but I can't remember why. I repeated my order. Needless to say, she was very angry with me. She did it three times before I accepted her poster.

Early one morning I heard my classroom door open. Then I heard a squeaky voice, "I won." I looked up and she was holding a trophy taller than she was! She had won first place for the whole city—she had competed with grades first through the fifth grade. Not sure if she even remembered how many tantrums she had, but I did.

Once I heard a teacher say she never had a student in her classroom who had been molested. The training I have had and a report of the "Victims of Crime" disagrees with that statement. One in five girls have been molested. The ages it most likely occurs is between the ages of seven and thirteen. That means if I had a class of twenty students, five girls could have been molested. One in twenty boys have been traumatized. With my life experiences I am sensitive to this issue on many levels.

The first time I had an instance where I had to deal with sexual abuse was in my second-year teaching. Hannah, was a vivacious, good student, and a high achiever. I bowled the same night as Hannah's mother, who was divorced. For no reason I could pinpoint, Hannah became hyper and she seemed to need a lot of attention which was unusual. During a test one day she started crying. Another day while sitting by a boy I noticed her hand rubbing the inside of the boy's leg. I asked her to stay in at recess. I told her I didn't know why she was getting upset all the time but I thought something was bothering her. I told her that Christmas break was close and when her dad came from California to take her back she needed to tell her dad what was bothering her.

One night I got a call from Hannah's dad from CA. He told me was going to sue me! He said Hannah had talked to me and I didn't do anything about what was bothering her. I explained I didn't force or coerce Hannah to tell me anything as I wasn't a qualified counselor. I told him that I told Hannah to talk to him, her father. He said he was going to call the police.

A couple of weeks later I was called to the principal's office. A policeman was sitting in the office with the principal. He introduced himself and asked me to have a seat. He said he was there in regards to Hannah, my student. He asked me what I thought was going on with Hannah. I told him I thought that Hannah had changed and I thought she was being molested. The policeman paused and then looked at me. He told me I was right. What a sense of relief I felt at that moment. Apparently, Hannah's mother's boyfriend had moved in with them. She had met him at the bowling alley while bowling. He was molesting Hannah after the mother went to work at night.

The father took Hannah back to California with him. A couple weeks later I received a letter at school from Hannah. She apologized for causing me trouble and she thanked me for helping her. Enough said.

I had another girl who was said to have been diagnosed oppositional defiant. Jenny was skillful in getting exactly what she wanted. During the book fair at school she brought a check supposedly signed by her mother. Jenny had gone to the drawer where her mother kept her checks. Jenny had the foresight of going to the bottom of the stack and getting a check for herself.

She had a crush on a boy and she couldn't keep her hands off of him. It was as though she was stalking him. There was a school rule which stated no spaghetti straps were to be worn by girls. As we were walking to our field trip one day—she took her blouse off. She had a spaghetti strap top on. I told her to put her blouse back on. She did, but complained the whole trip about how hot it was.

Many times, during class she would ask to go down the hall to the pencil machine to get a pencil. If I told her no, when another student entered the door on the east then she would nonchalantly go out the west door. I had to chase her down the hall several times.

During deer season the mother sent me a note and she said her husband wanted Jenny out of my class before he got home from hunting. We all met in the principal's office with the therapist. Jenny proceeded to climb into her father's lap and baby talk to him. He seemed uncomfortable but anyone (I could) tell that was a ritual for the girl and her father. The principal did not allow Jenny to transfer classes as she felt there was not a reason strong enough to justify for her to allow it. I told the therapist that I thought Jenny was being molested by her father. The therapist said Jenny never mentioned it to him. Case closed.

One night at the bowling alley one of my students came by my lane to say hello. Her brother came up behind her. Sheilah seemed a bit uneasy with her brother Tom, being so close to her. I had Tom in my class a couple years before. I was bowling with someone they knew and the sister and brother were sitting at a table behind me. The brother kept grabbing at his sister and her reaction was a high pitch giggle. It just wasn't right and I was uncomfortable. There seemed to be a tension in the air.

Sheilah had written in her science book; "He won't leave me alone." Her grandmother came in to pick Sheilah up after school. I had the book in my hand and I showed it to the grandmother. I said that I thought Sheilah was asking for help. The grandmother, a preacher's wife, waved me off and said that Sheilah was just joking. I told the principal about what I thought. I couldn't sleep. The nurse got involved. Finally, all the adults at school who were involved had a conversation with the Safe House. Safe House was a local agency who handled abuse cases. A lady interviewed us and someone came and got Sheilah and interviewed her. My worst fear was that the girl could have been pregnant. A teacher I knew spoke of sexual contact the girl had been involved in while living in another town. Sheilah was so developed for an eleven-year old. Perhaps, I was wrong but I did everything I could for Sheilah. I'm glad I did. I see Sheilah around town and she has two babies now. She is always happy and glad to see me. There's a feeling, an intuition about her I still sense. It's as though she knows I know. I have no guilt feelings. What I don't know now is out of my hands.

The saddest situation involving a student was with a boy. Even though I considered myself worldly I was a teacher of a student who probably was a transgender. I didn't know what that meant when I had him in my class. I'm sorry that I was ignorant of that situation. I won't assign a name, not even a fake one for him. And I am uncomfortable with describing some issues which led me to believe what I believed. The young lad was in the ninth grade or thereabouts when he committed suicide. If only I had known more or any of us "professionals" had known more, maybe we could have at least made his life less miserable for at least an hour or so. His mother wrote his obituary for the paper— it broke my heart. I never had read anything with so much pain dripping from words on a paper before, nor since.

The Rest of My Dog Tales

Most people want registered or purebred dogs (I found that is usually the topic of conversations when I talk to them anyway) I've had three; Sheba the German Shepherd, a birthday gift. Goldie, a cocker spaniel, a birthday gift from Ken which he traded a pistol for. Sophie, the one I'm going to talk about on this page, a Lab—a gift of sorts. I've never bought a purebred, myself. Mongrel dogs I have found seem to go that extra yard to give all the love and loyalty they have. I think purebred and registered dogs are overpriced. Truthfully, I think there may be a bit of snobbery for the human owners of such canines.

After my dog, Sam passed away I went to the dog shelter and adopted another female, Maggie. I had her for a couple weeks and she developed parvo. I took her to the vet as I was already attached to her and had her treated. Several hundred dollars and a week or so impounded she was deemed cured, and I brought her home. Her behavior was hard for me to figure out. She jumped the fence constantly. I read that using a toggle around a dog's neck would break them from jumping. That worked to keep her in the yard but her dragging a ten-pound toggle around the yard resulted in practically every flowerpot broken in the yard. When I took the toggle off she would go back to jumping the fence again.

As I was hanging out clothes one day I noticed a white Lab puppy in the yard next door. I didn't know my neighbors well, and to be truthful they were young and loud. I had only chatted with the woman mainly in passing. She told me she got the Lab puppy so her kids could have it to play with when they came to visit her on weekends.

One afternoon I heard Maggie yipping at something or someone. Looking out the window I saw that Lab puppy climbing the wire fence between my yard and the neighbor's yard. After a while I took the pup home and tied it to a railing on the neighbor's porch. Of course, loneliness drove that puppy in wanting to climb the fence and seek some company again. Once, I even took her for a ride. I took Maggie almost every day. Big mistake! That Lab was waiting for me every morning. I yelled across the fence and told the woman to come and get her dog as I was sick and tired of taking her back home twice a day. The neighbor came and got the Lab and threw her across her shoulder. That dog looked me straight in the eye—my knees buckled. She and I connected!

The next day a rerun of the day before except for me saying without even thinking, "If you don't keep that dog home I'm going to keep her!" Guess that's what I was thinking for quite a while.

"You can't keep my dog," she said angrily.

The next day the lady had to come and get her dog. I sort of apologized. I told her I spoke my mind and I shouldn't have talked so mean to her. Then I qualified my stance. "I'm a teacher."

"I know who you are," she replied. Seems as though I had her younger sister in my third-grade class a couple years before. The family had a reputation of having heavy drug usage and it was said they sold drugs. The mother came school and anyone could tell she was under the influence of something. The girl I had would try to sleep all during the day during class. She said she had to watch her baby brother all night long. The girl got a lead in a school musical that year. Another teacher was trying to get a student in her class to replace my student for that play. "Over my dead body," was the statement I made to the music teacher. I worked with that girl so she could learn her lines every chance I got. I held her hand while she finished her homework. We struggled and our work paid off. She was a star—for at least one day in her life.

A couple weeks later the owner of the dog told me to stay outside until she got back—I did. She brought dog food, a leash, and a paper which said the Lab was registered. "Take her," she said. "She won't stay with me anymore." What a gift! I named her Sophie.

Observing Sophie with Maggie I couldn't help notice the differences in the two dogs. One time, Maggie had jumped out of the bed of the truck. I had her chained and I heard the chain go over the side of the truck and I heard it snap. I stopped and carried her to the truck. I knew she was hurt but my reasoning was I had her treated for parvo and I wasn't spending any more money on her. I actually thought she would bond with me while she healed. I would carry her outside to relieve herself at night. I worked or talked to her constantly. When she could get around she went over that bloomin' fence again.

Watching the dogs in the backyard one morning I saw the strangest sight! Maggie was sitting with her toggle and Sophie was sitting by her; they both were looking at the lowest point in the fence. After a while, Sophie got up and jumped that fence. I swear I know better but Maggie was using mental telepathy or some kind of communication to tell Sophie to jump that fence. Sophie got caught on a barb in the fence and I took her to the vet as she had a deep gash. Life was getting complicated with those dogs and me. I was at my wits end.

Later that week I took both dogs up the Ocotillo Trail on the leash. Maggie literally pulled Sophie and me at a pace that we could barely keep up. Maggie's hyperactivity was too much for me to handle any longer. I had to make a decision. What to do about my predicament? I took the dogs home and got a rawhide treat. I then drove to the dog shelter. There were cages left outside for people like me I guess. I threw the rawhide inside and Maggie went after it. She never looked at me once. I told her goodbye, and left with a tear or two in the corner of my eye. I admitted failure with her.

Sophie and I would get up early and walk the Ocotillo Trail many times meeting Susan. It would be dark and I would let her off the leash and she would stay with me unless she saw a deer or a herd of deer. I got in trouble and received many a dirty look from some retirees who fed the deer everyday. I was amazed watching her running after a deer. I would liken her gait or stride to running water due to her smoothness and rhythm. I never really saw her chasing the deer as a problem; I knew she couldn't catch one but not everyone shared my thought. Once, she'd gone out of sight running a deer and I was mad at myself for a while. I decided that I would go get my truck and drive up the hill honking my horn as I thought she was lost. I literally ran down that hill, got to the truck, and there she was waiting on me—with her tongue hanging out of her mouth over the side of the truck. She was one smart dog. She loved everyone and everything except small dogs. She embarrassed me a couple times when she went after them.

One day I went home after school and Sophie was gone! My plan was to call the newspaper and put an ad in the paper "dog missing." The next day with the paper in hand I glanced at the ads. I read "Found; friendly Lab in Edwards Street area" with a phone number. Holding my breath, I called and it was early. A man answered and he said he had a dog—the dog was in bed with his wife! He asked me what her name was and I told him. "Hey Sophie, is that your name?" he yelled. He told me her ears shot straight up and he knew it was her. When I went to get her, he said she started following him and he took her home with him. He also said he and his wife were hoping no one would claim her. I surely understood that.

One Christmas break I was planning on going to Clovis to the museum. I spent a long time in Roswell and I was exhausted. It was cold outside and dark—I decided to spend the night in Portales. I pulled into the motel across from the college. The room was cold—I turned on the heater and took Sophie for a walk. I rushed her back to the room and I was uneasy about that place for some reason. A continental breakfast was advertised on the sign. Earlier, I had asked about the breakfast—the man behind the desk gave me a coupon for a coffee and roll down the street at a McDonald's.

I didn't take a bath—I just went to bed. The room was still cold and I motioned for Sophie to jump on the bed. There was a mirror on a dresser directly across from the bed. The mirror's reflection was distorted like a lot of old mirrors I've seen before. My mind was playing tricks on me I guess, because I thought I saw movement in that old mirror a time or two. Sophie jumped down from the bed, went to the bathroom door, stood there, while wagging her tail. I would watch her behavior for a while then call her and she immediately would come back and jump on the bed. She did that three or four times during that long night. Once I thought about my gun but I had left it in my truck. I sure wasn't going to get up and go outside and get it! The next morning, I left that place so fast and I thought, "the heck with my continental breakfast" and sped down the highway thinking about the night before.

One time, Sophie and I were walking the Ocotillo Trail. It was around noon and a thought came to me, "Was the reason I was happy or content as an adult because I had such a rough childhood?" I know I mentioned this before and my relationship with God is so vivid from my childhood. Was there a message I needed to figure out?

For some reason I had Sophie on a leash that day. I can't remember why. Perhaps we passed a small dog before. We were coming to the curve in the trail and Sophie was tugging on the leash. She was going out as far as she could to see around the bend. I wondered why—I remember thinking. We both saw the doe at the same time. Sophie didn't tug any longer she just stopped frozen to the spot. The doe turned and looked directly in my eyes and it was my mother's eyes! A message was sent to me via those soulful eyes. "I see you're doing just fine. I knew you would be," they said. That doe turned her head forward and went up the embankment in front of her. Sophie and I watched her until she was out of sight.

I've shared this story on Facebook on Mother's Day a time or two. Susan, a lady I walked with said I was in tuned to deer and animals and I tend to believe that too. I'm not afraid of them and they seem drawn to me for some reason. Am I a believer in ghosts or spirits? I can't readily say one way or another. But I can't deny that others believe in them. At this time of writing this book my boys and I have traveled many a mile to stay at haunted places and read about the mysteries of them. They really like the idea of the supernatural. I know my dog Sophie saw and responded to something in that motel room that night. I also know she sensed that doe was on the trail that day. I won't go so far as she knew the message I received from the deer but she sensed something. Perhaps, Sophie was a messenger, a medium psychic of some kind. I've thought many times I have a guardian angel; someone or something which has kept me safe all these years.

Early before daybreak, I was going towards Ocotillo Trail west on Pierce Street. I don't recall speeding but I won't/can't deny I wasn't. To my right, next to the curb I saw a form moving. Finally, my brain recognized it as a dog. He was going to run right in front of me. He looked at me and I simply reacted! Glancing in the rear-view mirror I saw that there was no traffic behind me. I swerved quickly and missed that dog. I forgot that Sophie was in the back of the truck. I had slung her out! I stopped—ran back and picked her up then carried her to the cab. I went on to meet Susan and we walked that hill. When I came back I thought my dog was in shock. I took her home, went to work and got the kids settled in my class. I asked if I could go home and see what I needed to do about Sophie. When I got home I could tell Sophie was in pain, but she did her best to let me know how glad she was to see me. I took her to the vet.

After school I went to the vet to check to see what needed to be done. Her hip was shattered and she needed surgery. The vet who was tending her said he wasn't sure he could do right by her. He thought I may want to take her to El Paso. He said he needed to put a spike in her leg and maybe that leg would be an inch or so shorter than the other ones. I told him I really didn't care and for him to do the surgery. The guilt I felt over that accident was heavy on my mind. Analyzing it my way, I decided that I couldn't hit that strange dog head on. I could have had Sophie in the passenger side of the truck but I didn't. The vet bill was over a thousand dollars. I didn't care I was responsible for her pain. That dog was ready to go home a couple days later. She wanted to tell the vet and all the assistants goodbye. Honestly, I don't remember her moaning once through that long ordeal.

The vet told me to gradually get her used to walking on that leg and not let her run. The not running part was like telling the wind not to blow. I had to restrain her or pull her back and it was exhausting. We walked around a block or two in the beginning. Her mind did not get that she wasn't supposed to run. I started walking her longer and longer. One day we overdid it. When we entered the house she just collapsed. Her eyes were rolling back in her head—I rushed towards the phone. While dialing the vet's number I saw her rouse herself to a standing position; what a relief.

It was Christmas break and I was invited to go to Queen with a couple, Ted and May. I had been several times before with them. Actually, I had spent a great deal of time with them. Sophie was always being humped by their dog and that was aggravating but off we went. It snowed that weekend and Christmas morning Ted suggested we walk to the road to get the dogs outside for some air. I started to get Sophie's leash but Ted said I didn't need it, so I didn't take it.

We were walking on the road and Sophie saw a male figure behind a little café on the road. She took off towards him. When she got to the man he ignored her and I yelled for her. She turned and started running towards me with the usual excitement glowing from her face. I heard a truck coming which was going rather fast for all the ice on the road. I began yelling at the driver to stop which in hindsight, was probably the worst thing I could have done. I distracted him –Sophie ran right in front of him! I started screaming and Ted told me to stay back. He was on his knees cradling Sophie and talking to her. The truck just kept going. Ted carried Sophie to their place and put her in a canvas bag. He buried her in the corner of his lot. That day was one of the saddest days of my life. That dog brought so much joy to my life and I had brought her so much pain. Not much of a trade the way I see it.

The refrigerator opens and there was not a nose touching my leg. There was not a clicking sound of paw nails on the floor following me— I was alone and I was hurting in my mind, my gut, and my heart; painful. The third day of moaning and crying I concluded that I had lived many years without another human in my home but I couldn't live without a dog. I picked up the newspaper and went to the want ads. Then I went to the dog shelter. Every dog which held an appeal for me at the shelter was spoken for. I decided to go to Roswell.

There were two shelters in that town and I went to both. Finally, giving up as I think I was looking for a Lab without success, I turned to leave. A rather large, golden dog jumped and stuck its paw through the enclosure. "Hey, he's kind of cute," I said to the attendant who had followed me the whole time I was looking around. He looked down at his clipboard and said, "That one is a female, a stray we picked up. Actually, we should have put her down yesterday." I looked into that dog's eyes and I saw a pleading look if I ever saw one. I was to blame for one dog's death—maybe, I could save another dog's life. "I'll take her," I said. I filled out the paperwork and he said I needed to sign and agree to get her spayed. I did and then I found out she was not the Lab I was looking for. I call her Amber.

Immediately, walking out the door I discovered she was a traumatized animal. She had to be carried to the truck and she was shaking all over. On the way home, I stopped to see if she needed to relieve herself—she just laid there in the snow. I talked to her on the way home but I did little to calm her down.

Retirement was near for me but I was going to be in and out a lot. Amber was going to be alone several hours a day. An idea of a "buddy" for her came to mind. I saw an ad for a small dog and I called the number. The man knew me and he said he knew I was a caring dog owner. His dog was not housebroken. His reason for that issue was that she was alone several hours daily. He used diapers on her. I hee-hawed in the conversation trying to get out of any promise of a commitment. I told him I was at a quilting retreat. Lo and behold, he brought that small dog where I was and knocked on the door. When I opened the door, she peed all over the sidewalk. I told him I had the retreat the next day too. Again, he was back at the place with that small dog.

Finally, I told him he could take the dog to my place under one condition; if Amber would accept her and if they got along. I found out Amber didn't like small dogs either. She growled at that small furry thing which was unusual for her behavior I found out. Well, that small furry thing jumped on Amber and was on top of her in a blink of an eye! I have to admit that impressed me. That man jumped in his car and took off. That little furry dog had been abandoned—she started whining and crying. I still feel pain of the way he left Abby, my other dog.

It was a good idea to get Abby. Rarely, is she scared of anything. Amber was scared of everything. Walking the two dogs was okay after I got a collar on Amber, then came the leash. If a big, noisy truck came down the street Amber would snap her neck and be out of her collar lickety-split. My thought was that she was somehow mistreated by someone in a truck or thrown from a truck. I took the dogs out in the desert a couple times but what an ordeal! When I went to get them back in my truck Amber would just lay down. There was a vast amount of distance from the ground to the backseat and I had to lift Amber; what a struggle.

Getting Amber spayed was another challenge. When I got her out of the truck she snapped her head and started running towards the traffic. I literally had to throw my entire body on her and hold her down. The receptionist came and put a choke collar on her. When I went to get Amber the attendant used the word 'bolted.' Amber was really an expert at that word. Needing help with Amber I went to a feed store as I heard there was a lady who was a dog trainer who worked there. I told her about Amber snapping her head out of the collar and bolting. The first thing she said was, "Don't take her to get her spayed yet!" Well, we all know I just did that. Confession time. She told me to get the metal choke chain with the spikes. She saw my reluctance, then she said Amber would get used to it. I didn't believe her but Amber remembered the walks, and she desperately wanted to participate in that activity again. I would hold the chain open, she would shut her eyes then she would stick her head inside—off we would go.

Amber weighed seventy-two pounds. I needed her to get in the truck on her own. One day, I pulled the truck in the yard and opened all the doors. Amber would go to the other side of the yard. I would throw treats in the back seat and Abby would get them (I had to lift her twenty-five pounds.) We did that for a couple weeks and I never forced Amber to do it. She needed to want to do it. Not sure how it happened but one day I threw the treat and she was in the back seat. I left all the doors open. A couple days later I got on the opposite side of the truck with the treat and I said her name. Just like I do when I'm diving off a diving board; she gritted her teeth, shut her eyes, and jumped. Occasionally, I see a fear come into her eyes but she overcomes the fear and she will jump in.

It took me a long time getting over Sophie and the guilt I carried, but Amber has been my therapy dog. She minds me better than any dog I ever had. She is totally devoted to me. If I tell her "it's okay" she will do whatever I ask of her. I've been known to say she would walk through hot coals for me but I would never ask anything like that of her and destroy the trust she has in me. She and I are kindred spirits.

We both had a rough start in life but we are now where we should be, together. Of course, little Abby is right behind us. Who knows; Amber and I may need her bravery someday.

Senior Olympics*

After the Alaskan cruise I went to the senior center. There was a sign on the desk advertising for ping pong players. There were men and women playing there and I was happy to have a group to play with. I met a lady, Jo who worked at the center. Boy, did she love the game. She wanted me to teach her how to play like I did. I explained that I would not be easy on her and she agreed wholeheartedly. That woman was one hard-headed gal. She traveled in her little truck with a camper through several states. She slept in Walmart parking lots without a dog or a gun in her truck. At one time during her life she had broken her back. She had to sit in a semi-reclining position even when driving.

Clyde was a retired educator and the leader in the state Senior Olympic Games. He participated in eight or nine events every year. He usually played mixed doubles in table tennis but that year his wife broke her toe—he asked me to be his partner. That year was my first year playing the games and I was excited. I think he and I placed second that year in doubles. I had signed up for singles. All the ladies knew each other and I was the newbie. I lost one game as my competitor slowed me down and I wasn't use to that type of playing. I won first place and surprised everyone including myself. I walked around with the thought that I was one of the best female players in the state in table tennis. The best memory I had that competition was hearing a male voice clear across that gym, "Come on, Sue!" I was so touched by Clyde's cheering for me. He later nominated me for the Eddy County Athlete representative. He treated me like his protégé—I liked that.

Every sport I do now has the same movement. That movement evolved from bowling and it's easy for me to adapt it to other sports. Horseshoes was similar to slow pitch pitching so I decided to try that event one year. When I arrived at the horseshoe pits a lady told me to go get my shoes. "I have to change my shoes?" (I guess my thinking reverted back to bowling). Everyone looked at me like I was crazy. She motioned to the fence where horseshoes were hanging. I got in the groove as I was sizing up my competitors. This was going to be easier than I thought. Several minutes later a van pulled up and there were about five muscular Native American women who piled out of that van. Apparently, they had made a wrong turn somewhere and they were late. They were penalized as they could only pitch the number of shoes from where we were at their time of their arrival. Goodness, they looked as though they could pitch horseshoes blindfolded and beat me. I barely won first but that was only because I got to add all my pitches and they couldn't. I didn't do the horseshoe again—I decided the competition was too tough.

Nine years ago, the strangest sound from a gym drew me inside. Gray heads were engrossed in a game which I had never seen before. I asked a lady sitting close by what was the name of the game I was watching. "Sit down, honey, and let me tell you about pickleball!" Fascinating. I bought into that game right off. When I came back home I convinced the ladies I played tennis with to try the game one day when it was raining. My enthusiasm for the game grew and grew. It is considered to be the fastest growing game in our country.

We have an old building which was a power plant at one time. It stood vacant for years. There were three floors with an elevator in the place. Kids use it for practicing many sports and it's a definite asset to our community. I applied for the ambassador position in SE New Mexico for pickleball. I've went to several tournaments with Margie. We usually have a respectable showing. When I decided to commit myself to the game I decided I had to do my best to promote the game. I've held classes for adults at the college. A group of us still play twice a week. I depend on tennis and pickleball for exercise to help control my diabetes.

Table tennis and pickleball were the two events I tried at the Sr. Olympics three years ago. Eventually, that plan didn't work out very well the last time I did that. I played singles in pickleball all morning— I was exhausted dragging myself to another gym to play table tennis with my male partner. We had played with each other for a couple years. Our first match was a tough one. We lost the first game. The table tennis ball is smaller than the pickleball one. I just couldn't get my bearings in the table tennis game after pickleball. The second game I decided I needed to be more aggressive. To do that I decided I should slam the ball more. So, to execute the next shot, I extended my arm way back but apparently my feet forgot what I was doing. My left leg went back behind my right leg and the right leg just stayed in the same position. I guess my left leg hobbled a couple hobbles as I don't remember—I went down. "Why is the ceiling leaking? I don't remember it raining," was my thought when I came to. Donnie, my doubles partner was dripping water from a thermos three feet above my face. "Can you play?" he pleaded. Shoot, I didn't know if I could walk! When I went down I had my paddle curved under my chin. In other words, I had a broken wrist. We taped it but it was too painful to play. That was my last game of competitive table tennis.

The partner I had before Donnie was Sid. He was married to a gal who was passive and did not speak up for herself at all. Sid and I played several years in the Senior Olympics. It was convenient for Jo and me to travel with the couple as he did the driving. For some reason Sid was always trying to impress me with all his "good ole boy" BS. Politics was a subject that we were miles apart in thinking and voting. That would have been okay but he was always trying to convert me to his way of thinking. That wasn't going to happen! He would get tutored by his good ole' boy clique and at the most ridiculous moment he would throw out a comment. His comments usually revolved around President Obama—that would bring out the fight in me. He would use a catch phrase and he would use it over and over. One that he used was "Obama was a Muslim, a socialist and of course the 'n' word.

Clyde played golf with a group of men, and he invited me to play with them. He would tell me it was more fun when I played. Standing around one day I made the comment that birds could be gay when we heard a flock of birds in the trees squawking. "Where did you hear that?" Sid demanded. "I read books instead of watching reruns of Bonanza!" I shot back. Clyde got shingles later on—he had to stay out of the sun—I quit golf too when he did.

A money issue was a sore point of mine involving Sid also. We were given money for our entry fee for the Senior Olympics by a club.

Sid was a member and so was I. Sid didn't approve of women, Hispanics, or Blacks being in that club. Go figure. He got the money, paid our fees and he kept the rest of the money. One night a group of us had dinner and Sid was going to pay the bill. I spoke up and said I wanted an apple dumpling dessert. Two other ladies said they wanted one too. Sid's wife looked at Sid in a pleading look—he shoved a dish of applesauce he had left over from his pork chop course towards her. I was fit to be tied! Later she had a nervous breakdown. I felt he was mentally abusing her but he sure was sly about it.

One day, Sid passed a paper around during table tennis practice. I picked it up and wrote on it. I told him I knew that he kept the money from our group. Watching as he read it, I saw he didn't even look around. The reason I even knew that fact was because I was at a meeting one night. I rarely went to those type of meetings except I had nominated two women that night for membership. They announced the amount they donated to the senior Olympic group. I heard the amount they designated for us to go to the Senior Olympics that year. When I added up the athletes' entry fees and there was over two hundred dollars left over that amount. I knew he pocketed that much that year—not sure how much the other years.

Our group has changed so much. In hindsight, they were like that all along. I just didn't see them as they were or I didn't want to see it until Obama's presidency. The biggest guy started carrying a gun around town. I've noticed the big men who are bullies are the ones who want/need guns. Clyde was really concerned about that. Sid would put the Hispanics down in our group when they weren't around. Sadly, they were the only ones who would golf with him.

. When I started teaching I had to decide for myself if I needed or should join a union. There were at least two teachers who were having legal issues with a student. The girl's mother had threatened a lawsuit against the teachers. The mother was claiming the teachers were picking on her daughter.

Lawsuits and the IRS are not in my comfort zone of living. I watched Jenny and the other teacher meeting with the teachers' union representatives constantly. I saw the stress they had to handle daily so that experience helped me decide to join the teacher's union, the NEA. I've never had to use but it was comforting to have it.

One of the teachers, Jenny, taught next door to me. At that time most of my social life revolved around friends I had before teaching; I was not quite comfortable with teachers. At first it was difficult walking in a building with all new faces, all of them had an education; it was going to take some getting used to. Gradually, I found myself going next door and chatting with Jenny after school. Jenny was a lovely woman who gave everything she had in her to her students. We didn't have a lot in common other than our jobs and we were both avid readers.

The men in our lives at that time had something in common though—they both had issues with alcohol. But Jenny and I handled the matter in our different ways. I left and Janice stayed in her marriage. I saw her agonizing over issues she had to deal with in her marriage. One day I made a comment, "Jenny, accept your situation, quit whining, or get the hell out!" We've discussed my comment several times. She's said I was right, she's said it hurt her feelings, and I felt she was angered also. Those words were exactly what I said to myself but I'm sure Jenny doesn't talk to herself like I talk to myself. Anyway, she stayed in her marriage and I didn't. I respect her decision but I'm glad I made my decision the way I did.

Jenny and I retired together. The staff had us a wonderful party. The principal, Myrl Moore, who hired me came to the party. At one time Myrl told me I would teach for a long time. He likened me to a teacher who had taught for over fifty years. I retired after just eighteen years. I still loved teaching, but something perhaps my gut told me it was time to retire. "Myrl, you told me I would teach for years," I reminded him.

"Sue, you're too smart to do that," he replied. I'm not sure what he meant by that statement. I have recalled it many times though, when I question my decision of retiring when I did.

Eight of us flew to Las Vegas for a final goodbye trip. That was a wonderful cap for the years we all worked together. The only sour note for me was the flying.

Thelma and Louise go to West Virginia

Right after I retired I was going through clippings, photos, etc. that I was going to put in a scrapbook. I came across a newspaper called BARN News. I was told later that was an acronym for Brush Creek, Ashford, Rumble, and Nellis. Once there had been a request in that paper from a person who was looking for me when I began teaching. My aunt answered the request and told the person I was in New Mexico. The editor of the paper was Judy Bowles McComas. I remembered a Judy Bowles from my early elementary years. I called the number listed on the paper. A female answered the phone and she immediately knew who I was—I knew who she was also. We chatted for a while and she told me about a reunion the following August, which was held every year. Mr. Elkins, my inspiring teacher, had passed away. Most of the people who attended the reunion had fond memories of him.

The more I thought about the reunion the more I wanted to go. One night I was at the club with Jenny, my friend. I told her of my decision to go to West Virginia to the reunion and she said she wanted to go. She said she hadn't ever been east of the Mississippi River. A couple days later my meanness kicked in. I got on the computer and made reservations for several places in Washington DC. I figured I would never have the opportunity of going there again, so going during this trip felt like a good idea. Jenny lost her cool for a while as I hadn't told her about the reservations—but I've learned a trick in dealing with Jenny. If I wait her out and let her say "Sue," then let her drag my name out the way she likes to do; then allow her to berate me a time or two; she gets over things rather quickly.

One night I got a call from Emil, a guy who had lived down the holler from me. Word had spread that I was coming back to the reunion. Apparently, Judy had given him my phone number and he called me several times. I thoroughly enjoyed listening to his stories—he had a way with words. His southern twang was like listening to music. His brutal honesty about people and places kept me in a laughter mode the whole time I listened to him.

He shared with me some of his memories of his mother. She was a bootlegger. She would take the bus to Madison and buy pints of liquor.

When she got home she divvied up the liquor out in to small bottles. When the drinkers around those hollers ran out of their moonshine they would buy her high price liquor and she lived off the profit of her sales during the time Emil was growing up.

Emil told me the last time he talked to me was a day he came up the holler to see Gabe. We walked out of the holler together and he told me we were talking about a hubcap in the creek. I have no memory of that. On the phone Emil told me he would have liked to have gone with me, but he thought we were cousins. His mom and Gabe were cousins, so we were definitely not cousins.

Emil did well for himself. He went in the Air Force and flew celebrities around. I remember Colin Powell but for the life of me I can't recall any others. When he called I thought he was in West Virginia but he lived in Kerrville, Texas. He owned airplanes and kept them in his hangars there. He suffered a stroke he told me so he had to give up his love—flying. He was on his second marriage. He divorced his first wife as he said "he didn't like her." Simple as that. Anyway, he told me if I was going to the reunion he would go too—he did.

Jenny had moved to Abilene to be near her kids so I drove there. She drove the rest of the way to West Virginia. We had fun impersonating the Thelma and Louise characters while driving. At Jenny's suggestion I had read the book, The Widow of the South. Somewhere along the way I guess we decided to go to battlefields and use the Civil War as our theme for the trip. We went to Carnton, the setting of the book written by Robert Hicks. The two parts of the book that had captivated my interest were when the surgeons threw body parts outside of the upstairs window—and the platonic love affair between the widow and a soldier. Neither of those two events happened. There was blood on the floor in a room upstairs where surgeries were performed. But the tour guide said if body parts were thrown out the window—the wounded soldiers would have run off. That made sense. The author made up the love angle to make the story more interesting. I sure was disappointed with the body parts and all the romance missing.

Jenny had a hissy driving over the mountains and competing with semis for her side of the road but we finally made it. On the way there I had Jenny drive around some places I remembered. We started up a mountain road and out of a 'Y' or an intersection came a big logging truck. Jenny had to back down the hill while using some colorful language, I didn't know she knew! "Sue" was sputtered at me again before she began cooling down. Needless to say, I didn't get to see that particular familiar place.

There was a bridge which had been dedicated to Mr. Elkins in Ashford—I wanted a picture of it. There was a post on Facebook with Frankie, his widow holding a plaque standing on the bridge. Jenny let me out on one side of the bridge then she drove across the bridge. I watched her as she pulled into a driveway of a house closest to the bridge. I saw a man come out the back door. I waved; I knew Jenny could handle herself explaining why she was trespassing. Janice told the owner of the house she was waiting for her friend. Jenny said he asked, "Is that Sue?" Jenny had pulled into Bryan Elkins's driveway who was no other than Mr. Elkins's oldest son. He had word I was coming from New Mexico, too.

We were to stay at my Aunt Adrenna's house. She was Mom's younger sister. She was the most educated of Mom's siblings and she was a Democrat. She had married a Republican though, and we considered them being well off. She had four kids, my cousins. They all came and visited us and Gary, my cousin, drove us to the reunion. Gary liked to share history of their state and we talked about his love of photography.

It was a potluck gathering in a park. Mr. Elkins's son, Bryan was there with Frankie Elkins, his mother. She was the widow of Mr. Elkins. She and I got to visit a long time. Before I came back she had sent me an email and had asked me why her husband was such a strong influence on my life. Being a retired teacher now, I know I always tried to remember the kids like I was in his classroom. He held me spellbound with his visions of other places, He was my cheerleader and the only one I had until I was sixteen. I tried to be a cheerleader for my students and to guide them to love learning just like he did for me. There was always a student who needed an extra push in their lives or a vision put before them. Sometimes a teacher is at the right place at the right time for a student. When that happens—magic. Frankie shared her life with me and we had a wonderful visit.

Bryan was a retired principal like his dad, and he related geography and the history of the place we had shared growing up. When he spoke, everyone gave him their attention. He had everyone's respect. Our friend Eddie was at the reunion. He was in politics and he had changed from the Democratic to the Republican party. It was said that his mother would have turned over in her grave if she knew he had done that. Seems as though the women I knew back there took their politics to heart. I sometimes wondered if it was due to their daddy's influence on their thinking and they were just loyal to his leanings. My first memory of Eddie had been in the Presbyterian church. We were practicing for a Christmas play and Eddie sang a solo. A feather could have knocked me over as his voice was so powerful. I guess that was the first time I became aware of someone I knew who could sing like that. Anyway, Eddy ended up being a Republican State Senator of West Virginia. Quite a feat for a guy from our small place of Ridgeview.

Politics is a strong identifier in my home state it seems. I remember Adrenna's husband my uncle, would get her all riled up just mentioning a politician's name. As I have been writing this thought occurred to me. I may have gotten my political views and passion genetically from Adrenna and Mom's side of the family. Anthony Bourdain did a show about West Virginia and its culture. There was a woman frying squirrel in an iron skillet and she had a hearty laugh like my Aunt Adrenna. My cousin Gary said while Jenny and I were visiting I had "that laugh" too.

Judy was the hostess of the event. She has done the reunion for years and she still does them years later. Emil arrived later and it was great to see him. It was nice to put a face with his endearing voice which I had listened to for so many hours during his telephone calls. His wife was friendly. Jennie was a real trouper listening to all of us reminiscing the whole day.

One guy I knew sent me emails and later we were friends on Facebook. Jack was his name, but we totally disagreed about everything. Politics was a subject I really took exception to the way we thought differently. That was during the time Obama was president. I'm not sure if he unfriended me or vice versa. But he was a man who liked to tell women what to do. Our friendship was put away finally for a lifetime. I'm rather glad he wasn't at the reunion after our serious discussions about politics and religion.

Another guy who didn't make the reunion was Marvin. He had been an arch foe of mine growing up. He had two brothers and we fought literally all the time growing up. Marvin denied that he was the brother who was the mean one, and we argued that fact many times. Sadly, it doesn't matter anymore and after sixty some years later I've gotten over our spats. Marvin is in a rest home now, and spending his golden years there. Marvin has a friend James Treadway, and he teased me many times about Marvin. We shared a lot of laughs over stories that we told about our fights long ago.

I spent several afternoons visiting with Aunt Adrenna. She had an old Bible on the coffee table. Once I had asked her at the time I went to West Virginia with Mom if she knew my father. That question was shot down real fast at that time by her. Aunt Nina is the one who told me about Mom's past and my birth. Adrenna was in another state working in a factory during the war and she claimed she didn't know anything about Mom's history. But there were pictures of me at six months old with Adrenna. A statement made by her still hangs in the air for me. She said Mom hated Gabe and she locked him out of the bedroom. I don't remember any doors in the houses we lived in. Mom would usually hang a sheet over the doorway. But what I got from that statement was—if she did lock him out that would have made me an easy prey. To sum up our "talks" Adrenna was loyal to her sister, my mother. She claimed the only thing she knew was gossip she heard, and I have to believe her. Whatever she told me I knew I was ready to leave her with her memories and it was time for me to let her be.

When I had made the reservations for the tours of Washington DC I figured Janice and I could take a bus out of Morgantown—so we wouldn't have to drive into the city. Bryan Elkins suggested that we drive all the way into the city as he had many times. That place was really a challenge for us but we made it to our old historical hotel right downtown. We were definitely centrally located at the Phoenix Park Hotel. I remember getting up early and looking down at the hustle and bustle of that city and it was as though I felt the energy radiating up to my brain to the third floor. I was impressed! What I was most thankful for was that knowing President Obama was in office at the time of our visit.

We got on the bus a half block from our hotel to Mt. Vernon. That historical place was located on the Potomac River—what a sight! What struck me the most about their farming practices was that water used on the crops was allowed to sit in the sun to be warmed. The reason for that: cold water could stunt the growth of young seedlings. I could have spent days there and I would have enjoyed every minute of it.

The Washingtons attended Trinity Church. I marveled at the gates between the pews. They were closed to control the coldness of the drafts after one was inside sitting down. Also, the parishioners would wrap hot bricks in cloth to put at their feet during church services. When I look at pictures of old churches now I scan for the little gates between the pews—I really enjoyed that history lesson.

The Capitol was another marvel we visited. We walked passed the White House. One evening we toured the Ford Theatre. We barely had a glimpse inside of the Smithsonian as it was humongous. Janice and I talked about all the history in that place and rarely did either one of us take a deep breath. We were in our element and we were enjoying it to the maximum.

The day we went to see all the memorials was a blazing scorching day. We made through all of them except for the Washington Monument. Just before seeing that monument we took a restroom break. Jennie and I both exited the stalls simultaneously as a female ranger burst through the door. "Get out!" she yelled. "Get out!" We thought there was a terrorist attack. All of the women, including us, were shoved outside to a grassy area. At 1:51 pm, August 23, 2011, there was an earthquake in Washington, DC. The Washington Monument was damaged during the quake and it was roped off immediately. The weirdest part of that day was that Jennie nor I felt any shaking whatsoever from that quake. I guess the potty was cushioned. Time to bid Washington DC adieu.

My book club had chosen the book Help just before we left town as Thelma and Louise. Janice had read the book. I bought the book on tape so I would know the story before our next club meeting. We listened to that tape for the many miles we traveled on the way to the mountains of West Virginia. When we finished listening to the last tape we were driving through Jackson, Mississippi the setting of the book Help. What a beautiful story. When we arrived in Abilene where Janice lived she looked in the paper and Help was showing in Abilene at the movies. We went to see it and that was like icing on the cake for our traveling venture. Perfect.

One night I was looking at the pictures we had taken back in West Virginia. On impulse I typed in the name Karen Messer Hill in Facebook. She was my half-sister who Mom wouldn't see. I knew the name because she had sent me a picture of her and her husband on their wedding day when I was a senior. Janice and I were in West Virginia in August 2011—the month I typed in Karen's name in Facebook was in November 2011. A page immediately came up and it was like a memorial page for Karen. She had passed away in Florida in September. I wrote a post on the timeline and explained who I was and why I was contacting the person who wrote the obituary for Karen. There were several pictures of Karen and she looked so much like our mother. The person who answered me was a person named Ellie. She would have been my niece. She wrote to me on Facebook and wanted to come and visit me. I was a bit leary about that for some reason. She wanted my phone number—I sent it twice. She then wanted travel money. I told her I didn't have much room in my small house and she should probably would need to stay in a motel.

When I talked to her on the phone she seemed to be really religious and I told her I was not a church goer. I didn't go to an organized church or any church for that matter. She began spouting scriptures and I told her I wasn't interested in hearing her out. I guess we talked on the phone a couple times, but truthfully, I did not want to see her. She called Karen's brother Lawrence, her uncle, as she wanted us all to get together. I told her to ask Lawrence about that and she did. He said he didn't want to meet me and that was fine with me as I understood. Finally, Ellie must have unfriended me. She was taking care of her mother-in-law, her daughter was in jail, and Ellie was raising her granddaughter. A lot of drama for sure. If Karen had been alive it may have been a good connection or maybe not. Anyway, I will never know.

Sue Brazeal

Dave and I Are Off to West Virginia

Over the years Dave had listened to my tales of my upbringing more than he wanted to I'm sure. Right after Janice and I returned from our Thelma and Louise trip Dave said he always wanted to go back to West Virginia with me. We decided we would go to the next reunion. We made different plans for our trip. I suggested we go by train since my trip to Seattle was a great memory. We made our reservations and we were to take Amtrak from Albuquerque to Charleston, WV. Dave was wanting to visit University of New Mexico where he graduated, so things were falling in place we thought.

We were at the train station bright and early on the day of our departure. They told us while checking in that they had tried to contact us. In August there were so many students going back to school and our trip would be delayed a whole day. That didn't work as I wanted to be at the reunion. The only way we could be there on time was to fly. Man, did I hate to fly but I had made so many arrangements. I had to decide what to do, so I conceded that I would fly, for my last time in my life.

Off we went from Albuquerque to Dallas. From there we were to fly into Charleston, West Virginia. The plane going to Charleston was much smaller, and it moved around a lot in the clouds which some call "turbulence" (fancy name for nightmare for me). I was sitting by a woman and we started scaring each other with our horror stories about flying. We were getting louder and louder. Everyone was looking our way except for Dave. He held his head down looking at a book—pretending he didn't know me. Looking down at the runway we were approaching I thought it looked rather short; thankfully, I didn't see any water.

The motor was roaring and my friend and I in panic mode couldn't hear each other. Really, I don't think either one of us cared if we heard each other or not. When we landed it reminded me of landing on an aircraft carrier. Not that I ever landed on a carrier before but I had seen them on the movie screen. When we hit, we stopped! It happened as quick as I just said the last sentence. I immediately rushed to the exit as I had to go to the restroom IMMEDIATELY! I was given dirty looks by many, but I didn't care. I didn't have time to explain myself.

We rented a car and got lodging in Charleston. There was a power outage so no air conditioner for a couple days. We contacted Judy Bowles McComas, my childhood friend. She was going to meet us at the Historical Nellis Church. My goodness, that woman had to wait on us a long time. I get lost in big cities all the time, but I have to admit I get lost in the mountains of WV, too. I drove all over those mountains with a broken arm. I guess that is not an excuse for getting lost though.

I had asked Judy if she would take us to places that I remembered from long ago. The first place we went was up the holler where I lived several years. Judy got permission for us to get out and walk around the place. That place held the most memories of my abuse. That holler recorded my prayers to God about the plight of my young life. The hair prickled all over my body. Eerie. We walked down the old railroad tracks which were corroded and no longer used—talking about Emil, the Bush boys, and others who popped in our minds. Dave just tagged along behind us taking pictures every once in a while. We tried to place the old cemetery in the holler without climbing the mountain. James Treadway agreed later that my memory was correct. We went to places like Dartmont, White Oak, Costa, Ashford and Rumble. I let a cousin know that Dave and I would be making the trip back there again. I didn't hear from anyone, so I did not seek them out that trip. I'm not sure but I felt there was some tension among the cousins. I guess everyone said what they wanted to say when I was there with Jenny. While I was writing this book, I got a message on Facebook that Aunt Adrenna had passed away. She lived into her nineties—a feisty old lady. I think she and others were uncomfortable with my plan to write all this down. I'm sorry about that, but it's my life, my choice.

Dave and I went to the reunion and things seemed a lot like when Jenny and I went. I got lost that day too. I swear those mountains move around just to confuse me. Frankie and Bryan Elkins attended that year also. Emil had called me and asked if I was going back that year. He said he would go if I did. He got sick right after that. He couldn't make the trip. It wasn't long until he passed away. Guess we are all getting older and time is stealing us away one by one. But at least I have some beautiful memories of the connections I had made from old friends. Not everyone has been as fortunate as I have been.

Mom used to talk about Hawk Nest all the time. Dave and I went there and had a lovely day. What beauty. We visited Babcock Park, the most photographed mill in the state. My skin gets prickly remembering the feeling of awe of that beautiful day. The New River Gorge Bridge is the most recent tourist attraction built and what a sight that is.

The fear of flying I might could handle if it was one way. But when I get to my destination I have to worry about my return trip; I feel it ruins my fun while visiting places. A low gnawing on my comfort zone is ever present, along with a sense of dread. That was my state of mind when we arrived at the airport in Charleston to return home. Then raw fear kicked in when I saw the storm that just hit the airport! I was walking, brooding, and fretting—in other words I was in a tizzy. Dave and I had a sandwich and I got an idea on how to relieve a bit of stress. I picked up the check and went to the bar to pay the bill. In a low voice I told the cashier I wanted a straight shot of vodka added to the ticket. As I watched her pour my request, I corrected myself; I told her I wanted two shots instead! She put them in front of me. I gulped them down before I had time to change my mind. I went back to the table.

After we boarded the plane the stewardess came by; I gave her the "woe is me look". She asked if I was okay. I started my long story and Dave said, "Give her a drink." Well, I wasn't going to argue with that. Not sure who, then someone said give her a double. I still didn't argue. We took off in flight running through deep puddles of water; lightning and thunder were in the background. The effects of the drinks, well, I used them up before we leveled off. I again made myself a promise I would never fly again!

My Politics

It was the morning of 9/11 and I had just entered the classroom. A teacher was running down the hall and telling us to turn on the television. I had my tv on just fifteen minutes ago—I didn't see anything alarming. Watching the planes hitting our landmarks took my breath away! I certainly was glad the students weren't in the classroom yet. For days we were all in shock—just going through the motions of teaching. Then it was time for the presidential election.

Truthfully, I had never taken elections too seriously before. I voted—I was always registered, but Ken and I were always at odds on each other's views. When Ronald Reagan was governor of California he put forth a rebate on something he wanted us to vote for. I can't remember what I was voting for—I just wanted the $500. I never heard the last of that from Ken. Of course, he helped me spend it.

I was at my wits end on who to vote for because I wanted our country to be safe. So, I decided I would go to Santa Fe. There was an educated couple I knew living there. I felt their advice on who to vote for would be my best bet. I will call them Barry and Glenda. They strongly endorsed George Bush and I'm sure I listened closely to their reasons but later I regretted my decision that I voted for him. Then and there I knew I needed to decide for myself so I would not regret listening to someone else about voting. I needed to study and research every candidate who was running. Later, when Obama was president Glenda spoke so negative of him and it finally dawned on me that the couple were die-hard Republicans. My interest in politics really went to the clouds after that. I became aware and I so wanted to know what was going on.

45 like sent me over the edge. Everything I was taught and felt—he went against. I guess I knew most people are racist to some degree, but it was put in my face by my friends and that really hurt. I had a friend who said #45 was a man of God and he would put our country back on track. Lordy mercy. There was a friend who believed in rocks. I'm making a joke, but she was told from a man of "God" if a rock was split and a semblance of a cross was in it, that was proof that Jesus was crucified at the minute the cross appeared. Another friend in her late sixties wouldn't sleep with a guy she was going to marry but she had not a problem with #45 being married to a porn star. Oh, and he just kept sleeping around while the porn star was having a baby. She did not have a problem with all the sex charges he had against him. That is where the "fake news" ploy came into \play. The revelation for me was that many of my ex-friends hated Obama and they had never uttered a word about that until the moment #45 was in office. He used "fake news" as a trick with anyone who had pulled the wool over their entire head and did deep breathing I guess.

After the Kavanaugh appointment and hearing the person in charge speaking of sexual assaults which he is accused of makes me angry! That has been a typical response to women like me. That person criticizing a person, especially a woman is as bad as the man in the house I was raised in. The only difference I see is financial. Those men are weak, insecure, and doubtful of their own masculinity and they prey on others who are weak and insecure in those predators' minds.

Sex to them is power and rarely has to do with an inherent need. They lie, overpower or buy what they want in the moment and leave lives and souls in ruins many times. Strength in women and a kid like me with a knife will always be a threat to them.

#MeToo

The #MeToo movement began while I was writing this book and it should have been put forward long, long ago. Maybe it is inching its way into the general public's psyche. Perhaps we will be made aware that the child in our classroom, our niece, our daughter, our neighbor, and of course the males in our lives will have an ear from us. We must be receptive and get help for the ones who are being abused. I've become aware of so many women my age who have been abused. All of us seem to handle it differently. Many have pushed it back and rarely acknowledge it out loud. One lady told me; "I know something happened but I know it will hurt if I think about it." She's right. We all have our reasons and timing and each have to deal with it in our own time. Not one of us should be penalized or criticized in any way about our subject or timing.

I had an older friend of mine say about the movement; "Why did those women wait so long if that happened so long ago!" she snarled. I snarled right back, "Because women like you wouldn't believe us!" I had wanted to say that to her for years. Good for me.

Sally Field just put her book out there In Pieces. She is seventy. The first time I began this book was thirty-five years ago. All of us have pain who have been abused. I'm thinking I have an advantage, as my mother and the abuser she lived with are both dead. I won't go to her grave as he is buried next to her. She's not there anyway is what I know, and I will do the best I can and go on.

There are a few regrets I have. I've found myself vulnerable and I acted out on my impulses at times. But the most soul-wrenching and guilt-ridden haunting I have had to deal with had to with Dora. Years of the sexual abuse I suffered I thought it was just because of me. I was a bastard and Gabe was not my father. I reasoned in my teenage years if I married and moved away that things would be alright for the rest of them. Dora told me once that Mom said I left to get away from the fighting at home. I really had not thought of that before because I was in the war zone all the time. I couldn't see the forest for the trees so to speak. On a trip back to New Mexico once Dora and I found ourselves in an upstairs bedroom. I don't even remember the address as I think they only lived there for a short time. Anyway, Dora said that Gabe was raping her! Eventually, I said. "I didn't think he would do that to you as you were his daughter, I thought it was just me being punished." Well, I now know that is not sane reasoning. Fathers do assault their own daughters! Even educated and wealthy fathers.

When Mom and the clan rented the two story the house that belonged to Ken's family there was an unfinished basement. By unfinished, I mean the ground was the flooring. Dora told me the saddest story. The entrance to the basement was lifting the flooring up in a bedroom. While Gabe was in the bathroom Dora would lift up the flooring and spend the whole day there until Mom got home from work. Thinking back, I was the lucky one—I ran to the mountains and spent the day there until I deemed it safe to go home. Many years ago, Dora and I had another conversation. She said her dad raped the boys too. The cue phrase he used was "sin, sin" for that act. Perhaps, he had been influenced by a church and he knew it to be wrong. When Gabe was ill and dying Doris spoke of him "speaking in tongues," another idea from a church. I've never known of Gabe going to a church but it impacted his life. Perhaps he did when he was young.

Hard Work Ahead

While I was teaching third grade I got the cutest little boy in my class, I'll call Terry. Sometimes he would have bouts of anger which would seem to rise up from nowhere. He hated to read at first but finally he got comfortable with his new-found skill and began reading.

One day I got a call I my classroom from a woman who wanted to talk to me about Terry. She told me she was a social worker and Terry was one of her clients. She said he and his mother stayed in a motel locally. She would lock Terry in the room while she would meet men for her profession, prostitution. The state had taken Terry and he was a ward of the courts. I didn't know any of this and there were issues brought up as to how she got directed to my classroom during class.

During that time dealing with Terry I decided I would volunteer and try to help kids who were surviving in conditions like he had been.

Terry's foster mom was a muscular, stout Hispanic woman and she had a biting tongue. She was married and she had five other foster children in her home. Terry did his homework and seemed happy enough leaving third grade. Several years later there was a write-up in the paper on a reading award and prizes Terry had received through the schools. Happy ending, right? No, that couple was abusing all the kids in their home and their foster care license was revoked right after that. They had received so many accolades for their care of children but it was all a lie! It's such a cruel world for so many kids in the system. But again, so many in their own home are being abused.

The training I received for dealing with abused and neglected children was in short—a revelation for me. The term dissociation was introduced in a class and it was like an envelope was handed to me telling me of my condition that I had been dealing with in my prepubescent years. Perhaps the price of the frustration that I went through those years dealing with my cases I was given keys I may have not have received otherwise. I'm truly grateful for the peace of mind learning about trauma, my trauma, from those classes.

We were taught by instructors from all over the USA. Washington instructors went into depth about sexual abuse. In that state convicted pedophiles give their permission to be tested. The subject would be monitored while watching videos of children. Sexual arousal would be evident by a penile device. Generally speaking,

pedophiles cannot be rehabilitated. A pedophile will change genders if he thinks he is being watched by someone. A pedophile may go through a dormant stage until he has grandkids. No two offenders are alike.

Choir directors, youth ministers, and other charismatic workers were shown how they attain the parents trust. They were also shown how they groom their victims. The pedophile is an opportunist we were taught. Whoever is around of either sex they will act on.

My first assignment was a shaken baby assignment. My stomach is turning now as my memory kicks in. The baby, or the young girl, is doing well in school. I do not stay in touch, as it's easier for me to move on. There were many disappointments for me in that case. I saw a social worker texting in during the trial of the abuser. No cell phones were allowed in the courtroom and she took hers to every court date. The abuser got out of jail and impregnated the mother of my case the second time. It was like watching a soap opera of which I had no control. I just had to let go. My way of doing that is usually completely.

My second case were with three neglected girls. My first visit was with the mother who was in jail. Our interactions were high energy and confrontational. The girls were placed in a behavior focused foster care home in another town. The foster mother, a teacher, was racking up thousands of dollars a month for her care. I'm not saying she did a poor job but she was rude to me and only relented her better self when she was directed to do so. I was especially disappointed as she was an elementary teacher. The parents cooperated and got their kids back. The last I heard of them the parents divorced and they moved back to Texas.

A Hispanic boy was my next case. He was struggling with sexual identity issues. His mother went to Mexico taking two of his siblings and leaving him with the father. Depression, anger, and his identity issues were bad enough but then his father died. The boy turned eighteen and aged out of the program. So sad.

My last placement was traumatized at an early age. Ross, I will call him had been placed in foster care but concerning issues surfaced after a while. It was decided that Ross needed professional counseling and daily monitoring long term. He was placed in a group home which used horse therapy for some of its clients. Ross rode and interacted with horses but I was told by his therapist that he did not benefit much by the horse therapy practiced at the ranch.

The trips to the Assurance Home in Roswell lasted for three years. I drove eighty some miles usually once a month. Some of the trips were through rain and snow storms. At times when I arrived Ross would be having a meltdown. Time was spent by me sitting and waiting for him to get himself under control. There were several medications which were prescribed for Ross but I did not know what they were. The first time I felt a connection with Ross was an evening he was told to sit with me. He was angry but I don't remember why. He covered his head with a blanket. I just started talking about World War ll. Ross was a very bright boy but his grades didn't back that statement up. I gave a background of the countries involved in the war as if I was giving a lecture. After a time, I saw an eye peeking out from the blanket. He was hooked! He would later say his favorite subject was history. He listened to the news and had opinions about politics. We talked a bit about natural disasters and I did my best to keep his interests in those subjects during my visits.

After I made the connection of the Assurance Home and horse therapy (sometimes listed as equine therapy) I remembered reading about it in Jaycee Dugard's book A Stolen Life. When Jaycee was rescued from her kidnappers and taken home she had a difficult time connecting with her mother after eighteen years. The young kidnapped girl could not bond or connect with her mother. The book told of Jaycee and her mother grooming the horse and talking. It was a focus outside of themselves. Jaycee has now founded the JAYC Foundation to help other traumatized children and their families reunite and connect using horse therapy.

I read another book Horse Boy by Rupert Isaacson. It spoke of a young father trying to connect with his autistic son. The scene I remember was the one where the boy was running wildly down a road. He meets a horse galloping towards him—just as they meet the horse stops and bows down. The father rode with his son and the boy responded well while riding a neighbor's horse. The father got the idea of going to Mongolia, the setting for the best horsemen of the world. Visiting a shaman and receiving insights was a wonder for me and the book spoke of the struggles of the young parents.

The subject would not be complete without speaking of Temple Grandin. She is an autistic animal behaviorist who explained that horses and autistic humans share "visual thinking." Since neither one uses verbal language the horse senses a connection with autistic humans. Amazing!

Ross made much progress but towards the end of my service I felt unnecessary. He went to college and for some reason my gut told me it was time to let the case go. It was as though I was interfering with his life. I felt like a nuisance he had to endure because it was required by the state. Another reason was that if Ross had a meltdown without professionals being there for my support I didn't know if I could handle that situation.

My assignments were hard but the organization I was volunteering for was a political and a religious ran machine. That organization was supposed to be a civic group but I found it not that way at all. There were conflicts constantly. The director was anti-gay and she wanted no part of having gay foster parents. She made crude remarks about President Obama. Me being me, had to always call her on it. She was "a good ol' boy" without being a male. She had 'pets' one day and the next day they would find themselves on her "shit list." While having a group dinner we had to say three prayers at least to let everyone know what good church-goers her, and her cronies were. I turned her in locally and she then assigned a new board president. On two different state surveys I complained about her political and religious statements to the state. Never was anything said to me or her I guess that I know of. My conclusion was that her views and actions were alright by them. That was not the case with me. A thought I have accepted for myself is I put myself out there to volunteer. At least I tried, and won't wonder about it years from now. My feet got wet but rocks collected between my toes.

Reading Coach / Board Member

My next volunteering endeavor was an organization which was formed to teach reading to adults. My vision was that I would teach reading one-on-one to an adult. Most, if not all were Spanish speakers. But with my background in teaching I was recruited to be on the board. That didn't suit my fancy at all. A male board member wanted the students to come to our homes. I was totally against that idea. Another kink I found was with the workshops they put on for the tutors. The instructor was threatened by tutors who had experience in reading. She was putting out a lot of information that just wasn't factual. She did not want any input. I felt the need to tell her I disagreed—she was a bit put out. I think they were in favor of experience but feedback from teachers was not welcomed. It's hard to feel included with that kind of atmosphere.

My first student was a lovely woman in her forties—she always was giggling. She didn't have papers but she wanted to learn to read so she could take her citizenship test and vote for President Obama. She worked really hard and I still see her and her family. Later, I got a couple of men who had gotten hurt on the job and they needed to learn English. They weren't inclined to attend class regularly and that was a hassle for me.

The board members were to help with writing grants for funding constantly and that was not a chore I was interested in. I gave my notice. Dedicated teachers at the building—and they had regular scheduled classes have left. When the election of 2016 was held and the new person was in the White House—those two teachers were told not to discuss the election with the students (Spanish speaking women). Again, politics and religion were a stronghold of that group. I no longer have a desire to volunteer in groups like that ever again.

Final Thoughts

Once I told Dave I had no fear of dying as I had had a good life. He corrected me and said, "Mom, HAVING a good life." I had to laugh as I had been talking in the past tense. I heard a man speak of dying the other day. He was a survivor of the priests in Pennsylvania who sexually abused over one thousand children including a child less than two years old. He said church goers are afraid of going to hell! He said he had lived in hell for years and he considers himself "spiritual." I've said the same things about myself. I'm sure I read that bit of wisdom somewhere. I was mouthing his words to myself as he was saying them during his interview. Perhaps he had read them somewhere too.

Many have commented on my sharp memory including Mom. She would test me in a way when I was young. She would ask me actors and actresses names and I always knew them. For some reason I don't remember lyrics of songs. When I hear music, I listen for the beat. I can still experience times in the past as if they were yesterday. I guess that's what they call long term memory. But I can actually feel sensations on my skin, my tongue and my taste buds can recall tastes. I can recognize people who I have seen move before from a long distance. Movement through space especially people I've seen move in sports I can readily identify seeing them in my mind. Sometimes, I recall telling myself I want/need to remember things and I can and do. Running down the railroad track—feeling coal cinders floating from the tipple hitting my face and my arms is a recurring memory. I was running home for lunch, so I could get back and to play volleyball. Most of those kinds of memories are when I'm passionate or euphoric about an upcoming event.

In my way of thinking or reflection I have overcome my long-ago nickname "Smut." Since I didn't focus on what I wanted, rather I focused on what I didn't want—made that possible I've come to accept. Perhaps the image of Smut coming up that hill that day with her old benefactor—I kept as a "visual" of who I didn't want to be. I willed that image far away in my long-term memory so it wouldn't haunt me. Not sure where my strong will has come from exactly. Perhaps just surviving my childhood has given me the strength to be who I am and to be darn proud of who I am.

Painful memories are only in my mind when I allow them to be present anymore. With age I have learned to push them back. But I have to admit it was painful to talk about some of the subjects I wrote about being raised the way I was. Moodiness was frequently my companion during this writing. Remembering that I have to get that jar down from the shelf and stir the memories once again was not what I wanted to do. Speaking of my outlook on life in instances of being brave I think, "I have little fear of anyone now as my abuser is dead. Then I think I've just had about every threat I can imagine. What else can anyone do to me other than kill me?" But what a price for my bravery!

I've done so many things and succeeded at most of them to some degree. One of my goals was to do a piece of art in my old age. I've taken lessons and self-taught myself in so many subjects—but none of the subjects held my focus long term as I wanted to move onto something else. Perhaps this memoir is my piece. Writing is a new passion for me. It was challenging and saddening, but it's done. Now, I'm ready for the next chapter of my life. Ironic, that today is Mom's birthday. Some things just work out the way they're supposed to. I'll just tuck this venture away and consider myself to be as blessed as anyone could possibly be in one lifetime.

Old Blue.

College days.

Graduation day with my boys.

My Buck.

Student teaching.

Third grade.